A Garland Series

The Modern Chinese Economy

Edited by
Ramon H. Myers
HOOVER INSTITUTION

The Revenue and Taxation of the Chinese Empire

Joseph Edkins

Garland Publishing, Inc., New York & London
1980

Bibliographical note:
this facsimile has been made from a copy in
the Yale University Library.

Library of Congress Cataloging in Publication Data

Edkins, Joseph, 1823–1905.
The revenue and taxation of the Chinese empire.

(The Modern Chinese economy)
Reprint of the 1903 ed. printed at the
Presbyterian Mission Press, Shanghai.
Includes index.
1. Revenue—China—History. 2. Taxation—China—
History. 3. China—Appropriations and expenditures—History.
I. Title. II. Series: Modern Chinese economy.
HJ2975.E4 1980 336.51 78-74331
ISBN 0-8240-4252-2

For a complete list of the titles in this series,
see the final pages of this volume.

All volumes in this series are printed on acid-free,
250-year-life paper.

Printed in the United States of America

THE REVENUE AND TAXATION

OF THE

CHINESE EMPIRE.

BY J. EDKINS, D.D.

SHANGHAI:
PRINTED AT THE PRESBYTERIAN MISSION PRESS.

ALSO SOLD BY

KELLY AND WALSH; BREWER AND CO., MR. E. EVANS, SHANGHAI, AND BY
P. S. KING AND SON, 2 GREAT SMITH STREET, WESTMINSTER, LONDON, S.W.

1903.

INTRODUCTION.

In ancient times the taxes were levied in field produce, in manufactured silk, and in copper cash. The public accounts were kept in this three-fold form, and this practice continued down to the time when paper curreney was adopted. The system of paper currency, combined with copper cash, prevailed in keeping the public accounts through the middle ages till the Ming dynasty. After the year 1368, when Chu T'ai-tsu became Emperor of China, the accounts began to be regularly kept in silver and copper cash. Paper currency was still recognised in the public accounts, but the main thing was silver from that time forward. Receipts and distribution of grain, silk stuffs, etc., were included. The public accounts being all drawn up in silver, the registers of taxes due are in every magistrate's office over this large country so constructed that silver always comes to the front. For example, now 1899, when the Bund at Shanghai has just been extended southward for a mile between the native city and the river those who had come into possession of the land newly recovered from the river were called on to pay for their occupation. Ten feet by five of land occupied for fifteen years was charged 300 taels. Occupiers for twenty years were made to pay 400 taels. Occupiers pay for foreshore which has come to them from the river. After fifteen and twenty years they will pay again for the new foreshore which by that time will have been made by silting. The obligations to pay taxes in the future are all carefully entered in taels of silver. The government suffers the loss of silver should it fall still further in value. On September 16th, 1898, an edict appeared in Chinese newspapers directing the Board of Revenue accounts to be published annually in the Gazette.

Taxes are paid in copper cash, silver, or grain. When grain is paid the magistrate has a granary in which to store it. What is entered in the public accounts is legal payment, whether cash or silver. In A. D. 1035 an order was made that taxes should be paid in strings of cash. But for Fukien, Kwangtung, and Kiangsi, silver was allowed to be paid. In Kiangsu silk goods of native manufacture could be paid. All these were at that time legal payment. But the foundation was in copper cash. This had been the national currency since the times of Confucius.

In certain cases copper cash are still mentioned as legal payment. For example in A.D. 1881 Corean farm emigrants within the Chinese frontier were ordered to pay 2,100 copper cash as a squatter's tax. In addition to this they were to pay annually 660 copper cash.

A Tartar dynasty began to rule North China A.D. 1115. They belonged to the same race as the Manchus. From Manchuria as a base sending in their armies they subdued the Chinese northern provinces and carried the Sung dynasty Emperors, both father and son, into captivity. In the chapter of the 金史 Chin-shih History of the Golden Dynasty on trade and taxation, it is stated that fifty taels of silver were changed for 100 strings of copper cash. If cut and beaten the price fell just as it is with Spanish dollars in recent times. There were one tael pieces, two tael pieces, five and ten tael pieces of silver. Each tael would be changed for two strings. When paper money was tried, it was found that silver seemed to rise in price and the paper money fell below its nominal value. Shopkeepers preferred to price their goods in silver and not in treasury notes for the reason that the notes did not keep their value. When paper and silk notes were made, as in A.D. 1215 by the Golden Dynasty, five years' trial was enough to show the government that it was impossible to keep the selling value of the treasury notes up to the nominal price. There was silver enough in circulation to carry the day against the notes. In A.D. 1222 the attempt was made to place in circulation a variety of silk and paper notes. Also at that time a string of large copper cash was given out as the equivalent of a weight of silver represented as fifty. (It is not said fifty of what denominator.) But copper fell and silver rose. The traders favoured silver, and the efforts of the treasury were fruitless. In A.D. 1224 silver only was acceptable to traders. It was just at this time that silver began to be of great importance in Chinese currency. Genghis Khan was fighting in the west and opening the communication with Persia and India. This brought silver into North China.

An old word coming down from the Han dynasty and meaning revenue is 帑 t‘ang or 帑款 t‘ang-k‘wan. Both these words are in the Shang-sheng. T‘ang means what is treasured up. It is that which is stored in a granary or treasury, Tsang-k‘u 倉庫. The tone shows that the word was applied in the sense government treasury in the Chow dynasty when that tone was in course of formation. Tang and tsang are really one word.

CONTENTS.

	PAGE.
Red Book Revenue Statistics ...	1
Gross annual revenue	2
Revenue of each province ..	3
Land and grain revenue ...	4
Silver from native customs ...	5
Grain tribute in A. D. 1732 ...	6
Expenditure	6
Board of Revenue Statistics ...	8
Government revenue, 1893 ...	10
Receipts from ordinary taxes, by new taxes, and by subscriptions	11
§ 1. Expenditure, 1893	,,
New expenditure	12
Revenue and expenditure in each province...	13
Coast and frontier expenditure	17
Army in each province ...	18
Miscellaneous sums	,,
Board of Revenue disbursements	19
Balance in Board treasury ...	22
§ 2. Receipts in Silver	,,
Land tax	,,
Miscellaneous taxes	23
Rents and profits	24
Grain commuted to silver ...	25
Melting and surplus tax ...	,,
Salt and native Customs ...	26
Likin and foreign Customs ...	27
Subscriptions and postponed taxes	28
Provincial savings	29
Loans in the provinces ...	30
Army expenditure	,,
Sums ordered to be paid to other provinces	31
Old balances in each province	,,
Receipts from old balances ...	32
§ 3. Expenditure	
Imperial tombs	33
Palace	,,
Sacrifices	,,
Public functions and salaries	34
Examinations and army ...	35
Courier service and bursaries	36
Rewards, charities, and repairs	37
Official purchases	38
Salaries	39
Subsidies	40
Native customs...	41
Purchases from foreigners ...	,,

	PAGE.
Payments of sums due from the provinces	42
Advances from the provinces...	,,
Government departments ...	43
Peking army	44
National army	,,
Help from one province to other provinces	,,
Annual deficit	45
Silver on hand in each province	46
Copper cash revenue	..
Expenditure in cash	47
Tribute grain received and distributed	48
Hay and straw received and distributed	49
Revenue and Expenditure ...	50
Mencius condemns levy of duties	50
Tithes in ancient China ...	,,
Tang dynasty taxation ...	,,
Loan subscriptions in 1898 ...	54
Revenue in 1899	,,
Subscriptions of Hwai-nan salt merchants	,,
Sir N. J. Hannen's estimate of Chinese revenue and public debt	55
Debt of England	,,
Chung-wai-pao statement of the revenue and expenditure of China	56
Memorials on Revenue	
Board of Revenue on the navy	58
Minche viceroy on frontier defence	60
Kiang-su governor and Hwai an Taotai	61
Précis of edict on revenue ..	62
German statement of the revenue of China	66
Japanese statement of the revenue of China	67
Jamieson's scheme for increasing the revenue	68
Payment of deficit in 1899 ...	69
Expenditure in 1558	70
Army expenditure in 1898, 1899	72
Naval expenditure in 1900 ...	73
Nanyang army. Relief distribution	75

	PAGE.
The three official companies ...	75
How to extinguish the annual deficit	76
Indemnities	82
The peace protocol	,,
Peace protocol and indemnity	,,
Remarks on the indemnity ...	90
Mode of payment	91
Reduction of army expenditure	92
Payment of loans	95
Military expenditure in West China, 97	95
List of foreign loans	97
Payment of loans by the provinces	100
Massacres of missionaries in 1900	102
Origin of indemnities and loans	103
Poverty of Kan-su	,,
The Yellow River	104
Payment of indemnities ...	,,
New coast defence subscriptions	108
Securities on loans	109
Russian loans	,,
British loan	110
Hongkong and Shanghai Bank loan	111
Annual payments of China from 1901 to 1943	112
French loan	,,
Native subscription loan ...	113
Payment of loans and indemnity	114
Return of Chinese loans, 1887 to 1898...	115
Payments from 1902 to 1940 ...	118
T'sen Ch'un-tsiuen's proclamation regarding Christian missions	123
Taxation in the Chinese empire	
Revenue in 1899	126
Right of taxation. Canons of taxation	127
Taxation forms	,,
Shanghai tax offices	128
Land taxation at different periods	130
Sale of titles to aid the revenue	137
Taxation of waste lands ...	,,
Change of grain tribute to silver	139
Taxation is light under the Manchus	141
Granary system	143
Tribute grain of Chekiang and Kiangsu	144
Conveyance of grain tribute to Peking has ceased	
Relation of copper and silver in its bearing in the collection of taxes	148 149
Contracting to levy taxes ...	155
Post dues or Loti-shui... ...	156
Tea tax	157
Japan land tax	160
Chinese local taxes on tea ...	162
Opium tax	,,
Sundry taxes	166
Barrier charges near Shanghai	169
Sung-kiang land tax	,,
Kiang-su taxes on grain ...	170
Tax on brokers	,,
Soochow taxation	171
Kang Yi's revision of taxes ...	,,
Tax on native opium	173
Shop tax	175
Timber yard tax	176
Distillery tax	177
Local taxes on opium	178
Tax on Chekiang wine ...	179
Shansi taxation	,,
Amoy native Customs' collection	180
Exemption from duty at Foochow	181
Revenue from salt	183
The salt administration of China	183
Early mention of salt, B. C. 600	187
Salt certificates...	188
Salt tax in the 18th century ...	,,
Commutation of salt tax to land tax	191
Salt lake in Shansi	194
Moral aspect of salt tax ...	196
Salt tax in Fukien	,,
Hwai-pei salt tax	200
Increase of salt tax	205
Salt at Tientsin	207
Salt smugglers	208
Salt in Hunan	,,
Salt wells at Hwai-pei	210
Hupei salt wells	213
Szechwen salt wells	214
Salt tax in various provinces...	215
Foreign salt if imported will cause much dissatisfaction ...	220
Contraband salt boats	221
Process for whitening salt ...	223
Chekiang salt in Kiang-su ...	224
Revenue from Likin	
Likin abolished by treaty ...	226
Origin of likin	,,
Likin in 1894	228
Szchwen Viceroy's report on likin	229
Likin as security for loan of 1898	230
Likin as guarantee for the Japanese war debt	231
Supplement	235

THE REVENUE AND TAXATION
OF THE CHINESE EMPIRE.

RED BOOK REVENUE STATISTICS.

The public accounts as they here follow are in the first instance extracted from the Red Book, a work in six volumes, privately issued each quarter with corrections and sold all over the empire, just as is the case with the *Peking Gazette*. The information contained in the Red Book and in the *Peking Gazette* is obtained from official sources, and both are virtually official. The Red Book states the amount for each city of the land and personal service tax in silver and grain, the quantity of stored grain in the granaries with the amounts of miscellaneous taxes and of salaries. Also the allowance for expenses is stated and the number of post horses.

Dr. A. Forke notices that the budget of Canton province in the Red Book of 1896 is the same as that of 1842 stated in Williams' Middle Kingdom. It appears to be the same as far back as about 1820. [Die Chinesische Finanz und Stenerwesen in the Transactions of the Oriental School of Languages. Berlin, 1900.]

The Red Book statistics which follow were then first published about eighty years ago.

MOUKDEN PROVINCE: Land, 38,708 taels; rice, 2,000,582 piculs; Banner lands rice, 32,390 piculs.

CHIHLI: Peking prefecture, Taels 154,173; land, Taels 2,334,475; miscellaneous, Taels 32,520.

KIANGSU: Land, Taels 3,116,826; miscellaneous, Taels 46,930; reed land, Taels 93,940.

ANHWEI: Land, Taels 1,718,824; miscellaneous, Taels 13,284; reed land, Taels 38,584.

SHANTUNG: Land, Taels 3,376,165; rice, etc., 353,963 piculs; salt, Taels 120,720; miscellaneous, Taels 47,890.

SHANSI: Land, Taels 2,990,675; miscellaneous, Taels 31,100.

HONAN: Land, Taels 3,164,758; rice, Taels 221,342; miscellaneous, Taels 12,650.

SHENSI: Land, Taels 1,658,700.

KANSU: Land, Taels 280.652; grain, 18,550 piculs; miscellaneous and salt, Taels 39,450.

SINKIANG: Grain, 276,051 piculs; silver, Taels 59,148.

FUKIEN: Taels 1,074,489; salt, Taels 85,470; miscellaneous, Taels 24,850.

CHEKIANG: Land, Taels 2,914,946; miscellaneous, Taels 10,650; tribute grain from Hangchou, Huchou, Kiahing, 612,720 piculs; white rice, 6,606 piculs; tribute grain of eight prefectures and salt, Taels 501,034.

KIANGSI: Land, Taels 1,878,682; miscellaneous, Taels 4,470; salt, 5,150; rice, 795,062 piculs.

HUPEI: Land, Taels 1,174,110; rice, 96,934 piculs; miscellaneous, Taels 58,780; soldiers' land, Taels 32,640; tribute conveyance tax, Taels 18,140.

HUNAN: Land, Taels 882,745; rice, 96,214 piculs; miscellaneous, Taels 30,530; soldiers' land, Taels 20,350; tribute conveyance, Taels 13,880.

SZCHUAN: Land, Taels 631,094; miscellaneous, Taels 20,520.

KUANGTUNG: Land, Taels 1,264,304; miscellaneous, Taels 5,990.

KUANGSI: Land, Taels 416,399; miscellaneous, Taels 25,880; salt, Taels 47,154.

YÜNNAN: Land, Taels 29,582; miscellaneous, Taels 127,626.

KUEICHOU: Land, Taels 101,268; miscellaneous, Taels 13,690; salt, Taels 6,234.

GROSS ANNUAL REVENUE.

Land tax ... ... Taels	29,227,402
Miscellaneous taxes	429,184
Kiangnan reed and rush tax	132,524
Hu-kuang soldiers' land tax	52,990
Hu-kuang tribute rice conveyance expenses	32,020
Peking share of salt tax	264,728
Peking prefecture special tax	154,173
Turkish province	59,148
Total,	30,352,169

In the *Shen-pao* of April 28, 1898, appeared the amount as stated in a memorial of Viceroy Liu of the land and personal service tax according to the returns of the Nanking treasurer for 1897 Taels 370,560 and of the Soochow treasurer Taels 731,373. Total Kiangsu, Taels 1,101,933.

This was more than the amount received in 1896 and 1894 and less than the amount received in 1895.

It may be noticed here that the receipts are little more than one-third of the Red Book amount as assessed by the Board of Revenue. The sum should be Taels 3,100,000. The actual receipts were Taels 1,100,000. The Viceroy adds that any sums received later he will report on a future occasion. This discrepancy between actual receipts and assessment is called 征不足額 Cheng-pu-tsu-ngo. Kang Chung-t'ang in the summer of 1899 in his memorial stated that at Soochow the discrepancy was two-tenths, 江蘇地粮比之原額常少二成, that is to say, the personal service and grain tax were together short of the assessed amount by two-tenths.

REVENUE OF EACH PROVINCE.

	Sent to Peking.	Reserved in each Province.
Chihli	Taels 2,939,941	Taels 621,811
Kiangsu	2,564,728	1,446,051
Anhuei	1,194,914	422,709
Shantung	2,730,736	691,140
Shansi	2,732,285	328,290
Honan	3,441.210	626,623
Shensi	1,344,548	265,498
Kansu	182,644	72,274
Sinkiang		
Fukien	1,055,209	288,050
Chekiang	2,287,346	687,277
Kiangsi	1,602,431	540,705
Hupei	776,173	333,543
Hunan	944,423	265,379
Szchwen	306,366	13,029
Kuangtung ...	919,307	339,143
Kuangsi	278,559	86,945
Yünnan	188,927	53,596
Kueichou	53,346	13,314
	Taels 24,313,093	Taels 7,095,378

Annual Amount of Land and Grain Revenue.

	Miscellaneous Taxes reserved.	Salt.	Peking.
Chihli ...	Taels 42,093	Taels 437,949	
Kiangsu ...	25,492		
Anhuei ...	46,611	2,085,282	
Shantung	22,711		
Shansi ...	51,844	507,028	
Honan ...	32,344		
Shensi ...	40,623		
Kansu ...	60,787		Taels 39,450
Sinkiang			
Fukien ...	27,775		85,470
Chekiang	38,437		501,034
Kiangsi ...	34,183		5,150
Hupei ...	22,554		
Hunan ...	14,813		
Szchwen ...	11,242		
Kuangtung	59,530	47,510	
Kuangsi ...	26,780		47,154
Yunnan ...	34,256		
Kueichou	13,742		9,234
	Taels 603,773		Total Taels 3,762,261

Common and white rice of Kiangsu and Chekiang ...	Total piculs	2,109,999
Common grain (usually rice) of Shantung, Honan, Kiangsi, Hupei, Hunan	Total piculs	1,563,515
Grain tribute of Shensi, Kansu, Kuangsi	Total piculs	722,227

Annual Revenue.

Shengking ... ...Taels	38,708
Chihli	3,21,168
Kiangsu	3,257,696
Anhui	1,770,692
Shantung	3,544,775
Shansi	3,021,775
Honan	3,177,408
Shensi	1,658,700
Kansu	320,102
Sinkiang	59,148
Fukien	1,184,809

Chekiang	3,426,630
Kiangsi	1,888,302
Hupei	1,283,670
Hunan	947,505
Szchwen	651,614
Kuangtung	1,270,294
Kuangsi	489,433
Yunnan	209,582
Kueichou	121,192
Total Taels	30,843,203

This has been included in previous statements. It is here tabulated to show the amount of silver actually received by the government each year to take the place of land and personal service taxes.

Silver from Native Custom Houses.

Shengking:	Shan-hai-kuan	Taels 28,200
Chihli:	Chang-kia-kou	10,000
	Tientsin Native Customs	40,460
Kiangsu:	Lung-kiang-kuan, Si-sin-kuan	33,684
	Hsü-shu	191,149
	Yang-chou	55,753
	Kua-yi	7,666
Anhui:	Huai-an	201,960
	Wuhu	194,026
	Feng-yang	79,820
Kiangsu:	Shanghai	25,516
Shantung:	Lin-ching	29,680
Shansi:	Sha-hu-kou	10,919
Shensi:	Tung-kuan	
Fukien:	Fuchou	73,549
Chekiang:	Pei-sin-kuan	122,664
	Nan-sin-kuan	26,500
	Ningpo	32,030
Kiangsi:	Kiukiang	173,880
	Kung-chou-kuan	46,471
Hupei:	King-chou	9,644
Kuangtung:	Yô-hai (Canton)	43,750
	Tai-ping	53,670
	Total Taels	1,490,991

The above amounts are from the Red Book. They are amounts fixed by the Board of Revenue.

Amount of grain tribute from Chinkiang, 431,100 piculs, sent by sea April, 1898.

Amount of grain tribute from northern Kiangsu, 133,070 piculs, should be sent north by canal April, 1898; a part of this, 30,000, was to be retained in Kiangsu. It will be used in relieving the famine. To this the Emperor added 10,000, so that the amount was reduced to 73,070 piculs in April, 1898.

Amount of Grain Tribute, A.D. 1732.

The grain tribute of Kiangsu in 1732 was 325,300 piculs. Chu-pi 硃批諭旨, ch. 36, p. 8. Soldiers' allowances were 102,200 piculs to be retained in Kiangsu for the soldiers in posts on the lower Kiang.

Special Expenditure.

When there is special occasion for expenditure at any point in the empire the Emperor orders a definite sum to be sent by the treasurers of adjoining provinces to the treasurer of the province where special expenditure is required. The expenses of a war are provided in this way.

In the year 1772, states the Tung-hua-hsü-lu, ch. 18, p. 18, a force of 60,000 soldiers was employed in Szchwen to subdue the aborigines who were in insurrection. The cost was Taels 7,127,000. At the time of writing this note more than a century ago the sum of Taels 3,500,000 still remained in camp not yet expended.

Regular Annual Expenditure.

A regulated sum is ordered by the Hu-pu as required by the Emperor to be sent by each province to Peking at certain times. The spirit of the legislation on revenue receipts and expenditure is seen in the appointment of definite amounts.

If the provincial treasurer fails to send the sum stated he is liable to punishment. The central government regulates its expenditure on these definite amounts as a basis. The required amounts of taxes are *fixed* high. In fact the receipts do not allow such large sums to be sent as are stated in the regulations. The expenditure needs to be limited from time to time accordingly.

In an extensive empire it is convenient to regulate the expenditure in Peking with a knowledge of the revenues which will be received from the provinces. This led to the adoption of the principle that the central government shall appoint the amount to be contributed to the revenue from each province.

BOARD OF REVENUE STATISTICS.

The Board of Revenue is the Chinese treasury, the centre of the national revenue and expenditure. It is called 戶部 Hu-pu, because it takes account of the population, 戶口 Hu-kou. In the Chow dynasty the management of the revenue was in the hands of the 天官 Tien-kwan, the heavenly officers. They, the revenue officers, belong to the fourth quarter of the year and make up their accounts then. These accounts were not publicly known till lately. Yet much information regarding the revenue is contained in historical works published at different periods.

The employment of Western foreigners in collecting the revenue has led to the periodical publication of the statistics of that portion of the revenue which passed through their hands. The regular publication of revenue tables is now in course of adoption in all the departments of State on the ground that it is usual in foreign countries, and some important advantages are secured by it.

The native Customs' revenue should be Taels 3,661,000. It is now short of this by one-fifth. This annual loss is represented by Chinese native writers as due to the effect of the foreign customs and the lekin combined. At least it has occurred since the collection of these duties.

The Canton contingent was Taels 899,000. It is now given as Taels 531,284. Mr. Jamieson * states it from the *Peking Gazette* as 156,000. It had recovered considerably in 1893, as the statistics now printed show.

Mr. Jamieson notes that the Shanghai native Customs' collection was only Taels 33,800 in 1893. In our statistics the entry is Taels 121,287, including the collection in six Custom

* The Revenue and Expenditure of the Chinese Empire, by Geo. Jamieson, Esq., H. B. M.'s Consul, 1897.

houses in the province of Kiangsu. The amount of the native Shanghai Customs' collection is not given in the treatise from which the statistics which follow are taken. This book is called 光緒會計錄, Collected Accounts of the Government Revenue and Expenditure in the Reign of Kuang Sü.

In the month of November of the year 1896 Li Hi-sheng published the treatise containing particulars of Chinese revenue at the present time. In the preface he remarks that in China the Sung dynasty spent most upon its army. Among foreign countries Russia has the most expensive army, China now has more than a million soldiers and volunteers in her army.

Those who in late years have done most to increase the revenue from grain were Tso Wen-siang in Hunan, Hu Lin-i in Hupei, Tso Wen-siang in Chekiang, Li Hung-chang in Kiangsu, and Li Ping-heng in Shantung. Several tens of thousands of taels were thus added to the revenue, and at the same time there was an equal gain to the people, because unscrupulous officials were not allowed to enrich themselves.

The lekin revenue has of late years somewhat suddenly diminished to the extent of five or six million taels. The reason of this is what foreigners pay for half duty paid transit passes. These are brought by Chinese traders. Only Chungching and Canton collect lekin dues at a less rate than the transit passes. On this account Sir Robert Hart proposed to allow native traders to receive transit passes. This the Yamên refused, fearing that the lekin collection would suffer. At present foreigners are allowed to manufacture native goods, and they pay five taels on goods valued at one hundred taels.*

* The native author is inaccurate here. Piece goods pay duty according to length and class of goods. Grey and white shirtings pay eight candareens a piece. Drills and jeans pay one mace, etc. The limits of length and width are stated in the tariff. Machinery from abroad pays five per cent ad valorem. Also leather, ship's lights, iron pans, medicated wines, iron nails, metal trusses to bind silk bales, musical boxes, pearl barley, shark's fins, refuse cocoons, Chinese soap, tea chests, telescopes, watches, softwood beams, camel's wool, etc., pay duty at five per cent ad valorem.

This is *lo-ti-shui;* and it exempts from lekin. This in the opinion of the author accounts for a heavy decline in the lekin annual receipts.

The revenue in the reign of Shun Chih was Taels 14,000,000. Last century it became about Taels 42,000,000. Now it is about Taels 80,000,000.

SECTION FIRST.—GOVERNMENT REVENUE AND EXPENDITURE, 1893.

REVENUE, TAELS 83,110,008.

The sources of revenue are the ordinary taxes, such as land tax, grain, and salt; the new taxes including the foreign Customs and lekin and additional contributions.

In the *China Mail,* October, 1898, it is said that the ordinary taxes might be easily raised to 400 million taels. If other financial reforms were adopted, it might be raised to 700 millions.

In the same journal it is said that in 1887 Taels 30,000,000 were set apart for the creation of a navy. The battle ships *Ting-yuen, Wei-yuen, Chi-yuen, Chen-yuen,* and *King-yuen* were paid for from this money. Later on it was decided to spend Taels 30,000,000 on the construction of railways. The railway built with this money was carried from Tientsin to Shanhaikwan. It is now being gradually completed to Moukden.

Total receipts 常例, ordinary 新增, additional 無關歲額 and extra tax	Taels	83,110,008
Total expenditure, ordinary, additional 補支, supplemental payments and 豫支 advances ...		73,433,329
Credit balance		9,676,679

1. Receipts from Ordinary Taxes.

地丁 Land and personal service	Taels 23,329,533.9.4.7
雜賦 Miscellaneous taxes	1,732,318.7.2.8
Gold Taels 24.	
Rents of State property—lands, ... houses, etc.	721,503.7.5.2
Grain tax collected in silver ...	4,447,763.6.7.7
Hao-hsien silver exchange tax ...	3,036,735.9.0.2
This tax is partly to meet loss in exchange and in part to supplement expected deficit in the treasurer's accounts. It is an old Ming dynasty tax.	
Salt tax	7,679,828.9.9.5
Native customs' collection	2,844,374.8.2.9
	Taels 43,792,059.8.3.0

2. Receipts by Newly-imposed Taxes under two Heads.

(Lekin and Foreign Customs, 1893).

Lekin total collection	Taels 14,277,304.2.3
Foreign Customs' collection... ...	16,801,179.7.4.2

3. Receipts by Contributions or Subscriptions.

Subscriptions to purchase titles ...	Taels 4,090,171.0.4.1
Postponed payment of taxes ...	2,093,992.5.1
Disbanding troops and other reductions in the expenditure of each province cause an increase in the amount received, that is, an unexpended balance in hand is credited to the Board	2,055,301.4.2.2
Total revenue, silver	Taels 83,110,008.7.7.9

REGULAR EXPENDITURE OF CHINA IN 1893, SILVER.

Imperial tombs	Taels 92,219.3.5.1
Palace	280,000.0.0.0
Provincial sacrifices	255,112.6.8.7
Ceremonial functions in provinces. Imperial Household, Banqueting Court in Peking are included ...	45,069.4.8.8
Pensions in Peking and in the provinces	3,845,116.0.0.7

Examinations	113,852.3.1.2
Army and army horses	18,495,269.8.5.8
Post courier service	1,830,905.8.9.4
Bursaries to undergraduates ...	117,113.6.1.7
Rewards and charities to widows and orphans, etc.	1,463,897.8.6.1
Repairs of buildings	3,300,316.2.1.1
Purchases	4,122,983.9.5.9
Imperial factories	1,400,388.4.5.7
Salaries	5,144,951.7.4 8
Miscellaneous expenditure	300,616.2.0.2
常例 Total expenditure, silver	39,807,914.6.5.5

New Expenditure.

Army Boards in the provinces ...Taels	17,069,920.3.3.6
Expenditure of native custom houses and boards	3,181,741.0.6.1
Paid to foreigners for articles purchased	3,598,449.8.2.2
新增 Total	23,850,111.2 2.1

Additional Expenditure ... ...Taels	5,315,671.7.2.1
Advances	1,881,435.2.5.7
Total additional, with advances	7,197,106.9.7.8

Maintenance of Peking departments, Taels	2,578,196.2.7.1
New expenditure, with additional and advances	23,850,111.2.2.1 7,197,106.9.7.8
Regular expenditure	39,807,914.6.5.5
Total expenditure, 1893	73,433,329.1.2.7
Board of Revenue balance in hand, silver	9,676,679.6.5.2
Total revenue, 1893	83,110,008.7.7.9

Revenue collected in 1893 in copper cash	5,050,568	strings	744 cash
	719,779	„	109
	4,257,529	cash	
	3,208,633	strings	219

Expenditure in copper cash...	4,466,879 strings	189
	4,823,179 „	974
	3,285,017 „	117

Grain revenue	4,493,075 piculs	34 pints
Grain distributed from granaries,	4,239,624 „	2,557
Remainder in granaries,	253,450 piculs	93

Hay and straw received	4,822,612 bundles
ditto	19,599 catties
Distributed	8,191,129 bundles
ditto	19,599 catties
Remainder in store,	3,368,517 bundles

Old silver remainders in the Board treasury ... ...Taels	3,421,254
Four-tenths of foreign duties ...	232,459.5.6.6
Coast and frontier defence	3,288,967.1.9.4
Army expenses	3,670,000
Total of the above four items, Taels	10,612,681

Remainder resulting from saving by change of scales ... ...Taels	939,456.8.0.7

CHIHLI.

長蘆 Lutae salt	Taels	88,411.7.0.7
do. army		437,157.7.8.2
Salaries returned to officers		4,000
Red paper and stationery generally...		9,218.4.7.4
Ha-ta-men duties		100,864.4.8.2
Pa-keu duties		436.6.2.2
Ta-tsz-ken		145.3.5.4
Kwei-hwa-ch'eng reductions ...		321.4.0.2
Sha-hu-ken		16,847.8.5.5
Urhada		1,322.4.1.0
Dolonor		14,163.0.6.1
San-tso-t'a		1,580.3.1.6
Tientsin customs		66,051.2.3.8
do. army of Peking		66,034.6.7.6
Shan-hai-kwan reductions		9,515.7.1.5
Additional military salaries		12,000
Total revenue received from Chihli by the Board of Revenue	Taels	827,171.0.9.4

Shantung.

The Board received in silver revenue	Taels	1,143,702.1.2.4
Peking military expenditure ...		848,318.8.1.0
Ku-pen additional army expenditure		60,000
Salt		210,000
Chefoo Customs' troops		25,000
Lin-ch'ing customs		3,830,000.3.1.4
Remainder left in Shantung after deductions.	Total Taels	3,829,616.9.9.0

Honan.

The Board received in silver revenue	Taels	320,136.1.2.6
Peking military expenditure ...		84,000
Empress jubilee contribution ...		29,200
Silver received for grain		160,000
Duties		11,936.1.2.6
Ku-pen pay for troops		20,000
Chefoo Customs' contribution as an addition to salaries		15,000

Shansi.

Silver revenue received	Taels	1,088,887.7.9.4
Peking military expenditure ...		771,431.0.0.7
Province military expenditure ...		115,000
Additional bannermen expenditure...		200,000
Tax on native opium		2,456.7.8.7

Shensi.

Peking military expenditure ...	Taels	109,627.7.9.3

Anhwei.

Silver revenue received	Taels	983,038.4.4.9
Peking military expenditure ...		313,595.9.9.2
Silver for grain tribute		130,000
Additional returned salaries to officers		10,530.1.5.2
Wuhu Customs		311,236.3.2.1
Foreign opium		163,826.1.4.6
Feng-yang customs		53,849.8.4.0

Note.—In September, 1898, Anhwei sent 80,000 taels of silver packed in wood to Shensi and Kansu to pay troops in those provinces. See *Hu-pao*, September 8th, 1898.

KIANGSU.

Silver revenue received ... ... Taels	2,601,671.4.7.1
Peking military expenditure ...	1,011,595.6.4.5
Province military expenditure ...	45,000
Additional returned salaries to officers	8,250
do (probably sent from Soochow)	125,476.2.7.7
Salt subscription	500,000
Salt tax	370,000
Shanghai Customs' additional returned salaries to officers	10,000
Shanghai Customs' duties	148,642 7.9.1
Chinkiang Customs' additional military salaries	42,500
Returned salaries to officers... ...	1,250
Customs	40,000
Yangchow Customs	30,000
Hwai-an Customs	120,000
By grain superintendent silver sent in place of grain	26,456.7.5.8
Nanking bannermen added pay ...	222,500

KIANGSI.

Silver revenue received ... ... Taels	1,422,621.3.2.1
Peking military service	400,000
Province pay to troops	19,663.2.9.9
Silver in place of grain tribute ...	690,000
Kiukiang Customs	132,445.7.1.4
Kung-chou native Customs	40,512.3.0.8
Lekin	50,000

CHEKIANG.

Silver revenue received ... ... Taels	1,107,701.4.9.7
Peking military expenditure ...	633,745.3.4.1
Salt	220,000
Ningpo foreign Customs	152,193.7.8.1
Silver for grain	19,226.6.0.9
Extra salaries for military	66,000

WENCHOW.

Foreign Customs ... ... Taels	16,535.7.6.6

FUKIEN.

Silver ... ... Taels	935,420.7.5.7
Troops of the province	65,000

Peking military expenditure ...		115,500
Salt		108,654.3.2.9
Foochow Customs for Peking military expenditure		266,411.4.8.4
Foochow Customs' duties		192,000
Additional for military expenditure		26,000
Foochow copper freight		10,366.5.2.0
Duty on tea		151,488.4.2.4

Hupei.

Silver revenue received	Taels	1,472,589.4.2
Peking military expenditure ...		803,237.0.3
Military expenditure in the province		65,000
Silver for tribute grain		95,352 3.9
Hankow Customs' duties		154,000
Hankow Customs by economies ...		5,000
Added salaries for military officers...		200,000
Salt and lekin		150,000

Hunan.

Silver revenue received	Taels	67,940.6.7.8
Peking military expenditure ...		430,490.9.1.1
Troops in the province		60,000
Silver for tribute grain		148,915.1.6.7
Salt and lekin		40,000

Canton.

Silver revenue received	Taels	1,241,846.2.0.2
Peking military expenditure ...		230,000
Troops in the province		120,000

In the *China Mail*, October, 1898, it is said that the Nankin revenue amounts to $240,000 a year. The Emperor receives $20,000.

Bannermen	Taels	118,489.3.8.3
Salt		305,165
Additional pensions and troops ...		117,800
Canton foreign Customs		224,000
Tai-p'ing Customs' (Macao) Peking military expenditure		30,000
Additional returned salaries to troops		43,600
Macao Customs		5,279.1.8.2

SZCHWEN.

Silver revenue received ... ...Taels	572,397.8.1.0	
Peking military expenditure ...		431,600
Troops of the province		60,000
Additional returned salaries to troops		2,400
Chungking Customs		78,397.8.0.1

MOUKDEN PROVINCE.

Silver revenue received ... ...Taels	226,525.0.6.8	
Economies		120,044.0.2.5
Salt and Lekin		106,481.0.4.3

Total from Provinces, Taels 14,732,742.9.9.5

Received four-tenths of the foreign Customs' revenue from	
Kiukiang ... ...Taels	126,086.3.2 4
Chinkiang	49,324.4.7.2
Total, Taels	175,410.7.9.6

COAST AND FRONTIER EXPENDITURE.

Kiangsu ... ...Taels	70,000
Kiangsi	130,000
Hankow Customs	70,000
Shanghai Customs	100,000
Chekiang	170,000
Kiukiang Customs	50,000
Anhwei	150,000
Shantung	170,000
Canton Customs	120,000
Foochow Customs	100,000
Hwai-an salt	120,000
Hunan	80,000
Szchwen	260,000
Canton	80,000
Hupei	90,000
Fukien	40,000
Shansi	100,000
Kung-chou Customs	9,597.1.3.7
Total,	1,909,597.1.3 7

MONEY FOR ARMY EXPENDITURE.

Fukien	Taels 80,000
Kiangsi	150,000
Canton Customs	120,000
Chekiang	460,000
Foochow Customs	120,000
Canton	200,000
Kiangsu	20,000
Anhwei	40,000
Hankow Customs	240,000
Shanghai Customs	140,000
Nanking	20,000
Total, Taels	1,590,000

SUBSCRIPTIONS, MISCELLANEOUS DUTIES, AND OTHER MISCELLANEOUS SUMS.

Miscellaneous sums in various departments	Taels 120,227.8.0.6
Subscriptions...	270,996
New subscriptions for coast defence	93,416
Expenses for food, etc.	136,370.0.6.7
Returned from the Granary Yamên	12,400
A sum intended to pay for copper and lead, but transferred to the regular expenditure fund to be used in paying the Peking troops	500,000
Silver transferred from the grain commutation amount to regular expenditure fund	300,000
Silver transferred from the regular expenditure fund to be used in buying copper and lead ...	1,212,608.9.2.5
Silver of the coast and frontier defence fund transferred to the regular expenditure fund ...	600,000
Silver transferred from the regular expenditure fund to fund for congratulating the Dowager-Empress on the occasion of her jubilee ...	132,024.7
Salt subscription of Hwai-an transferred to the regular expenditure fund	100,000
Total, Taels	3,481,043.4.9.7

Total sum received in the provinces. Taels 21,888,791.4.2.7

BOARD OF REVENUE TREASURY DISBURSEMENTS.

Western and eastern Imperial tombs Taels	49,144.2.9 8
Troops	1,708.8.0.0
Purchases and work—Chung-hwa-kung and Household	1,484,389.4.1.6
Purchases and work—Porcelain tiles	77,608.6.1.6
Palace—Amount forwarded by Board	280,000
Outlay—Household. Amount petitioned for and forwarded ...	960,000
Salaries—Household expenses ...	45,975
Purchases and work—Moukden felt and thread 盛京*	5,539.9.6.2
Imperial clan records	36,000
Grand Secretariat—Pensions, Chinese	123,215 1.1.9
Additional pensions	1,000
Cabinet and salaries of the keepers of the three treasuries	31,316.1.4.4
Cabinet rewards	3,000
Guards	10,000
Board of office salaries	10,000
Colour and silk and satin treasuries; instead of colours and silk, silver was given	606,927.0.4.7
Board of Ceremonies salaries ...	3,500
Board of Ceremonies rewards to Corea	3,186
Board of War courier service—Hay and beans	12,266.4.4.7
Board of Punishments—Return of expenditure 奏銷	6,000
Board of Works	147,180
Board of Works—Powder materials	30,723.4.6.5
Li-fan-yuen Tartar dependencies rewards	55,699
Tartar Li-fan-yuen courier service ...	85,000
do. pensions of Mongol Princes and Dukes	130,907.5
do. Lamas	29,107.4.6.5
Additional to Lamas...	1,420

* Sheng-king is the Manchu southern province. The prefecture named Feng-tien-fu is the capital of the province.

Additional straw and beans, Li-fan-yuen courier service	15,952.4.1.6
Metropolitan drilled soldiers ...	15,600
Board of Sacrifices	10,627.2.8.2
Banqueting Court	1,600
do.	32,941.6.9.5
Stables, pensions, east and west wings	1,380
Stables, pensions, east and west wings	25,395
Imperial academy	8,400
do. banner schools	32,000
Carriage repository	214,510.8.9.6
Chief of police	579,453.3.9.5
do. silver for grain	6,566.6.7.5
Carriage depository	5,000
Canals	40,814.1.0.4
Tsung-li Yamên expenses	9,800
Navy Board "	500
	1,000
New coast defence subscriptions ...	275,559
Board for printing the statutes—Paper	10,000
Household wheat commuted for silver	19,600
Eunuchs of the Eight Banners ...	63,500.4.2.0
Stables, pensions	442.5.0.0
do. straw	44,000
do. troops	12,759
Workmen in Metropolitan mints ...	196,216.1.9.2
Eight Banners' pensions of Princes and Dukes	878,700.5.4.8
Metropolitan mints	39,883.5.8.4
Eight Banners' salaries	19,111.2.5
Army rewards	32,599
Eight Banners' military expenses ...	4,675,969.7.0.8
Iho* park rewards	57,142.5.0.0
Eight Banners' rice commuted to silver	1,108,441.7.1.4
Shen-chi-ying pay for troops ...	811,560
Arms	12,000
Chihli drilled troops	579,671.1.0.0
Chahar pensions, officers	57,694.8.6.9
do. soldiers	209,484
Mi-yün troops, officers	25,439.1.4.9
do. soldiers	61,275.1.8.3

* Colloquial name Wan-show-shan. This park has for the time taken the place of Yuen-ming-yuen as an Imperial residence.

Jehol, officers	65,390.4.9.9
soldiers	107,556.2.5.3
Horses	12,465.8.0.0
Shun-tien-fu and Chihli rewards ...	480,000
„ charities	145,000
„ soup kitchens	2,000
Feng-ch'en-yuen park expenditure ...	32,000
Purchase of copper and lead for coining	1,718,094.6.1.1
Appropriation for purchase of ditto...	1,258,094.6.0.0
Hwai-an salt contractors' subscription	100,000
Grain commuted to silver	300,000
Imperial kitchen	120,000
Board of Works	13,793.1.0.3
Buildings—Wages for work done ...	39,392
Amur province addition	22,476
Empress-Dowager's jubilee	129,813.5.1.0
Total of the above 81 items, Taels	18,928,686.6.3.7

As an illustration of the above payment to Jehol, it may be mentioned here that in the *Sin-wen-pau* of September 11th, 1898, the Jehol military authorities are said to have sent an officer to Tientsin to take charge of Taels 15,000 of silver forwarded by the Viceroy of Fukien and Chekiang from Foochow. It was taken from the foreign Customs' revenue at that port and was entrusted to two native banking firms 蔚泰厚 Yu-t'ai-hoa, 源豐潤 Yuen-feng-jun.

Mi-yun-hsien is 140 *li* north, north-east of Peking.

The Chahar tribes are Mongols. They are scattered over the grass land beyond the Great Wall north and north-west of Peking.

Kirin drilled troops (from $\frac{4}{10}$ths foreign Customs' receipts) ...	280,000
Frontier defence—Pei-yang pay to troops	440,000
Kirin frontier pay to troops ...	836,572.8.3.0
Passed to regular expenditure account	600,000
Amur province pay to drilled troops	330,000
Navy Board subscriptions	1,369.1.9.0
Total of the above six items, Taels	2,487,942.0.2.0

Provision for troops' fund, Shun-tien-fu charity	Taels	100,000
Chihli, river repairs		100,000
Railway expenditure		700,000
Si-chih-men stone road*		300,000
Wan-shou-sz monastery buildings* ...		134,739.9.0.1
Carriage repository, silver for boots and shoes for the army ...		40,000
Total of the above six items	Taels	1,374,739.9.0.1
Total expenditure		22,791,368.5.5.8

BALANCE REMAINING IN THE BOARD TREASURY.

Regular revenue, grain commuted to silver, and various items ...	Taels	2,706,355.7.9.1
Four-tenths of foreign Customs' receipts		127,870.3.6.2
Frontier expenditure		2,990,622.3.1.1
Military "		3,885,260.0.9.9
Total		9,710,108.5.6.3

Remainder resulting from a saving of six per cent. in expenditure by change of scales to the Ching-p'ing 京平	Taels	586,992.3.6.2

SECTION SECOND.—GOVERNMENT RECEIPTS.

RECEIPTS IN SILVER.

LAND AND PERSONAL SERVICE.

Shengking	Taels	31,240.6.4
Fengtien		75,496.4.2.1.7.4
Chihli		2,150,838.0.4.6.8.7.3
Shantung		2,986,895.1.9.5
Honan		2,813,414.8.9.9
Shansi		2,751,792.7.4.7.7
Shensi		1,314,130.9.3.3

* The 西直門 road leads from Peking to I-ho-yuen. The Empress when going there by this road stops for luncheon at Wan-shou-sz, which is half the distance.

Kansu	204,180.3.6.9.1
Anhwei	984,009.7.7.3
Kiangsu	1,700,214.4.3.5
Kiangsi	1,291,288.1.5.3
Chekiang	1,958,683.6.1.8.7.5.5.2
Fukien	1,006,727.7.3.6.9
Hupei	862,673.1.6.1
Hunan	1,064,531.4.7.1
Canton	916,788.3.6.8.8
Kwangsi	334,308.4.3.7.6
Szchwen	669,101.0.0.2.0
Kweichou	49,418.0.0.8.0
Kirin	127,892.7.3.9.6.4.1
Suiyuench'eng	35,907.7.9
Total Taels	23,329,533.9.4.7.1.0.9.2

MISCELLANEOUS TAXES 雜賦.

Shengking	Taels 133,271.9.3.8
Fengtien	387,748.0.3.3.7.5.7.7
Chihli	102,506.8.1.4.9.0.1
Shantung	14,946.1
Honan	154,897.3.3.4
Shansi	67,539.9.9.7
Shensi	30,755.1.9.4
Kansu	22,164.6.8.6
*(Gold tax, Tls. 24.)	
Anhwei...	40,333.1.1.5
Kiangsu	193,492.8.4.6.7
Kiangsi...	69,809.3.1.2
Chekiang	68,852.5.8.6
Fukien	51,130.0.8.2
Hupei	16,880.7.8.9
Hunan	7,333.1.3.9
Canton	10,431.5
Kwangsi	31,328.9.3.1.6.7.5
Szchwen	194,593.5.0.8.4.3.6
Kweichow	1,928.3.7.3
Kirin	99,949.2.5.2.4.5.8.4
Heilungkiang	32,425.1.9.6.2
Total Taels	1,732,318.7.2.9.1.2.8.1
Gold tax, Taels	24

* Probably this came from Mahommedan gold hunters.

RENTS AND PROFITS.

Under this heading are included lands, produce, and houses which pay rents on account of their being owned by the State as confiscated or otherwise.

Shengking	Taels	41,545.9.8.4
Fengtien		84,950.9.0.2.6.7.6
Chihli		329,527.1.4.7.7.4.2.9
Honan		3,653.1.4.0.9
Shansi		26,984.1.7.5
Shensi		12,417.4.3.4.5
Kansu		4,995.2.3.4
Anhwei		287.7.5.6
Kiangsu		30,269.6.5.3.3
Kiangsi		1,100.4.8.7
Chekiang		15,488.7.8.7.5.1.5
Fukien		8,738.7.5.2
Hupei		1,147.9.2.2.6.9.5
Hunan		513.6.3.5
Kwangtung		25,356.2.2.4.8 8
Kwangsi		1,449.4.7.3
Szchwen		10,666.5.0 8.8
Kirin		111,134.7.8.5.2.2
Suiyuench'eng		11,275.7.4.8
	Total Taels	721,503.7.5.2.2.2.8.9

SHENGKING 盛京. The Moukden commandant as Tsung-tu receives a salary of Taels 8,000. The Vice-Presidents of the five boards under him receive Taels 300 each. There is no board of civil office at Moukden. The governor, under the Manchu commandant, is the Feng-tien-fu-yin. This higher kind of prefect, 府尹 Fu-yin, receives a salary of Taels 6,000. The Peking and Moukden Fu-yin are the only two in the empire. There is a Manchu commandant at Kirin who discharges the duties of governor. There is another who presides over the Hei-lung-kiang province, and is also governor. The Shengking military commandant is also Tsung-tu of the three provinces.

Revenue from Grain commuted to Silver.

Shengking	... ... Taels	8,151.7.4.8
Fengtien	... ...	1,001.3.5.8.1.0.3
Chihli...	... ...	18,632.7.3.9
Shantung	... ...	87,139.7.1.2
Honan	... ...	439,897.0.0.5
Shansi	... ...	6,058.7.1.0.9
Shensi...	... ...	15,918.0.6.5
Anhwei	... ...	517,578.0.2.9.3
Kiangsu	... ...	786,785.7.2.5
Kiangsi	... ...	880,510.1.2.6
Chekiang	... ...	743,922.6.7.2.2
Hupei...	... ...	512,318.1.2.2.2.7
Hunan	... ...	286,221.1.9.4.4
Kuangsi	... ...	33,090.3.7.1.2
Szchwen	... ...	754.7.6.5
Kweichou	... ...	28,135.0.1.4
Kirin ...	... ...	1,052.9.9
Heilungkiang	... ...	75,260.1.8.2.4.2.9.5
Suiyuench'eng	... ...	5,335.0.5.7.8.5
	Total Taels	4,447,763.5.8.7.6.5.2.5

Melting and Surplus Tax.

Fengtien	... ... Taels	52,474.6.6.2.8.9
Chihli	... ...	274,266.0.0.0.4.0.7.3
Shantung	... ...	429,567.5.5.0.7
Honan	... ...	353,729.8.4.7
Shansi	... ...	344,315.7.0.8.1
Shensi	... ...	193,889.7.1.5
Kansu	... ...	30,749.6.4.7.1
Anhwei	... ...	120,060.7.3.6
Kiangsu	... ...	180,140.9.7
Kiangsi	... ...	145,422.0.7.5
Chekiang	... ...	124,060.6.9.6.2.5.2
Fukien	... ...	145,052.4.9.2.2
Hupei	... ...	98,409.3.1.9
Hunan	... ...	109,573.4.0.5.8
Canton	... ...	198,808.1.1.6.9.3.2
Kwangsi	... ...	32,481.7.6.9.1
Szchwen	... ...	175,220.3.2.0.7.7.9.8
Kweichou	... ...	20,932.4.4.7
Kirin	... ...	6,179.5.5
Suiyuen	... ...	1,437.7.4.6
	Total Taels	3,036,772.7.7.5.2.6.1.1

Salt Revenue.

Chihli...	Taels	851,223.3.5.2
Shantung		202,116.0.2.1
Honan		1,884.6.9.6
Shensi		15,627.5.6.2
Kansu		9,219.7.9.6
Kiangsu		4,185,292.7.3.9.8.5
Kiangsi		30.
Chekiang		357,512.7.3.0.7.5.2.8
Hunan		93,682.9.0.3
Canton		676,974.8.2.2.8.1.4
Kuangsi		72,979.9.2.7.2.9.3.3
Szchwen		823,670.9.1.7.1.5.4.6
Yunnan		389,613.5.2.7.4.0.0.0
Total	Taels	7,679,828.9.9.5.2.6.4.7

Native Customs' Collection.

Fengtien	Taels	118,789 3.0.2
Chihli...		351,165.8.2.7.9.7.4.5
Shantung		119,160.5.9.2
Shansi		25,822.2.6.5
Anhwei		230,300.1.3.3.7
Kiangsu		121,287.9.1.7.2
Kiangsi		355,171.9.5.2.5
Chekiang		33,778.9.3 3
Fukien		193,408.9.4.7
Hupei...		302,863.4.6.3.3
Hunan		16,964.6.7.6
Kuangtung		531,284.2.8.4
Kuangsi		178,130.8.3.9
Szchwen		72,076.8.6.3.5.7.6
Yunnan		90,576.2.2
Kirin		81,255.9 6.9 9.2.2.4
Suiyuen		22,336.6.4.3.3
Total	Taels	2,844,374.8.2.9.4.7.2.9

This amount { by the Hweitien should be Taels 4,500,000
by the Board Regulations Taels 3,661,000 }

Total of the above seven tables of taxes ... } Taels 43,792,059.8.3.2.6.9.9

LEKIN COLLECTION.

Shengking	Taels	674.9.2.7
Fengtien		535,546.0.0.5.9.9
Chihli		276,299.3.0.7.6.2.2.7
Shantung		166,523·7.0.5.5
Honan		74,152.0.6.3
Shansi		192,342.5.4.3
Shensi		297,991.1.5.5.7
Kansu		294,117.5.5.5.7
Anhwei		410.504.2.5.0.5
Kiangsu		2,132,935.8.3.3.3.4.2
Kiangsi		1,079,000.2.2.8.5
Chekiang		1,925,079.6.5.6.2.8.3.5
Fukien...		1,328,167.6.2.8
Hupei		1,044,166.5.3.3.4.9.3.4
Hunan...		869,832.5.2.9.1
Canton...		1,676,800.1.6.7.6.9
Kuangsi		519,478.8.1.5
Szchwen		1,074,684.0.9.7.1
Yunnan		252,394.7.0.7.3
Kueichou		126,612.5.2.5.3
	Total Taels	14,277,304.2.3.5.1.2.1.6

FOREIGN CUSTOMS' COLLECTION.

Fengtien	Taels	489,543.5.9.2.1.0.1.7
Chihli		703,747.7.5.0.8.8.0.4
Shantung		331,161.7.6.8
Shansi (Russian trade) ...		1,108.9.6
Kansu (Russian trade) ...		177.4.0.8.5
Anhwei		630,870.1.9.6
Kiangsu		6,789.943.6.0.6
Kiangsi		1,031,531.1.7.2
Chekiang		1,480,472.5.7.5.1
Fukien		2,846,485.3.0.7
Hupei		2,305,287.9.0.1
Kuangsi		10,252.8.6.8
Szchwen		179,188.4.5
Suiyuench'eng (Russian trade)		1,408.1.8.7.5
	Total Taels	16,801,179.7.4.2.0.8.2.1

These, added together, give for Lekin and Foreign Customs	Total Taels	31,078,483.9.7.2.2.0.3.7

SUBSCRIPTIONS.

(N.B.—The Amount is fixed by the Board of Revenue.)

Board of Revenue treasury ...	Taels	3,481,043.4.9.7
Chihli		15,938.4.1.8.0.5
Honan		29,475.1.4.2
Shansi...		14,227.4.3.2
Shensi		1,641.2.9.5
Kansu		52,062.4.1.9.3
Anhwei		2,994.1.5.9
Kiangsu		63,905.8.3.1.5.6.1.2
Kiangsi		39,996.1.1.6
Chekiang		332.5.8.9
Fukien		250,019.3.8
Hupei...		16,409.3.4.5
Hunan		611.7 5.5
Canton		76,056.1.6.1.6
Kuangsi		1,264.4.1.9
Szchwen		20,715.4.2.5.6.2.2
Yunnan		18,700
Kueichow		1,253
Suiyuench'eng		3,523.8.3.5
Total Subscriptions		4,090,170.2.2 0.1.3 3.2

Money for special objects, such as repairs of the Yellow River embankments, are met by levying it upon rich salt farmers or other men having large property.

POSTPONED TAXES.

Fengtien	Taels	14,290.9.1.3.6.3.0.1
Chihli		91,526.8.1.3.7.7.9
Shantung		346,892.7.3.0
Honan...		95,502.6.2.9
Shansi...		224,956.0.3.7.1
Shensi		11,857.7.2.4.5
Kansu		1.373.1.9.8
Anhwei		97,326.9.8.4
Kiangsu		192,032.7.1.1.2.8
Kiangsi		65,977.1.6.3
Chekiang		388,861.1.2.6
Fukien		16,127.5.0.8.8
Hupei		148,882.9.5.7.5
Hunan...		17,689.8.4.1.7

Canton	177,015.1.0.5.3.5.8
Kuangsi	19,479.1.0.4.3.9.3.5
Szchwen	79,844.5.0.7
Kueichow	100,807.8.1
Suiyuench'eng	3,547.6.4.5
Total, Taels	2,093,992.5.1.0.3.0.2.6

PROVINCIAL SAVINGS DRAWN ON BY THE BOARD.

Shengking ... ... Taels	112,793.4.4.3
Fengtien	19,136.3.8.2
Chihli	27,342.0.8.2.9.4.8.5
Shantung	58,749.2.9.3.8.3.3
Honan	276,989.2.3.6.5.6
Shansi	257,705.8.4.7.8
Shensi	161,462.8.0.6.3.4
Kansu	273,448.5.5
Anhwei	58,304.2.2.4.6
Kiangsu	125,954.0.1.4.3.2.4.9
Kiangsi	5,152.0.3.2
Chekiang	20,816.6.8.9
Fukien	113,693.6.3.1.4
Hupei	56,088.2.3.8.6.7.7
Hunan	49,125.1.3.5
Canton	19,778.3.5.5.2
Kuangsi	35,842.9.6.8.3.5
Szchwen	82,352.6
Kueichou	20,372.8.4.9.4.2
Kirin	274,094.7.4.9.9.7.4
Heilungkiang	5,903.9.0.0.0.7.0.8
Suiyuench'eng	194.3.9.1.4.8
Total, Taels	2,055,301.4.2.2.7.7.0.4

When reductions are made in expenditure in any province the amount not expended is a surplus on which the Board can draw. The amounts in the preceding table are the amounts thus drawn.

The total of the preceding three tables—(1) subscriptions, (2) deferred taxes, and (3) reductions in expenditure, amounts to Taels 8,239,464.9.7.4.2.0.6.2

The three totals—regular taxes, new duties, and additional amounts, *i.e.*, Ch'ang-li, Yang-k'wan, with Lekin and the three tables just entered, amount in all to Taels 83,110,008.7.7.9.0.1.9.8.

MONEYS RECEIVED FOR LOANS IN THE PROVINCES.

Chihli	Taels	799.4.2.3
Shantung		20,037.0.5.0.2.4.0.8
Honan		503.5.2.6.8
Kiangsu		155,237.5.4.6.1.0.8.5
Kiangsi...		182,462.1.3.2
Fukien		781.4.5.4.4
Hunan		125,134.9.8
Suiyuench'eng		1,300.3.0 0.7
Total received for loans in the above eight provinces	Taels	486,256.4.1.3.2.4.9.3

These loans are made from public money in one province to another province. Advances are made by the treasurer before the right time. In such cases the amounts advanced have to be returned.

EXPENDITURE ON THE ARMY.

Fengtien	Taels	1,679,724.3.2.7.5.1.8.2
Chihli		3,651,126.4.5.1.1.2.2.7
Shantung		827,431.4.9.2.0.1.3.6
Honan...		462,312.1.8.6.5.7.9.1
Shansi...		187,248.5.1.9
Shensi		483,638.6.0.2
Kansu...		820,144.7.5.4.5
Anhwei		448,953.2.3.0.4.5.9.5
Kiangsu		3,901,036.8.0.3 2.7.1.9
Chekiang		903,921.2.9.9.0.8.6
Fukien		1,167,970.2.9.9.6
Canton		993,423.1.5
Kuangsi		827,089.2.3.9.3.6
Szchwen		32,027.2.1.9.0.4.5
Kueichou		683,872.7.6.8.5.8
	Total, Taels	17,069,920.3.3.6.9.1.2

Receipts under the head Po 撥 Shou 收. Instead of being sent direct to the Board they are paid to another province by order of the Board.

Shengking	Taels	176,913.4.8.6
Fengtien		553,742.7.9.9.3.6.6.8
Chihli		201,169.2.0.2.9.1.6.9
Shantung		108,013.8.7.3.9.4
Honan		150,165.1.4.6.5.2
Shansi		981,646.0.5
Kansu		76,999.4.7.2
Anhwei		240,289.1.0.1.6.2.0.6
Kiangsu		405,196.3.8.8.5
Chekiang		413,514.5.1.8.8.0.7.2
Fukien		1,118,309.0.6.7.7.8.8.9
Canton		444,739.4.2.1.8.2.2.0
Kuangsi		459.2.7.2
Szchwen		904.800.5.7.9.2.2.7.5
Kueichou		683,872.7.6.8.5.8.0.0
	Total, Taels	1,769,920.3.3.6.9.1.2

RECEIPTS FROM 舊管* OLD BALANCES IN EACH PROVINCE.

Treasury of Board of Revenue, Taels	10,612,682.6.9.6
Shengking	556,322.8.5.1
(Gold, 4,034.1.1.7)	
Fengtien	779,893.8.1.6.9.9.1.4
Chihli	4,204,696.5.4.9.6.5.5
Shantung	600,049.1.0.4.3.8.0.3
Honan	1,461,148.0.5.1.6.8.9.4
Shensi	1,027,027.6.1.9.5.1
Kansu	4,101,233.3.6.8.8.3.4
(Gold, 272.8.4.9.2)	
(Gold ore unmelted, 5.4.2)	
Anhwei	715,796.7.1.1.3.9.0.5
Kiangsu	3,478,632.0.7.6.8.0.4.2
Kiangsi	543,099.4.8.2.4
Chekiang	1,299,839.2.9.3.4.0.1.6
Fukien	1,162,111.6.2.4.5.1.5.4

* Example of old balances.—Viceroy Liu says in a despatch, *Sin-wen*, August 12, 1898: Chiu-kuan Taels 224,061 to the credit of the Ch'en-fang-chü 籌防局, had accumulated from February, 1896.

Hupei	1,115,374.7.2.9.7.2.7.8
Hunan	219,779.6.1.8.3.8
Kuangtung	891,642.2.3.2.0.8.3.2
Kuangsi	274,182.8.7.3.6.2.7.2
Szchwen ... ... (Gold, 2.9.8)	2,507,579.4.7.6.4.2.6.6
Yünnan	83,802.6.0.7.8 4.2
Kueichou	792,616.5.8.8.9.5.8
Kirin	52,723.4.2.5.7.8.4.7
Heilungkiang	42,346.9.1.5.3.2.3
Suiyuench'eng	276,781.3.5.1.0.8.6
Total, Taels	39,906,248.1.3.0.0.1.0.3

Gold Taels	4,309.9.4.6.2
Gold ore Taels	5.4.2

RECEIPTS FROM OLD BALANCES WHICH SHOULD BE ON HAND IN THE PROVINCES.

Fengtien ... ... Taels	9,204.8.6.6.5
Chihli	17,311.4.0.3.6
Shantung	2,226.6.3.1
Honan	381,534.9.9.8
Shensi	1,941,791.7.1.6.2.3
Kansu	293,569.4.3.2.4
Anhwei	81,308.3.2.6.1
Kiangsu	1,684,721.6.3.5.7.8.7
Kiangsi	2,780,231.7.3.5.8
Fukien	448,852.2.9.2.4.9.6
Hunan	9,411,921.0.6.5
Canton	159,553.0.1.4.1.7.8
Kuangsi	4,708.8.5.6
Szchwen	3,086,763.0.9.6.6.2.0.2
Kueichou	7,554,566.8.0.9.2
Total, Taels	27,858,265.8.7.8.9.7.7.2

Supplemental receipts arising from the sums fixed by the board not being reached. 不符收款, literally, not agreeing with the sum received.

Canton ... ... Taels	2,304.4.3.3.5
Total of the preceding six supplemental amounts } Taels	105,943,413.1.6.4.7.8.6

Total of Gold ... ... Taels	4,309.9.4.6.2
Gold ore unmelted	5.4.2

Total revenue in A.D. 1893, Taels 189,053,421.9.4.3.7.2.8.4

Gold ... ... Taels	4,333.9.4.6.2
Gold ore unmelted	5.4.2

SECTION THIRD.—GOVERNMENT EXPENDITURE.

Expenditure on Imperial Tombs.

Board of Revenue ... ... Taels	50,853.0.9 8
Chihli	41,366.2.5.3.8.3.5.9.5
Total, Taels	92,219.3.5.1.8.3.5.9.5

Palace Expenditure.

Board of Revenue ... ... Taels 280,000

Expenditure on Sacrifices.

Board of Revenue ... ... Taels	10,627.2.8.5
Shengking	2,241.9.9.1
Fengtien	16.
Chihli	4,357.4.2.9
Shantung	6,859.4.1.6
Honan	17,434.1.9.8
Shansi	10,196.7.1.3.9
Shensi	10,914.5.4.7
Kansu	7,413.4.1.7
Anhwei	8,555.7.1.4
Kiangsu	13,919.9.9.8
Kiangsi	13,425.8.3
Chekiang	22,196.1.0.5
Fukien	11,825.7.6.3
Hupei	12,274.6.1.6.2.5
Hunan	73,407.5.4.2
Kuangtung	14,922.8.8.7
Kuangsi	2,313.2.0.1
Szchwen	10,327.
Yünnan	283.2.2.9
Kueichou	1,018.4.2.2
Kirin	396.1.7.6
Suiyuench'eng	184.5.1.7.7
Total, Taels	255,112.6.8.7.8.5

PUBLIC FUNCTIONS.

Board of Revenue ... ... Taels	21,200.
Chihli	603.
Shantung	176.5.8.5
Honan	519.
Shansi	15,637.5.3.6.1
Shensi	604.4.5.4
Kansu	149.6.2
Kiangsu	1,562.6.7.2
Kiangsi	1,070.8.6
Chekiang	1,986.9.0.3
Fukien	623.7.5.2.8
Canton	447.6.3
Kuangsi	415.4.5.7
Szchwen	328.6.3.7
Kueichou	132.
Suiyuench'eng...	13.8.0
Total, Taels	45,069.4.8.8.9

The amonnt Taels 21,200 is made up of Nei-wu-fu Taels 19,600 and Kwang-lu-sz Taels 1,600.

SALARIES.

Board of Revenue ... ... Taels	1,783,518.6.0.2
Shengking	199,732.7.8.1
Fengtien	31,481.4.2.7
Chihli	56,708.8.6.1.5.5
Shantung	256,559.2.1.4
Shansi	74,689.4.1.8.5
Shensi	103,009.2.1.6
Kiangsu	13,207.4.0.6.5
Anhwei...	102,814.8.5.2
Kiangsi	92,395.4.6.2
Fukien	88,952.4.9.1
Chekiang	138,246.7.6.2.8.2.4
Hupei	88,854 8.9.8.2.2
Hunan	62,416.0.6.9
Kansu	72,512.8.2.5.6
Szchwen	149,598.4.1.8
Kuangtung	114,934.4.9
Yünnan...	38,403.6.7.6.9
Kueichou	29,251.0 5.5
Kuangsi	88,492.6.6.3
Sinyuench'eng	288.
Total, Taels	3.845,116.0.0.7.3.9.6

Examinations.

Fengtien	Taels	281.
Honan		5,120.9.6.4
Shantung		2,349.8.9.3
Shensi		11,000.
Kansu		11,662.8
Kiangsu		2,607.7.9.9
Kiangsi		20,859.0.5.9
Chekiang		10,608.2.5.6
Fukien		21,169.5.7.9.2
Hupei		7,970.3.4
Hunan		3,625.4.4.4
Kuangtung		9,436.3.1.2.1.1.1.2
Kuangsi		211.8.6.6
Kueichou		5,950.
	Total, Taels	113,852.3.1.2.3.1.1.2

Army.

Board of Revenue	Taels	7,322,245.9.1.2
Shengking		371,338.7.0.2
Fengtien		57,968.7.5.1.4.4.5.2
Chihli		275,437.8.7.1.7.7.0.6
Shantung		503,124.7.6.8
Honan		335,652.4.8.3
Shansi		641,938.5 8.1
Kiangsu		775,942.4.4.0.0.6
Anhwei		99,571.5.5.4.3
Kiangsi		73,581.9 8.3
Fukien		975 575.7.5.8.0.2.4
Chekiang		1,209,052.5.0.3.8
Hupei		1,122,532.3.7.5.8.8.2
Hunan		425,335.3.1.6
Shensi		523,893.5.0.6.2.2
Kansu		514,853.3.8.9.4
Szchwen		1,001,362.5.9.1.2.1
Kuangtung		953,523.1.8.1.8.6.8.7
Kuangsi		227,233.6.9.7
Kueichou		120,595.6.2.1
Kirin		530,072 1.0.3
Heilungkiang		208,564.8.3.7.4.4
Suiyuench'eng		225,971.9.3.1
	Total, Taels	18,495,369.8.5.8.4.2.0.5

Courier Service.

Board of Revenue Treasury ...	Taels	157,218.8.6.3
Shengking		27,443.9.9.9
Fengtien		6,753.4.9.4
Chihli		5,707.3.4.3.0.4
Shantung		151,358.3.1.5
Honan		282,388.6.0.5
Shansi		191,939.4.2.6
Shensi		191,939.4.2.6
Kansu		144,097.3.6.7
Anhwei		63,720.7.2.9
Kiangsu		99,031.4.5.9
Kiangsi		69,371.4
Chekiang		64,226.1.8.2
Fukien		29,315.4.2
Hupei		114,293.0.7.8
Hunan		62,227.4.7
Canton		10,428.4.4.7
Kuangsi		3,461.3
Szchwen		34,784.8.2.4.8
Kueichou		61,316.6.2.4
Kirin		75,607.1.1.6.6
Heilungkiang		18,681.5.6.3
	Total, Taels	1,830,905.8.9.4.6.4

Bursaries to Able Bachelors of Arts.

Board treasury	Taels	8,400.
Chihli		2,654.8
Honan		11,959.6.0.1.7
Shensi		11,052.1.7.7
Kansu		4,494.6
Anhwei		4,613.2.1.3
Kiangsu		19,887.0.8.2
Kiangsi		3,991.4.9.8
Chekiang		9,368.3.1.6
Fukien		13,551.3.4.0.4
Hupei		5,409.1.8.5
Hunan		1,795.1.8.4
Kuangtung		5,514.4.0.4.4
Kuangsi		3,060.8.3.4.1.2
Szchwen		10,559.6.2
Kueichou		538.7.6.2
Heilungkiang		263.
	Total, Taels	117,113.6.1.7.6.2

Rewards and Charities.

Board treasury	Taels	854,484.
Shengking		5,459.3.6.3
Fengtien		16,592.8.3.7.8.2.2.2
Chihli...		36,479.0.9.5.0.1
Shantung		19,916.9.4.8
Honan		7,743.3.9
Shansi...		215,659.2.4.3
Shensi...		29,825.6.5.2.0.8
Kansu		7,348.6.8.1
Anhwei		8,204.4.2.6
Kiangsu		17,935.0.2.7.4.2.5
Kiangsi		19,340.0.4
Chekiang		51,734.1.8.5.3.0.3.8
Fukien		38,679.2.4.1.6
Hupei...		15,481.1.4.9.6.9.5
Hunan		20,828.4.6.1
Canton		30,621.9.6.8
Kuangsi		534.4.7.6.1.2
Szchwen		32,933.5.8.2.0.3.5
Kirin		28,120.9.6.0.4
Heilungkiang		3,726.2
Suiyuench'eng		2,249.
	Total, Taels	1,463,897.8.6.1.9.8.1.6

Among the rewards are the honours decreed to officers who have died in battle, 陣亡員弁 chen-wang-yuen-pien; gifts of money to soldiers, 出力兵勇 chu-li-ping-yung, and to persons having hereditary titles, 世襲 shih-hsi. Asylums for the aged, for foundlings, for widows, and gifts of food for the poor and for beggars, are assisted from this fund.

Repairs of Walls and Public Offices 修繕.

Shengking	Taels	41,278.4.2.3
Fengtien		26,422.7.4.6.2.5.2.2
Chihli		404,920.4.5.9.9.6.5
Shantung		647,529.2.5.2
Honan		687,477.2.4.8
Shansi		712.1.4.6
Shensi		376.8
Kansu		1,419.4.5.1
Anhwei		28,396.5.7.4

Kiangsu	319,357.7.1.2.6.1.4.6
Kiangsi	13,361.4.7.2
Chekiang	28,892.9.6.9.7.5
Fukien	5,164.3.6.7
Canton	4,408.2.1.5
Kuangsi	10.1.6.4
Szchwen	88.8.2
Kirin	84,520.6.5.5.5
Heilungkiang	4,581.9.9.7.3.6
Suiyuench'eng	1,396.7.3.8
Total, Taels	2,300,316.2.1.1.4.4.1.8

Charges to this account are made for repairs of city walls and moats, magistrates' offices, temples to the dead, roads, wayside booths, forts, river embankments, sea walls, and bridges.

OFFICIAL PURCHASES, 採辦 T'SAI-PAN.

Board of Revenue ... ... Taels	2,792,134.5.1.1
Shengking	10,863.6.3.1
Fengtien	14,163.4.1.2.5.1.5.2
Chihli...	37,456.0.0.3
Shantung	200,666.7.8.0.0.3.2
Honan	43,836.0.0.3
Shansi	20,779.1.2.4
Anhwei	64,956.9.9.7
Kiangsu	696,628.1.8.7.9.3.3
Chekiang	16,146.5.7.1.5.5
Hupei	77,746.5.0.6.7.7
Hunan	29,992.0.1.4
Canton	16,335.7.4.2
Szchwen	65,122.9.6.1.6.6.3.7
Yunnan	34,785.5.8
Kirin	1,369.9.3
Total, Taels	4,122,983.9.5.9.4.6.3.9

The purchases of the Board of Revenue refer to materials bought for the Imperial household. The building of the palace called 重華宮 Cheng-hwa-kung was very costly. It was a residence for the inferior wives of the Emperor. The expenditure was Taels 1,500,000. The manufacture of porcelain tiles cost Taels 77,000. The manufacture of gunpowder cost Taels 30,000. The repair of the road outside the west city to Hai-tien cost Taels 300,000.

Soochow Imperial Factory, for silks and satins, Taels 1,081,425.3.3.8.9.

This sum includes the expense of the Nanking Imperial Factory for satins.

Hangchow Imperial Factory for silks, 318,963.1.1.8.2.5.2.9

Total, Taels 1,400,388.4.5.7.1.5.2.9

Official Salaries.

Board of Revenue* ... ... Taels	227,552.8.9.4
Shengking, Salaries of Officers at Moukden	8,141.5.2.4
Fengtien Prefecture, Moukden	245,822.9.4.2.6.3.1
Chihli	398,551.9.6.8 2.9.2
Shantung	157,253.2.6.5
Shansi	286,948.6.7.7.3
Honan	284,453.1.5.4
Kiangsu	365,984.4.6.3.4.6
Anhwei	183,381.4.7.1
Kiangsi	147,743.8.1.9
Chekiang	285,599.3.8.9.5.7.5
Fukien	250,236.5.7.6.6
Hupei	192,809.8.2.9
Hunan	224,921.1.9.9.6
Shensi	205,461.0.2.7
Kansu	254,048.5.5
Canton	197,552.2.9.7.4
Kwangsi	153,210.0.0.7.4.5
Szchwen	588,415.1.8.3.8
Yunnan	337,404.9.9.8.5.0.8
Kweichou	40,229.0.4.9
Kirin	74,313.6.1.7.0.2.6.8
Heilungkiang	24,049.8.7.2.8.6.0.8
Suiyuench'eng	10,865.9.7.2.2
Total, Taels	5,144,951.7.4.8.7.2.8.6

* This is the cost of salaries for Peking officials.

MISCELLANEOUS EXPENDITURE.

Chihli	Taels 16,302.2.4.4.2
Shantung	157,616.7.2.5
Shansi	38,553.0.2.7
Kiangsu	8,299.8.6.3
Kuangsi	673.6.0.6
Szchwen	65,262.9.9.4.8.8.1.2
Suiyuench'eng	13,907.7.4.2.0.6.6
Total, Taels	300,616.2.0.2.1.4.7.2

It may be noticed here that one-half of the miscellaneous expenditure belongs to Shantung, then governed by Li Ping-heng, but afterwards by Chang Ju-wei.

Total of fifteen items ordinary expenditure, 1893.	Taels	39,807,914.6.5.5.8.8.9.6

SUBSIDIES TO BOARD OF REVENUE AND TO EACH PROVINCE CONSTITUTING A SUPPLEMENTAL REVENUE.

Board of Revenue	Taels 18,407,750.9.2.8
Shengking	461,953.0.5.2
Fengtien	41,320.9.6
Chihli	3,807,170.2.2.7.9.2.0.4
Shantung	270,108.8.6.4.4.8
Honan	8,000.
Shensi	3,529.0.8.4
Kansu	4,944,911.9.2.2
Anhwei	154,011.5.9.2.8
Kiangsu	999,908.8.9.5
Fukien	307,526.4.7.1.4.1.7
Hupei	122,800.
Kuangsi	148,262.5.4.8.8.6.2.5
Kueichou	1,714,413.7.4.8.3.0.5
Kirin	83,134.
Heilungkiang	119,000.
Suiyuench'eng...	210,918.4.9.9
Total, Taels	31,804,720.7.9.3

These supplemental revenues in each province are accorded to them by old rule. For example in Chihli there are Hwang-ch'ai or imperial special duties requiring pecuniary outlay to support the persons appointed. Kansu receives a large amount because it is a frontier province. Kueichou receives a subsidy because it is thinly populated. The Board of Revenue receives, in order to send forward, probably for the Manchu establishment and the army, eighteen million taels. The remaining thirteen are from the provinces.

LOCAL EXPENDITURE ON NATIVE CUSTOM HOUSES AND BOARDS.

Fengtien	Taels	95,991.1.0.5.3.2
Chihli...		865,667.1.3.4.4.7.7.9
Shantung		140,889.4.3.9.2.1.1
Shansi		8,932.
Shensi...		39,842.1.3
Kansu		44,171.0.5·5.7
Anhwei		73,122.3.3.3.8.4.5
Kiangsu		612,950.8.1.2.7.0.2.6
Kiangsi		111,964.2.3.5
Chekiang		274,709.4.7.2
Fukien		152,938.8.5.8.7
Hupei...		552,536.5.6.1.2.9.6.4
Hunan		2,115.5.0.7
Kuangtung		45,969.4.2.2
Kuangsi		46,819.3.0.5.2.1.6
Szechwen		48,513.0.3.1.1.9.8.8
Yunnan		51,947.3.1.7.6.1.7.8
Kweichow		12,661.3.4.0.7
	Total, Taels	3,181,741.0.6.1.9.8.5.5

PAYMENTS IN EACH PROVINCE TO FOREIGNERS FOR ARTICLES RECEIVED.

This is headed 洋欵等項.

Chihli...	Taels	59,214.6.3
Shantung		10,315.8.3
Anhwei		58,438.5.7
Kiangsu		1,390,294.8.9.3.6.4.7.2
Kiangsi		87,000.
Chekiang		311,996.5.8.5.3
Fukien		1,356,785.8.1.8.3.0.9.7
Hupei...		262,041.6.6.4.8.9
Kwangtung		62,361.8.3.0.2.4
	Total, Taels	3,598,449.8.2.2.3.8.6.9

These payments are probably chiefly for artillery.

Total of three items of new expenditure, Anno 1893,	Taels 23,850,111.2.2.1.2.8.4.4

PAYMENTS FROM EACH PROVINCE OF SUMS DUE.

These payments are headed 補支支欵, expenditure on account of deficiency in previous years.

Chihli...	Taels	243,217.3.2.4.3.4.8.6
Shantung		274,486.8.2.2.9.4.6.1
Honan		33,952.3.2.9
Shansi		154,673.3.1.4.3
Shensi		3,824.1.8.5
Kansu		76,985.2.5.3.8.8
Anhwei		136,020.4.0.1.7
Kiangsu		904,805.1.5.3.9.1.7.2
Kiangsi		477,755.6.9.8
Chekiang		616,255.3.9.1.2.0.1.8
Fukien		997,553.1.2.2.1.7.5.2
Hupei...		207,531.4.7.5.8.3.6
Hunan		71,929.7.9.4
Kuangtung		106,393.8.1.0.8
Szchwen		770,677.3.7.9.7.5.0.8
Kweichou		239,610.2.6.4.4.1.2.9
	Total, Taels	5,315,671.7.2.1.2.6.8.6

The Chinese system allows postponement in paying taxes when there is inability to discharge the debt to the government at the due date.

ADVANCES MADE BY THE PROVINCES TO THE GOVERNMENT.

Chihli...	Taels	14,247.7.1.2
Honan		367,694.7.2.6
Shansi		22,324.1.4.7
Shensi		60,055.4.4.0
Anhwei		381,611.3.7.2
Kiangsu		143,526.9.2.5
Kiangsi		128,423.2.2.1
Chekiang		656,194.0.5.4
Hupei		221.2.0.0
Hunan		10,647.7.4.3
Kuangtung		1,139.2.8.2
Kuangsi		4,900.7.7.6

Szchwen		90,256.1.6
Kweichou		192.4.9.2
	Total, Taels	1,881,435.2.5.7

Expenditure repaid and in advance ...	Total, Taels	7,197,106.9.7.8.2.6.8.6

AMOUNT SENT FROM THE PROVINCES TO MEET THE EXPENSES OF GOVERNMENT DEPARTMENTS IN PEKING.

Fengtien	Taels	28,188.9.6.0.9.2.5.6
Chihli...		171,022.1.5.3.8.8.0.4
Shantung		138,861.6.1.9
Honan		33,011.0.7.3.6.2.5
Shansi		6,755.4.0.1
Shensi		4,700.
Kansu		23,226.7.1.3
Anhwei		246,948.4.8.6
Kiangsu		657,659.0.9.4.2.2.4
Kiangsi		182,504.0.4.1
Chekiang		152,931.2.3.5
Fukien		705,629.3.1.6.5
Hupei		71,542.0.5.9
Hunan		3,704.9.5.1
Kuangtung		136,560.
Kuangsi		2,492.2.9.1
Szchwen		9,050.6.8.9
Suiyuench'eng		3,408.1.8.7.5
	Total, Taels	2,578,196.2.7.1.7.5.5

The preceding four totals make the expenditure for 1893 in all ...	Taels	73,433,029.1.2.7.1.9.7.6

CONTRIBUTIONS FROM THE PROVINCES FOR THE PEKING ARMY, 解京餉 CHIÊ-CHING-HIANG.

Shengking	Taels	120.
Fengtien		22,203.4.6.9.8.2
Chihli		278,471.7.7.8.9.7.6
Shantung		785,475.5.8.6
Honan		352,600.
Shansi		1,080,367.0.1
Shensi		75,623.8.9.1
Anhwei		1,208,657.6.0.3

Kiangsu	2,205,025.1.3.2.6.9.2
Kiangsi	1,872,100.5.6.7
Chekiang	1,386,695.6.2.5.9.1.6
Fukien	1,256,046.8.7.4.9
Hupei	1,230,224.9.6.2.2.8.3
Hunan	639,409.7.4.7.9
Kuangtung	848,977.3.3.7
Szchwen	578,000.
Suiyuench'eng	202.3.9.1.4.8
Total, Taels	13,820,201.9.7.7.9.6.7.9

Contributions in Aid for the National Army.

Board treasury ... ... Taels	1,941,452.8.5.3
Shengking	271,953.0.5.3
Fengtien	226,197.1.9.7.4
Chihli	138,453.0.3
Shantung	359,250.4.1.7.4.7.1
Honan	1,397,214.5.2.7
Shansi	2,868,207.1.5.7.3
Shensi	276,759.9.1.1
Kansu	3,565,192.6.6.7
Anhwei	504,844.1.5.4
Kiangsu	4,549,972.4.4.4.1
Kiangsi	631,612.9.1.5
Chekiang	914,409.6.3.5.8
Fukien	399,094.5.6.2.3
Hupei	1,159,789.1.2 9.4
Hunan	280,951.9.0.6.6
Kwangtung	320,488.5.5.6
Szchwen	531,800.
Suiyuench'eng	32,687.2.1.1.4
Total, Taels	20,370,328.6.0.7.9.6.9

Amounts from the Provinces transferred by Order to other Provinces.

Board treasury ... ... Taels	7,341,680.5.4
Fengtien	9,213.6.5.0.5
Chihli	2,266,702.3.8.5.0.7.6
Shantung	343,132.8.0.2.7
Honan	336,767.9.0.5
Shansi	930,392.4.7.3

Shensi	2,481,351.1.0.5.2.1
Kansu	335,660.2.9.1
Anhwei	61,379.1.7.6.1
Kiangsu	1,633,750.6.4.8.2
Kiangsi	3.990,578.5.7.4.8
Fukien	395,140.5.6.4.3.9.6
Hupei	504,766.6.5.6.8.1.4
Hunan	10,148,470.0 5.0.1
Kuangtung	1,042,720.7.9.2.3.2.3
Szchwen	3,332,319.5.1.0.4.0.4
Yunnan	230,180.
Kueichou	8,301,841 4.7.7.4
Kirin	96,116.9.0.5.7.4
Total, Taels	43,782,165.5.0.8.7.7.3.6

In explanation of this system of transference of funds it may be observed that Szchwen, a rich province, was ordered to transfer Taels 180,000 of the salt and likin collection to Kweichou, a poor province. Kweichou has to maintain a large military force. The collections from taxes, duties and likin amount to Taels 395,000. Kweichou, according to Mr. Jamieson's statistics, received in one year from Szchwen, Taels 350,000; from Hunan, Taels 30,000; from Chekiang, Taels 10,000; from Shantung, Taels 28,000 ; from the Shanghai Customs' collection, Taels 320,000; from Kiukiang Customs, Taels 58,000 ; from Canton Customs, Taels 10,000. Total, Taels 1,381,000. This sum was expended in the province of Kweichou for salaries, for the army, for the support of boards, and other requirements.

Revenue Insufficient for Expenditure.

Chihli	Taels 1,800.
Kwangsi	146,895.1.2.8.4.6 1.8
Total, Taels	148,695.1.2.8.4.6.1.8
The preceding four totals—Peking army, national army, amounts transferred, and deficiencies—make in all	Taels 78,121,391.2.1.6.0.0.0.2
Grand Total, Taels	151,554,720.3.4.3.1.9.7.8

Silver in Hand in Each Province.

Board Treasury ... ... Taels	9,710,108.5.6.3
Shengking	584,294.6.0.2
(Gold, 4,034.1.1.7)	
Fengtien	702,118.6.9.5.3
Chihli	4,453,695.9.7.3
Shantung	760,333.2.1.5.9.9.5
Honan	1,444,629.1.1.3.5.6.5.3
Shansi	1,245,431.6.2.3.4
Shensi	548,574.7.9.2.2.6
Kansu	4,425,821.6.1.7.8.5.4
(Gold, 296.8.4.9.2)	
(Gold sand, 5.4.2)	
Anhwei	599,784.2.3.1.6.0.6.6
Kiangsu	3,692,237.9.3.6.6 2.1.8
Kiangsi	533,701.5.8.2.4
Chekiang	1,457,081.9.1 0.7.7.0.1
Fukien	1,129,878.6.6.9.4.8.7.4
Hupei	977,276.7.9.4.5
Hunan	211,136.9.4.9.1.8
Kuangtung	891,775.3.2.0.6.8 9.3
Kuangsi	189,887.4.6.7.2.9.0.1
Szchwen	2,530,582.8.0.4.9.5.4
(Gold, 2.9.8)	
Yunnan	142,082 8.0.4.9.5.4
Kueichou	913,848.1.1.1.0.9.0.1
Kirin	56,390.1.3 3.3.7.3.7
Heilungkiang	15,500.7.2.3.1.6.8.5
Suiyuench'eng	282,528.7.0.3.5.7
Total, Taels	37,498,701.6.0.1.5.3.0.5
Gold Taels	4,333.9.4.6.2
Gold sand Taels	5 4.2

Revenue Received in Copper Cash.

Board of Revenue	270,447	strings	174	cash
Good cash	1,099,696	„	866	„
Shengking*	147,654	„	621	„
Small cash	1,309,695	„	752	„
Fengtien, good cash	152,734	„	815	„
„ small cash†	1,898,937	„	467	„

* In strings of 660 cash each.
† In strings of 330 cash each.

Chihli	2,392	strings	809	cash
Shansi	2,697	„	286	„
Shensi	2,444	„	855	„
Anhwei	243,993	„	749	„
Kiangsu	3,998,866	„	933	„
Chekiang	9,934	„	719	„
Fukien	5,590	„	320	„
Hupei	2,997,134	„	377	„
Hunan	357,420	„	585	„
Kirin	15,300	„	—	„
Heilungkiang	702,086	„	300	„
Large cash	10,403	„	446	„
Suiyuench'eng...	1,556	„	527	„
Total,	5,050,568	„	744	„

Additional receipts in copper cash	719,779	strings	109	cash
Further receipts	4,257	„	529	„
Small cash received	3,208,633	„	219	„

Expenditure in Copper Cash.

Board Treasury	195,246	strings	949	cash
Other receipts	1,263,491	„	—	„
Shengking, large cash* ...	133,835	„	230	„
„ small „ † ...	1,309,639	„	752	„
Fengtien, large strings ...	210,219	„	288	„
„ small „ ...	1,975,377	„	467	„
Chihli	1,666	„	740	„
Shansi	4,060	„	857	„
Shensi	7,439	„	909	„
Anhwei	654,021	„	369	„
Kiangsu	4,161,842	„	890	„
Chekiang	11,627	„	600	„
Fukien	6,284	„	285	„
Hupei	2,290,512	„	701	„
Hunan	340,972	„	671	„
Kirin	15,876	„	226	„
Heilungkiang	831,140	„	116	„
Strings of 660 each ...	9,573	„	584	„
Suiyuench'eng...	1,031	„	430	„
Total	4,466,879	„	789	„

* The large are in strings of 660 cash each.
† The small are in strings of 330 cash each.

Additional	848,683 strings	82 cash	
"	4,823,179 "	974 "	
Strings of 330 each,	3,285,017 strings	219 cash	

TRIBUTE GRAIN RECEIVED.

Fengtien	Piculs	101,041.0 0.2.0.2
Chihli		86,727.2.3.6.0.7
Shantung		345,462.9.1.3.8
Shansi		87,841.1.5.1.8
Shensi		120,201.9.3.7.2.5
Kansu		383,191.1.8.0 3
Anhwei		241,141.2.1.3.3.9
Kiangsu		1,223,973.4.2.2.5
Chekiang		605,295.0.7.6.7
Fukien		91,031.3.7.9 2.1
Hupei		8,360.9.8.5.5
Hunan		82,441.1.6
Kuangtung		342,303.7.0.8.8
Kuangsi		89,832.6.0.7.5.9
Szchwen		17,518.8.4.5.8.7
Kirin		43,163.5.1.9.6
Heilungkiang		28,231.6
Suiyuench'eng		9,065.8.0.2.4
	Total,	4,493,075.3.4.8.7

TRIBUTE GRAIN DISTRIBUTED.

Fengtien	Piculs	99,139.0.7.9.7
Chihli		81,701.7.0.2.2
Shantung		320,679.9.7.8.1
Shansi		77,143.3.7.6.3
Shensi		141,754.1.5.4.5
Kansu		193,954.1.9.1.4
Anhwei		272,217.0.3.5.4
Kiangsu		1,223,973.4.2.2.5
Kiangsi		584,211.6.4.6.6
Chekiang		534,857.3.8.6.8
Fukien		88,457.1.1.5.3
Hupei		6,291.6.3.6.6
Hunan		81,515.6.6
Kuangtung...		326,016.2.3.1.9
Kuangsi		109,797.4.6.4.9
Szchwen		11,509.8.7.4.8

Kirin	43,268.9.1.2.6
Heilungkiang	30,844.2.8.2.8
Suiyuench'eng	12,331.2.0.3.3
Total,	4,239,624.3.5.5.7

Tribute Grain in Hand, ... Piculs 253,450.9.9.3

HAY AND STRAW RECEIVED.

Fengtien...	453,060	bundles
Chihli	685,483	,,
Shansi	859	,,
Shensi	109,883	,,
Kansu	3,573,327	,,
Szchwen	19,599	catties
Total, bundles	4,822,612	
Catties	19,599	

HAY AND STRAW DISTRIBUTED.

Fengtien...	261,031	bundles
Chihli	82,714	,,
Shansi	856	,,
Shensi	108,873	,,
Kansu	7,737,655	,,
Szchwen	19,599	catties
Total, bundles	8,191,129	
Catties	19,599	

Hay and Straw in Hand, ...Bundles 3,368,517

REVENUE AND EXPENDITURE.

Views of Mencius on Customs' Duties.

Mencius advocated the abandonment of all barrier taxes as being unrighteous exactions. In Book 3. part 2, chapter 8, he states this in reply to Tai-ying-chï. This great officer of the Sung dukedom said to him: "I am not able at present to be content with a tithe on the produce of land. I cannot abolish the barrier and market tax, but I ask if you will approve of my diminishing the tax in the meantime and wait for a year before taking strenuous measures." Mencius said: "It is always wrong to steal a neighbour's fowl. A good man will not say, this year I will take only one fowl; next year I will cease the practice."

Origin of Tithes.

By the Hia statutes, B. C. 2000, every husbandman received fifty mow of land and paid the produce of five mow to the government. The Yin statutes, B. C. 1600, gave a ninth part of 630 mow to each of eight husbandmen. The remaining seventy mow were cultivated by the eight farmers for the government. The Chow dynasty, B. C. 1100, gave 100 mow to one family. Ten families cultivated 1,000 mow and paid one-tenth to the government.

Tang Dynasty Taxation.

In the year A. D. 763 there was an edict stating that when there were three in a family two only should be taxed, and the land tax was two pints of grain to the mow. If we assume that two piculs represent the grain produced, it thus appears that the tax was only one per cent. of the value.

From A. D. 763 and onward on account of the defects in levying the three kinds of taxes known as Tsu-yung and T'iau an edict decided that a summer and autumn tax should be levied on land according to area. In the next reign, A.D. 780 to 805, when Yang Yen was minister, it was decided that the summer tax should be levied in July and the autumn tax in December.

昭信股票王公大臣滿漢官員認領清單.

FIVE PER CENT. LOAN CONTRIBUTIONS IN 1898.

		部庫收數.
Prince Kung (deceased)	恭忠親王	Taels 20,000
Prince Kung	恭親王	3,000
Prince Su	肅親王	5,000
Prince Ch'ing	慶親王	20,000
Prince Twan	端郡王	6,000
Lien, son of the Fifth Prince	濂貝勒	3,000
Lan Kung	瀾公	1,000
Yung Lu	榮中堂	10,000
Hsü Ch'ung	徐中堂	2,500
Kang Yi	剛毅	10,000
Sun Chia-nai	孫家鼐	2,000
Ching Sin	敬信	10,000
Wang Wen-shao	王文韶	20,000
Ch'i Siu	啟秀	10,000
Hsü Ying-kwei	許應騤	2,000
Liao Shou-heng	廖壽恒	4,000
Hsü P'u	徐郙	2,000
Ch'ung Li	崇禮	10,000
Chao Shu-ch'iau	趙舒翹	1,000
Ch'ien Ying-p'u	錢應溥	5,000
Hwai Ta-pu	懷塔布	2,000
Hsü Shu-ming	徐樹銘	1,000
Chung Kwang	崇光	10,000
Hsü Yung-i	徐用儀	2,000
P'u Shan	溥善	1,000
Li Shan	立山	10,000
P'u Liang	溥良	2,000
Chang Ying-lin	張英麟	1,000
T'ang Ching-ch'ung	唐景崇	1,000
P'u T'ing	溥頲	1,000
Wen chih	文治	1,000
Hsü Hwei-feng	徐會灃	1,000
Hsü Cheng-ü	徐承煜	500
Shih Shü	世續	5,000

Chang Tsui	長萃	1,000
Ch'ung Kung	崇公	1,000
Sun Yü-wen	孫毓汶	1,000
Chang Shun	長順	3,000
Wen Lin	文琳	2,000
Hu Yü-fen	胡燏棻	1,000
Wu T'ing-fang*	伍廷芳	10,000
Lü Hai-hwan†	呂海寰	6,000
Lo Feng-lu†	羅豐祿	3,000
Yang Ju†	楊儒	3,000
Yü Keng†	裕庚	3,000
Hsü King-ch'eng†	許景澄	3,000
Weng T'ung-yü	翁同龢	10,000
Li Twan-fen	李端棻	1,000
Chang Yin-heng	張蔭桓	10,000

Total	共銀	243,000
	Officers of 1st, 2nd, and 3rd button 三品以下各官共銀	35,500

Total 二共合銀, Taels 278,500

The preceding are the amounts actually received in the treasury of the Board of Revenue. Probably one-third of the subscriptions are patriotic gifts. The remainder have been or will be repaid. It was the indemnity to Japan after the war of 1896 that led the government to make this appeal to the nation. Interest at five per cent. was promised to all subscribers.

昭信股票外省官員認領清單.

Special Contributions in the Provinces.

Chihli	直隸		316,200
Shansi	山西		130,000
Kwangtung	廣東	海關在內	251,600
Fukien	福建		180,000
Hunan	湖南		90,200
Kansu	甘肅		100,000
Shensi	陝西		200,000
Honan	河南		308,400

* 出使大臣 Minister abroad in America.

† 出使大臣 Minister abroad in Germany, England, France, and Russia.

Yellow River Superintendent	東河	34,000
Kwangsi	廣西	48,700
Shantung	山東	130,600
Sinkiang	新疆	154,300
Grain Transport Superintendency	江甯江蘇漕屬 {將軍織造在內}	427,305
Hupei	湖北	80,000
Anhwei	安徽	73,900
Kweichou	貴州	50,000
Chekiang	浙江	210,000
Szchwen	四川	433,160
Yünnan	雲南	59,200
Kiangsi	江西	284,900
Chahar General	察哈爾都統等	12,000
Foochow "	福州將軍等	23,600
K'ingchou "	荆州將軍等	15,600
Canton "	廣州將軍等	4,900
Amour "	黑龍江將軍等	27,150
Kirin "	吉林將軍等	112,650
Jehol "	熱河都統等	7,300
Moukden "	盛京將軍侍郎等	250,000
Sian "	西安將軍等	7,000
	Total 統共收銀, Taels	3,992,660

Revenue in 1899.—This is, in an (*Chung-wai-pao*, November 17th) essay on the grain tax, stated to be

Land and personal service ... ... Taels	23,000,000
Foreign Customs	16,000,000
Likin	14,000,000
Salt, regular duties, miscellaneous melting and compensation, grain commutation	20,000,000
	73,000,000

In this, extra taxes 例外抽納 are not included. Also the sums paid as taxes beyond what the law stated, and short payments of taxes due, are not taken account of.

CONTRIBUTIONS OF HWAI-NAN SALT MERCHANTS.

In the *Shen-pao*, April 29th, 1899, the Hwai-nan and Hwai-pei merchants are stated to have undertaken to pay one million taels for certificates. The time when this sum should have been paid has passed. The commissioner 兩淮鹽運司, who resides at Yangchow, has received a despatch from Viceroy Lieu stating that he learns from the Pay Office 支應局 of Nanking that the Soochow and Shanghai Likin Boards owe to four foreign States Taels 92,500. The Shanghai Custom House will not be able to continue for a long time to lend this sum. They ask me to direct the Hwai salt commissioner to pay back this loan out of the subscriptions of the Hwai-nan salt merchants. The salt commissioner replied that the amounts received under the head of subscriptions were quite limited and altogether insufficient for this purpose. Could the viceroy find the required sum elsewhere? In this difficulty the viceroy gave orders to the Pay Office (Chi-ying-chü) and the Defence Board (Ch'ou-fang-chü) to undertake this responsibility. They replied that out of the million taels' subscription of the salt merchants two hundred thousand from the Hwai-pei administration had been received and paid out by the salt commissioner. Out of the eight hundred thousand due from Hupei, Hunan, and Kiangsi only 180,000 had been advanced. What of the remaining 600,000 taels? The salt administration of the three provinces mentioned should advance each a portion of the sum, Taels 92,500. Let each be required to pay 20,000 Taels. Then the salt commissioner can apply for a proportionate amount to the Anhwei salt department, and this, with the collection due from the conveyance merchants (運食各商), will make up the deficiency, so that he will be able to send the Taels 32,500 needed to the Shanghai Customs to pay the foreign loan. The Shanghai Customs' department writes that last year they had lent this money, and this loan could not be continued. The result was that the salt commissioner at

Yangchow found 30,000 Taels in the treasury and added two thousand five hundred from elsewhere. He entrusted the San-tsin transmission bankers with the amount for immediate conveyance to Shanghai and wrote despatches to the viceroy and to the Chï-ying and Ch'ou-fang offices informing them that he had done so.

Sir N. J. Hannen estimated the annual revenue to be: Land tax, 25,088,000; grain tax, Tls. 6,563,000; salt gabelle, 13,659,000; likin, 12,952,000; Customs, foreign, 21,989,000; native, 1,000,000; duty and likin on native opium, 2,229,000; miscellaneous, 5,500,000. Total, 88,979,000, or about £14,829,000.

Revenue and expenditure, 1896, about £14,850,000.

Total debt, 40,000,000; gross Customs' revenue, £3,751,023.

Yearly interest due, about £2,500,000.

Total imports, £33,764,999; total exports, £21,846,903.

Imports from the United Kingdom, £5,179,767.

Exports „ „ „ „ 2,684,722.

The public debt of England was £638,266,482 on March 31st, 1898. Less Suez Canal shares and other assets, £25,241,799, it amounts to £613,024,683.

The *Daily News* of April 26th, 1901, states from the *Chung-wai-pao* the following statistics of the revenue of China.—

1. Land and personal service of eighteen provinces, Taels 29,000,000. Of late years they do not exceed Taels 24,000,000.

2. Supplementary taxes from eighteen provinces should yield Taels 3,000,000. The actual amount has been Taels 2,500,000.

3. Customs, Taels 1,600,000 have been collected.

4. Grand Canal traffic.—The amount levied should be Taels 1,930,000 per annum. The actual amount has been Taels 1,300,000.

5. The value of tribute rice on the Grand Canal should be Taels 2,169,000. Actual receipts, Taels 1,800,000.

6. Salt taxes and additional salt likin.—Total receipts have been Taels 13,400,000 per annum.

7. Likin, Taels 16,000,000.

8. Miscellaneous duties, Taels 1,000,000.

9. Ordinary Customs' duties, Taels 2,700,000.

10. Foreign opium duties, Taels 17,000,000.

11. Foreign opium likin, Taels 5,000,000.

12. Native opium likin, Taels 1,800,000.

Total, Taels 88,000,000 per annum received by the Chinese government.

EXPENDITURE OF THE CHINESE GOVERNMENT.

1. Land and poll taxes retained in the eighteen provinces for local expenses, Taels 5,450,000.

2. Supplementary taxes retained in the provinces for local expenses, Taels 2,500,000.

3. Miscellaneous taxes and duties retained in the provinces for local expenses, Taels 1,600,000.

4. Income on Grand Canal traffic deducted, Taels 1,300,000.

5. Value of tribute rice on the Grand Canal retained, Taels 1,800,000.

6. Soldiers' pay for Manchu Banner men and Green Flag regiments in the eighteen provinces, Taels 12,000,000.

7. Soldiers' pay for troops, specially raised for coast and river defence, Taels 18,000,000 to 19,000,000.

8. Customs' duties retained for local expenses, Taels, 445,000.

9. Salaries of foreign Customs' staff, Taels 3,168,000.

10. Expenses of the Imperial Household, Peking, Taels 600,000.

11. Additional expenses of the Imperial Household, Taels 500,000.

12. Railway construction and maintenance, Taels 800,000.

13. Additional military outlay in Kansu, Taels 480,000.

14. Manchurian provinces:—Salaries of officers and pay of troops, Taels 490,000.

15. Peiyang and Nanyang imperial navy should be Taels 500,000. Actually expended, Taels 400,000.

16. Legations abroad.—Paid by the Customs, Taels 1,000,000.

17. Shantung coast soldiers' pay, Taels 600,000.

18. Yungting river repairs in Chihli, Taels 340,000.

19. Foreign loans, principal and interest, inclusive of additional amounts to compensate for loss by gold exchange, Taels 23,000,000 to 24,000,000.

20. Salaries and soldiers' pay:—Peking army expenditure, 8,000,000.

21. Frontier defence, Taels 2,500,000, inclusive of Taels 500,000 recently added.

22. Reserve for military expenses, Taels 200,000.

23. Board of War.—Salaries and pay for officers and men, Taels 1,200,000.

24. Banner organizations, Taels 660,000.

25. Additional pay of Manchu troops, Taels 1,380,000.

26. Additional salaries and wages, Taels 260,000.

Total annual expenditure, Taels 101,400,000.

MEMORIALS ON REVENUE.

Hu-pu Memorial on the Navy.

The Board beg to present a return of the ensuing year's expenditure. In April, 1895, the naval administration prayed the Emperor to direct that the payment of the officers of the navy and other items in the navy expenditure should not be made separately. It is better that all money should come to the Board. The Board can purchase ships and arms. The Board can supply the Nan-yang and Pei-yang expenditure and pay the new-drilled troops of Hei-lung-kiang. This was ordered, and we in a memorial prayed the Emperor to require the viceroys, governors, and superintendents of Customs to send all money for the navy to the Board. This new arrangement was to begin with 1895. This does not affect the retention in the provinces of a certain proportion by the system hitherto in use. The sum formerly set apart for General Lui Cheng-kwan may in the new heading be classed as frontier defence expenditure. The amounts of subscriptions for coast defence in each province and the native opium likin should now be transmitted to the Board of Revenue. Out of the native opium likin the Board will each year appropriate Taels 300,000 to the Feng-chen-yuen* and other offices in the capital. In 1896 by edict we were commanded to appropriate a sum for the Yuen-ming-yuen repairs in addition to those at Wan-shou-shan. The sums sent us to spend on naval administration since this change took place have been few. In the provinces it appears to have been felt that the naval department is practically abolished and that the money of the Board remains unused

---

* The Feng-chen-yuen (奉宸院) is a yamên in Peking which is manned by the Nei-wu-fu slaves. They supply requisites for the place, such as food and clothing.

in the treasury. It is not considered in the provinces that we give out sums to the military department. The military expenditure is less than before, but the Amoor province expense is not small. The drilled force there has to be paid as before. The Board gives monthly pay to the new Tientsin land force in barracks outside Shan-hai-kwan. The Board pays the Pei-yang Brigade (毅軍). In all we pay Taels 2,000,000 a year in this way. The amounts sent from the provincial custom houses would have been better able to meet these calls had there not been a falling off during late years in Customs' receipts. We pray the Emperor to direct the heads of the provincial administration in each instance as also the Customs' superintendents to forward promptly the amounts due to the Board for the year 1899 on account of the military and naval expenditure of the Nan-yang and Pei-yang department. We also pray that the superintendent of Customs may be directed to distinguish carefully in returns the year and the particular account headings to which the expenditure in each case belong. This will be a real aid to us in our system of accounts.

Appropriation of Likin Funds.

The following arrangement was made for supplying funds to the navy administration for 1899, including all amounts now transferred to the Board :—

Kiang-su likin collection, Taels 400,000, eight-tenths to be forwarded to the Board and applied to the Nan-yang expenditure.

Chekiang likin, Tls. 400,000, eight-tenths to be forwarded to the Board for Pei-yang expenditure.

Kiangsi likin, Taels 300,000, to be forwarded to the Board; Taels 200,000 for Pei-yang expenditure, Taels 100,000, for other uses.

Canton likin, Taels 300,000, retained in the province.

Fukien likin, Taels 300,000, retained in the province. Here follow the foreign Customs' accounts.

Kiang-su and Chekiang. Amount not fixed. Four-tenths and a half are to be forwarded to the Nan-yang and Pei-yang departments.

Shan-hai-kwan Customs. Four-tenths.

Chefoo. Amount not fixed. Pei-yang.

Canton and Swatow Customs. No fixed amount.

Fukien Customs. No fixed amount.

Chekiang Customs. No fixed amount.

Fukien foreign opium and likin, Taels 240,000. The amount formerly forwarded for the New Land Brigade (新建陸軍) is now to be applied to the New Volunteer Central Brigade (新募中軍) to the extent of 100,000 Taels. The remainder, Taels 140,000, is forwarded to the Board treasury.

Memorial of Min-che Viceroy Regarding the North-east Frontier Defence.

In the *Chung-wai*, September 6th, 1899, appeared a return of deficits in the contingents for North-east Frontier Defence from various provinces. The deficit in Chekiang from 1883 amounted to Taels 690,000. The deficit in Fukien from 1882 to 1898 amounted to Taels 662,000. In 1894 the Fukien and Chekiang viceroy in a memorial stated that the Fukien province defence was important and the funds available for military expenditure were deficient. He begged that the deportation of funds to the north might be delayed. This was in the time of the war with Japan. The Board of Revenue supported his petition, which was granted. Whenever there was a surplus it must be sent, so that the required amount might be paid by instalments. At present it is needed, and the whole deficit ought to be forwarded.

Memorial of Kiangsu Governor.

Deficit in the amount due from the Kiukiang customs:—The whole amount due from 1882 to 1895 was Taels 331,200. In 1895 the governor of Kiangsu in a memorial pleaded for delay. He needed to wait for a large collection of duties. This was allowed. In 1898 the Board asked the Emperor to require an investigation on the part of the governor into the state of the provincial treasury. Could he or could he not pay the deficit? The governor's reply was that the Customs' receipts were not sufficient to allow of the required payment. The loans negotiated with four foreign countries had to be met. There was also the payment of Arnhold, Karberg & Co.'s loan to the Nanyang administration. A part were at four per cent. interest and another part at $5\frac{2}{10}$ths per cent. The governor asks that he may be permitted to delay the payment of the amount due for the north-eastern frontier defence until the foreign loans are paid. By the annual payment of the Customs' receipts, whether they amount to more or less in a year, he will be able to forward all that is due.

Native Customs' Revenue.

The *Sin-wen-king-pao*, August 17th, 1899, prints a memorial of the Customs' Taotai for Hwai-an. The fixed amount is Taels 254,363.6.0 1. The 盈餘 surplus tax is Taels 110,000. The last superintendent from February 2nd, 1898, to May 30th, that is, in 120 days, received in the three custom houses—Hwai-an, Hai-chow, and Su-chien—Taels 7,704.7.2. The present occupant from May 31st to January 22nd, 1899, that is, in 240 days, received Taels 33,609.8.1.3. The tax remitted on account of scarcity in Kiangnan and Shantung was Taels 7,164.7.0.5. In all, the Hwai-an Customs received Taels 35,635.5.1 in a year and remitted Taels 5,906.4.7. The Su-chien Customs received Taels 5,458.1.7.4 and remitted Taels 1,258.2.3.5. The Hai-chow Customs received Taels 220.2.4.9. The total receipts of three native custom houses were Taels 48,478.6.3.8. The deficit in the fixed surplus was Taels 315,884.9.6.4.

Beside this the Hwai-an Customs' granary account has a total collection of tea duty of Taels 13.3.9.4. The Hai-chow Customs' tonnage on sea-going junks Taels 459.1.1.1. According to the Board regulations all that has been collected has been forwarded to the Board.

The deficit on the surplus tax has been compensated by drawing on the ordinary tax 正項 collection a sum amounting to Taels 14,443.3.1. In 1897 the harvest was limited by constant floods and drought. In addition, the Transit Passes issued by the foreign Customs 洋單 diminish the receipts at the native custom houses and barriers. There is also much smuggling at the towns named Tsing-er and Shao-pe. Through the operation of these causes the Customs' receipts have fallen off considerably. The memorialist, a Manchu, Kin Sheng, regrets to be obliged to add that the weather in 1898 was most unpropitious. Such was the distress that viceroys and governors united to ask for remission of duties and likin. There was a great lack of money for traders to use, and business in consequence languished. There was also a rebellion at Wo-yang and Tang-shan which further contributed to limit the receipts at these custom houses.

In Peking, says the *Hu-pao* of October 27th, 1899, the Customs' receipts are less by Taels 138,106 than in the previous year. The amount was then Taels 176,858; collection counts from the beginning of the Chinese year to the 1st of the ninth month.

Precis of Revenue Edict.

On July 11th, 1899, an edict on revenue said that corruption abounds in the Customs' (native) lekin and salt departments. A remedy must be applied. Such was the language of a former edict which required the Grand Secretaries, Cabinet, Six Boards, and Nine Bureaus to consult and report on this matter. Yesterday memorials were received which said that a bold and insatiate spirit of corruption everywhere prevailed. A way must be found to terminate the present habit of receiving presents and wrongful appropriation of funds. Beside the united memorial there were separate memorials by Sü T'ung, Chun Liang, Yuen Ch'ang, Kao Khe-hwei, I Ku, and Chang Chung-hin. Some recommend an increase in taxation; others advocate some change of special importance. A second conference took place, and some excellent suggestions were made. (Such being the language of the edict it is clear that in this document while the Emperor speaks, and the Empress-Dowager approves, the ideas of the edict on revenue are the result of the conference of the chief ministers and their colleagues. When their ideas appear to the Emperor to deserve separate consideration, they are separately stated and approved or condemned. A common phrase to use at the end of a memorial is, we beg the Emperor to carry out by edict this suggestion.) This is a time when difficulties bristle in our path. The army needs money to maintain it. Every officer, high or low, should exert himself on behalf of the State. But instead of this in the Customs, lekin, and salt departments abuses are always on the increase. The officers in those departments are influenced by selfish cupidity and not patriotism. The Manchu generals, viceroys, and Governors have their favourites, and gloss things over. They are listless and care not for the welfare of the State.

On account of the fertility and wealth of Kiang-nan, Kang Yi was sent to improve the revenue in the three departments—Customs, salt and lekin. He will not fear the voice of calumny, and he will be able, in conjunction with the Manchu general, the viceroy, and the governors, to discover the real facts. The actual amounts of collected taxes under the treasusers, superintendents, and local tax offices, together with subscriptions of traders, will be learned and all abuses probed to the bottom. It will then become possible to terminate the misappropriation of funds and to apply all available money to aid the revenue. Within three months memorials must be sent from each responsible high officer.

There is another feature. Though money does not go to the State or to the trader altogether, it may go to companies. This is adverted to by Sü T'ung. The companies intended are the China Merchants' Company, the Telegraph Company, the Kai-ping Mining Company. So long as their profits remain in their own possession the State is not benefited. It is hereby ordered that within three months these companies, especially those managed by Shêng Siuen-hwai, shall present to us an accurate statement of receipts and expenditure, with the amount to be placed at the disposal of the government and asking for the imperial decision.

In the same way the Chihli viceroy is hereby ordered to prepare statements of the receipts and expenditure of the Kai-ping coal mine and the Mo-ho and Chien-an gold mines. Mo-ho receipts have fallen off. Let this matter be set right. Regulations for the new Chien-an gold mine should be drawn up. The whole should be reported to us for decision. The only railway that pays is the Tsin Lu. But it is a short line, and borrowed money has to be paid back before revenue is available. The money used is partly official and partly belongs to private persons, who must be reimbursed. The great profit will be that of the Lu Han line when it is finished.

Chun Liang thinks railway construction should be vigorously prosecuted. We do not agree to this, for the present at least. Yuen Ch'ang thinks the lekin needs to be collected on new principles. He proposes six changes, of which some can be accepted. The suggested extra expenditure can be referred to the Board. The collection at barriers and various local offices can be made either by government servants or by selected gentry, as the Manchu general, the viceroys and the governors regard as most advisable.

The Peking official memorialists have named Ch'eng I-lo and other Taotais as suitable to take office. This may be arranged by the high officers of the provinces to which they belong.

I Ku recommends that there be an increase in the Customs and salt duties and in the lekin. There is no objection to placing these collections in the hands of traders, so far as the Lo-ti tax is concerned. But traders cannot manage the collection of taxes on goods going to or coming from other provinces.

I Ku and Chang Chung-hin suggest an addition to the taxes. To this proposal we say no. We will not be less liberal than our ancestors for 250 years. The country prospered with light taxation. We prefer to rely on the patriotism of the people and the gratitude of the high officers who owe their position to imperial favour. We look to them to do their utmost to increase the revenue in the present crisis. Why should they weary and vex the people by demanding more from them than they now pay?

The gentry and people should know our intentions. Let the Manchu generals, viceroys, and governors inform them by proclamations. The directors of companies and office managers should assist in making this known. The government does not wish to take all the fish in the lake and leave none behind. What is required is that all balances of money should be faithfully transferred to the State treasury.

German Statement of Public Revenue in China.

(From the *King-shï-wen Sin-pien* 8, p. 22.)

Land tax. 地稅.	Amount properly due. 戶部應收常例.	Actual amount received. 各省實收中數.
Chihli	3,029,644	2,200,000
Shantung	3,380,052	2,600,000
Shansi	3,056,407	2,600,000
Honan	3,250,263	2,316,000
Kiangsu	3,277,971	1,468,000
Anhwei	1,655,454	1,046,000
Kiangsi	2,077,645	1,118,000
Fukien	1,248,200	1,010,000
Chêkiang	2,794,340	1,400,000
Hupei	1,124,700	950,000
Hunan	1,162,736	1,150,000
Shensi	1,627,513	1,550,000
Kansu	231,104	204,000
Szchwen	668,482	2,390,000
Kwangtung ...	1,279,903	1,600,000
Kwangsi	393,703	500,000
Yünnan	210,531	300,000
Kweichow	31,581	125,000
Manchurian provinces	221,774	560,000
Total, Taels, 合計	30,721,003	25,087,000

Revenue of China. 通國進欵.

1. Land tax	地稅銀	25,088,000
2. Grain „	米糧銀	6,562,000
3. Salt	鹽稅銀	13,659,000
4. Lekin	釐金銀	12,952,000
5. Maritime Customs	洋關稅銀	21,989,000
6. Native „	土關稅餉	1,000,000
7. Opium lekin ...	土煙釐稅	2,229,000
8. Miscellaneous duties	雜項稅餉	5,500,000
合計 Total, Taels, 共進銀		88,979,000

RICE CHANGED FOR SILVER. 漕糧折銀.

	Kinds of grain. 米色.	擔數.	Commutation Rate. 每擔折銀.	Amount changed for silver. 共折銀.
	Coarse rice and white rice.			
Kiangsu	漕白米	850,000	Changed for silver at two taels.	1,700,000
Chêkiang	漕白米	450,000	do.	900,000
Kiangsi				600,000
Hupei				270,000
Anhwei				750,000
Hunan				240,000
Honan				300,000
	Millet.			
Shantung	粟米	200,000		280,000
	Total, piculs,	1,500,000		5,040,000

JAPANESE STATEMENT OF THE REVENUE OF CHINA.

INCOME.

Land tax ... ... Taels	24,000,000
Personal service commutation tax ...	2,500,000
Miscellaneous taxes in the provinces ...	1,600,000
Miscellaneous collections in the provinces	1,000,000
Grain commuted to silver	4,100,000
Salt	13,500,000
Lekin	16,000,000
Native customs	2,700,000
Imperial maritime customs	22,000,000
Opium tax	1,800,000
Total, Taels	88,200,000

EXPENDITURE.

Government	10,000,000
Manchu soldiers' pay	1,380,000
Palace	1,100,000
Administrative expenditure in the provinces	20,000,000
Land army	300,000
Navy	5,000,000
Legations abroad	1,000,000

Foreign Customs	3,600,000
Yellow River	940,000
Railways	800,000
Payment of foreign debts	24,000.000
Special expenditure (預備費)	3,300,000
Total, Taels	100,112,000

Mr. G. Jamieson's Scheme for Increasing the Revenue of China.

(*Shen-pau*, September 12th, 1901.)

By abolishing the lekin and increasing the foreign customs' collection the annual amount realized will be Taels 22,000,000.

If the Chinese native customs are administered by the foreign customs' staff it will be expedient to limit the jurisdiction of each custom house. Thus Kiangsu and Chekiang have one system of collection. The province of Kiangsi and the vicinity of the Poyang Lake form the area of a second custom house. The third custom house will have jurisdiction over the Tung-ting lake and the provinces of Hunan and Hupei. Szechwen forms a sufficient area for the collection of duties by one custom house.

Customs' Collections by Land:—Custom houses are established and customs' collections made on three principal routes: 1. From Poyang Lake to Kwangtung. 2. From Hunan to Kwangsi. 3. From Kiangsu to Shantung. If railways do not pass out of the area over which the custom house has jurisdiction, they should not pay taxes.

Imports, Tls.	167,380,000=	Duties, Tls.	5,730,000	Additional Duties, Tls.	20,836,000
Opium	=	"	5,477,000	" "	5,477,000
Exports	147,037,000=	"	5,405,000	" "	5,961,000
		Total Tls.	16,612,000	Total Tls.	32,274,000

By the absorption of the native customs in the foreign Imperial Maritime Customs the revenue of the latter will be increased.

Imports, Tls. 68,000,000,	Duties, Tls. 1,184,000	Additional Duties, Tls.	8,500,000
Native opium	,, 477,000	,, ,,	477,000
Exports	,, 2,901,000		
Re-exports	,, 1,717,000		
Tonnage	612,000	,, ,,	612,000
Likin	14,000,000		
Native customs	20,500,000	,, ,,	6,000,000
	Total Tls. 39,003,000	,, ,,	47,863,000

Payment of Hupu Deficit in 1899.

(The *Chung-wai-pau*, June 28th, 1899.)

Hupei Province.—Smuggling prevention expenditure, amounting to (sent to Wuchang to await orders from the Board)...	Taels 50,000
Increased tax, on Chang-lu salt, to be levied from July 8, 1899. (This will yield, if seven-tenths are assigned to the revenue), ...	200,000
Chekiang.—No addition is made to the salt tax. Traders offer as a free gift (pau-hiau) 報効 for 1899	60,000
After 1899, by instalments spread over five years, traders will give	150,000
Shensi.—The addition to the salt tax amounts to	80,000
The Sheng-king pawnbrokers' tax for 1897, still due, will yield	32,300
The same tax for 1898 will be	28,520
In 1897 the grain tax outside of Feng-t'ien province, after subtracting the diminished soldiers' pay appropriation and three-tenths of the magistrates' salaries, amounts to	5,211
In paying the regular amount for frontier defence to the Kirin Taotai, the Board deducts (being the remainder due to the Board still in the hands of the said Taotai)	24,490
In Hei-lung-kiang, when soldiers' pay for autumn is asked for, the sum to be deducted on account of tobacco tax and brokers' license tax amounts to	40,684

The Hupei fixed contingent of tribute grain is piculs 30,000. The tribute grain Taotai should send it. The value, with estimated expense of conveyance, is Taels 70,000. This amount has, on account of the Board of Revenue treasury being empty, gone to pay foreign loans. The tribute grain Taotai prays the viceroy and governor to memorialize the throne, asking that further time may be granted him for payment. (*Chung-wai-pao*, August 26th, 1899.)

Expenditure in A.D. 1558.

In the year 1558 it was ordered that one million taels of silver should be given over for the use of the palace, in addition to the Emperor's special expenditure. This was the result of the influence of the eunuchs at that time. In addition there were 400,000 taels, the confiscated property of delinquent officials and penalties for offences against customs' regulations. The eunuchs grew bold. They would send despatches to the Board of Revenue for silver, and they did not take the trouble to say for what purpose or to what amount silver was required. This is stated in the history about 1567. To this the Board objected. They petitioned the Emperor to check the eunuchs, but without success.

Shen Tsung came to the throne A. D. 1573. In his eighth year (Wan-li 8) the treasury was yearly receiving Taels 4,500,000 of silver, (Ming History 79, 10,) Taels 200,000 beyond the amount recognized as suitable in A. D. 1436. Soon after Taels 70,000 were added for feed of horses, and the treasuries of the Board of Revenue, that of the Imperial Banqueting Court, and of the Imperial stud, were nearly empty.

The Board of Works had a treasury for the produce of silver mines. The president of the Board paid workmen with this silver. The Emperor rebuked him and ordered him to replace the amount so used by other silver. From this time all the silver of this treasury was applied to palace expenditure. The eunuchs at this time were court favourites. They were of low origin and without Confucian education. Their cleverness pleased the Emperors and aided them in many ways. There was always a feud between them and the Confucianist class. They cast covetous looks on the silver that was now fast being added through foreign trade and the working of mines to the stores accumulated by the Mongols in their wars.

The salt administration in the Ming dynasty is connected closely with the history of the currency. According to the method pursued at the close of the fourteenth century, salt farmers manufactured salt within fixed territorial limits. Each salt certificate, or yin, represented 200 catties, and this was equivalent to one hundred catties of rice. It is singular that at present (July, 1897) twenty-five copper cash will buy one catty of rice and in places half a catty of salt, but salt is usually much cheaper than this. Thus, at Canton salt and rice are nearly equal in price, because Canton is on the sea where salt is cheaply manufactured, whereas on the river at Hankow and beyond it, in fresh water districts, the people suffer from a too heavy taxation of an article so necessary as common salt. I am told that at Nanking the price of rice and of salt is much the same per catty. Beyond this up the river westward the expense of conveyance adds to the price of salt.

A certificate 引 yin means 675 catties (Giles). At Tientsin one large bag of salt, carried by four bearers, weighs 640 catties. Such bags are made of rush mat. In A. D. 1436 the Kiangsu salt was sold so far away as Kweichow, but a few years later, 1465, the salt of Pakhoi, on the Canton coast, was carried to the cities of Hunan. At the same time the Kiangsi cities near Canton province made use of Canton salt.

Military Expenditure in 1898.

In the *Shen Pao*, January 6th, 1898, the governor of Chekiang sends a return of the estimated expenditure for 1899 for Manchu and Chinese troops, the garrisons at Hangchow and Chapu, the guard of the governor, general, major, and colonel, as also the Imperial factory, Taels 761,861.1.7.2.

To meet this there are only Taels 85,000 and another 5,000. The governor asks that the Board of Revenue will send the remainder, with the required rice amounting to 150,962 piculs, 4 teu.

Peiyang Military Expenditure.

There are three brigades under the Peiyang administration. Forty regiments (毅 軍 i-chiün) are commanded by General Sung Ching 宋 慶, the Szchwen provincial general.*

Thirty regiments of the new land force (陸 軍) are commanded by Yuen Shi-kai 袁 世 凱.†

Thirty regiments of the Chihli land force are commanded by the Chihli provincial general, Niê Shi-ch'êng 聶 士 成.

The normal number of each regiment is 500 men. They compose therefore an army of about fifty thousand men, raised since the Japanese war.

This army is additional to the ordinary army. It was commenced in 1883, on account of the war with France in 1881. In 1889 Yü Lu mentioned in a memorial that the amount to be annually expended was decided upon.

In *Chung-wai*, November 17th, 1899, a memorial of Yü Lu, the Peiyang viceroy, states that to meet the Peiyang expenditure Taels 1,100,000 are contributed by the lekin of Kiangsi and Chekiang and from the foreign Customs at Shanghai, Ningpo, and Chefoo. Of this amount 800,000 have been actually received.

* For many years he has been stationed at Shan-hai-kuan.

† He was formerly minister to Corea and is now Viceroy of Chihli.

To this should be added three-tenths of the Chihli coast defence fund, that is to say, Taels 400,000. Total, Taels 1,200,000.

Expenditure.—School, torpedo regiment, batteries, dock, arsenal,	Total Taels 700,000
To meet the naval current expenditure there is a remainder of ...	„ 500,000
To meet the expense of thirteen new vessels we need...	1,000,000

and only the 500,000 are to be depended on. We need 500,000 more. The China Merchants, telegraph, and mining companies might advance Taels 300,000 toward our naval expenditure. I propose that 120,000 should be applied from Hwai army reduction fund, and 80,000 from the drilled army reduction fund. [The Emperor grants these requests.]

Naval Expenditure Taels 4,000,000.

(*Chung-wai*, January 27th, 1900.)

The name Hai-chiün-sin-tseng-ching-fei 海軍新增經費 is now changed to Sin-kien-lu-chiün 新建陸軍. The amount is one million taels, made up in the following manner :—

Shanghai opium lekin	Taels 260,000
Kiukiang	160,000
Chinkiang	80,000
Canton, Swatow, Kiungchow, and Pakhoi	300,000
Cowloon and Kungpei	200,000

For 1899 these sums, after subtracting amounts used on Nanyang, Peiyang, and provincial account, are to be forwarded to the Board.

1. General Lei's appropriation.—He was T'i-tu for Shensi and Kansu. He died last year in Shansi, and was called Ku-yuen 固原 t'i-tu, because he resided at the city of that name. His appropriation is placed under the heading Naval Administration Expenditure.

Kiangsu	Taels 20,000 monthly.
Chekiang	9,000 „

These amounts are to be sent monthly to the Board.

2. Subscriptions for 1899 due to the Board, with two exceptions. The brigade of Niê Shi-ch'êng 聶士成 is to be paid in accordance with Chihli memorial. He is Chihli T'i-tu. The famine relief is to be reserved in accordance with Kansu memorial.

3. Native opium duty and lekin for 1899 is all due to the Board. Of this sum Taels 300,000 are appropriated by the Board to the Feng-chen-yuen and Wan-shou-shan. The remainder is applied to Yuen-ming-yuen expenditure. Feng-chen-yuen is a Yamên within the Tung-hwa-men.

The money which supports the river, military, or naval expenditure is collected at eight lekin stations. See *Shen Pao*, August 10th, 11th, and 12th, 1899, which gives 900,000 as the amount needed to support the 長江水師年餉 Chang-kiang river naval expenditure. This amount is given in a memorial by Yung Ch'ang, on reforms in the native customs and lekin. He says the use of transit passes seriously diminishes the receipts of the lekin stations. The collections diminish while the foreign customs' collection increases. The remedy is found in a return to an old system. Barriers are set up in busy market towns at two, three, or four places in each district. The head lekin office at the provincial capital appoints upright scholars or rich traders to contract for so much a month. They collect a goods tax and examine the books monthly of the leading shops, exacting five per cent. on the profits. In reporting to the Board of Revenue the system commenced by Tseng Kwo-fan and Tso Tsung-t'ang is followed. To prevent illegal charges a tariff of taxes is posted in public places in each city. The memorialist recommends that the lekin charge may be lightened, so that it may compete with the foreign customs' passes. He adds that successful and honest collectors should be rewarded, and those who are faulty punished by the provincial treasurer.

Nanyang Army.

The *Tsz-lin Hu-pao*, August 10th, 1899, says that Kang Chung-t'ang has memorialized the Empress, saying that 100,000 soldiers will be needed for the southern army—twenty thousand guard Woosung; twenty thousand are stationed at Fu-shan, fifty miles up the river from Woosung; twenty thousand are stationed at Kiangyin and twenty thousand more at Chinkiang. Beside these, about 20,000 are stationed between Hwai-an and Tsing-kiang-pu on the Grand Canal.

Relief Distribution.

The treasurer of a province, in cases of drought and flood, is in communication with the Board of Revenue. That Board authorises famine distribution for a certain limited time. If the distress continues beyond the limited time the treasurer asks the Board to allow an extension. In the *Shen-pao* of January 12th, 1899, it is stated that in Hupei drought had lasted three years. The limit was the China New Year of 1899. The treasurer, feeling assured that there will be great distress in the spring, consulted with Viceroy Chang. They agreed to ask the Board to allow another year. To this the Board consented.

The *Shen-pao* of May 6th, 1899, mentions that at Kiukiang a Weiyuen inspector of ships of war died in great poverty. The superintendent subscribed $30 for his burial expenses. To this friends added other sums.

Hu-pu Memorial on the Three Official Companies.

Sü T'ung,* President of the Board of Revenue and Ta-hio-shï, in his memorial printed in the *Shen-pao*, August 5th, 1899,

* Committed suicide, when the foreign army captured Peking, at Pao-ting-fu in August, 1900.

says the Steam Navigation Company, the Telegraph Company and the Railway Administration are flourishing. Yet they pay nothing to the State. They ought to share their profits with the government. He asks that Director-General Sheng and Yü Lu be required to present within two months a clear statement of railway accounts: also that the Steam Navigation Company and Telegraph Administration, as well as the Mining Companies prepare returns of receipts and expenditure within two months for presentation to the Emperor. He observes that the China Merchants' Company can compete with Messrs. Butterfield & Swire and with Messrs. Jardine, Matheson & Co. in prosperity. Why should not the State share in the profit?

Payment of the Hupu Deficit.

The *Chung-wai-pao* of June 26th, 1899, publishes the replies of the fourteen subordinate departments of the Board of Revenue to the demand of the president as to what measures should be taken to increase the revenue and diminish the expenditure of the Board. The deficit amounts to Taels 20,000,000.

Chekiang department.—The import duty on foreign wine, cigars, cigarettes, instead of being 10% *ad valorem*, might be 20% *ad valorem*. This would amount to Taels 10,000,000.

The Chekiang imperial factory might, compared with the sum expended about 1864, expend Taels 100,000 less on silk and satin fabrics for the use of the court. The expenditure on maintaining the sea wall of Chekiang province may be reduced to the extent of three-tenths. This will add to the revenue Taels 50,000.

The expenditure in the form of travelling expenses allowed to civil and military graduates proceeding to Peking to the final examination, may be temporarily withheld.

Honan department.—The miscellaneous taxes may, by investigation and revision, be made to yield many thousand Taels more than at present. By diminishing the postal charges many thousand taels may be saved. Also the surplus tax (han-sien) remaining in the treasury. This will amount to 50,000 or 60,000 taels.

The Chang-lu salt department should send each year to Honan, for Yellow River repairs, Taels 8,000. This is the result of money put out at interest. This sum should go to the Board of Revenue. Several regiments of the drilled troops might be disbanded. There are seven in all. The volunteer defence regiments cannot be disbanded. Many thousand taels may be saved by disbanding drilled troops. The seven regiments are not all required.

The allowance for the Yellow River repairs, Taels 120,000, might be placed at the disposal of the Board.

Canton.—The profit from sand field taxes, amounting each year to Taels 200,000, might go to the Board.

Six-tenths of the deed tax surplus for sales of land and houses should go to the Board and four-tenths remain for the salaries of military officers. The regulation amount is Taels 100,000. The Board should receive Taels 60,000.

The Lo-ti, or import local tax surplus, amounts by the regulation rate to Taels 50,000. Six-tenths should go to the salaries of civil officers and four-tenths be at the disposal of the Board.

The lekin tax on all goods must amount annually to Taels 2,000,000. The collectors must be so diligent in their duty that there may never be a less collection than this. The lekin office has hitherto applied one-tenth of the collection to office expenses. We propose that the Board reduce this expenditure to six-hundredths. The saving will amount to Taels 80,000 a year.

The money lent by the Board of Revenue to the Tientsin telegraph office has been long since returned in full by the payment of messages. We recommend that beginning from this year there be no more payment for messages sent by the government. The trader still pays for his messages and loyally aids the government by his support of the telegraph service. The money lent was Taels 3,000,000. It was in response to a memorial of Li Chung-tang, about the year 1863, that the two empresses, then ruling, approved of this expenditure.

There may be a reduction of two-tenths in the salaries of the (Wei-yuens) managing officers of the Peiyang and Nanyang arsenals, the Tientsin pay office, the Canton coast defence office, and the Canton Shan-how office. This will amount to a saving of Taels 2,000,000.

Szchwen.—The Hupu department for Szchwen replies to the president that the deed tax for sale of houses and land might yield Taels 1,000,000 if an order were sent to that effect. Independently of two-tenths left in the province treasury for expenses and Taels 180,000 contributed each year as hitherto, there would then remain Taels 600,000 which could be credited to the Board.

The same department recommends that orders be sent to the Szchwen province to modify the lekin returns sent regularly to the Board. Instead of a return in one round sum each lekin office throughout the province should report what its rules and its tariff are and the duties collected, great and small, should all be accurately stated, so that the Board may be able to decide what additions can be made to the revenue.

The Kiangnan department of the Hupu, in its reply to the president, first refers to the lekin collection. The amount collected each year has been calculated at 1,500 or 1,600 cash a tael. The Board may order the lekin management to calculate the cash at 1,200 or 1,300 to the tael of silver. Each year the sum stated in silver will be increased by Taels 40,000 or 50,000. The lekin on salt may also be increased by Taels 80,000 or 90,000. In each province throughout the empire it will also be possible to make a large addition to the revenue by estimating lekin receipts in cash at the current rate in silver. This should be done in the case of the lekin tax on ordinary goods, on salt, and on the additional charge specially made on each catty of salt; orders should be promulgated requiring this to be done in every province.

Two years ago the order was given that from 1897 and onward the Nanyang expenditure on war vessels propelled by steam should be reduced by Taels 1,600,000 each year. In 1899 the saving in fact amounted to Taels 360,000. The Nanyang administration memorialized the Emperor asking that this amount should be retained to be applied to the construction of swift steamers and steamers adapted to ram other vessels. But this expenditure would not be required at once. When the time came for these new vessels to be built and paid for the Board could make the appropriation.

In 1897 the governor of Anhwei stated in a memorial addressed to the emperor that measurements having been made to determine the proper amount of land and grain tax, the addition to the revenue in that province would be Taels 60,000; after the second year an addition of Taels 100,000 would be reported. At present it will then be possible to obtain an increase in revenue at the rate thus indicated. The Board can direct this amount to be used in a way to be stated by them.

The provinces of Kiangsu and Anhwei have each several boards, some of which are not needed. The Board for manufacturing silver dollars may be abolished and silver dollars may be obtained from other provinces; or the mint board of Kiangnan may be amalgamated with the arsenal of Kiangnan. The Nanking and Shanghai mints may both be abolished.

The same economical change may be made in other provinces. Anhwei is near Hupei, and can obtain dollars from Wuchang. [September, 1901.—At Shanghai, no dollars are made at present. At Nanking the mint is still working.]

In the year 1897 there was a reduction in the number of piculs of rice sent from Kiangsu to Peking, amounting to piculs 300,000. The silver value was Taels 900,000. This amount of silver was used in paying a foreign debt. In 1898 the amount due on account of foreign loans is not great. What we propose is that 300,000 piculs less of grain be sent from Kiangsu as in the year preceding. Less will be required to pay for loans and a remainder of rice will be in the granaries. This will be at the disposal of the Board.

The Kiangsi department of the Board of Revenue sent a very brief reply. Each province keeps back a certain proportion of the regular and miscellaneous grain tribute. The salaries and pensions of officers have to be paid, but some officers are degraded, and there are punishments, fines, and vacancies. The amount thus saved in the expenditure ought to be credited to the Board. In all the provinces the same rule should be followed.

During the summer of 1899 certain secretaries of the Hupu, acting for the provinces of Kiangsi, Hukwang, and Fukien, reported on the taxes in those provinces available for the needs of the treasury in Kiangsi. In this province a balance in hand of the grain and miscellaneous grain taxes, of salary and pension allowances and of fines for misconduct may be applied.

At Wuchang four taels tonnage is paid by each vessel 25 feet in length, and a waste tax of Taels 0.4.0. If the vessel is 24 feet long the tax is Taels 3.7.0, waste tax taels 0.3.7. The Board may secure a share.

Hukwang.—The Hukwang department reports that in the Hupei lekin there is what is called the Shen-ch'wen 申串

cash to the number of 6,000 strings which are set apart for use in rewards each year. This may be applied to the revenue.

Hupei Broker's License Contribution.—Of this a very large amount is due. It is called 牙帖捐 Ya-t'ie-kiuen.

Hupei Small Pawnshops.—They can all be required to pay the pawnbrokers' license tax just as it is levied on the large pawnbrokers and becomes one of the miscellaneous taxes in the treasurer's (Fan-tai) returns.

In Hunan and Hupei the field tax, house tax, pawnbroker's tax, and miscellaneous tax may be made the subject of inquiry, and an exact report being presented the collection of these taxes may be increased through the two provinces.

Hunan Lekin.—There is an annual remainder of Taels 30,000 not forwarded. The whole of this may, in each year's return of taxes, be added to the public revenue. Besides, the rule has been in Hunan to expend ten per cent. on local needs. This may be made eight per cent. as it is in Hupei. This will be equal to a saving of Taels 20,000 a year.

Fukien.—This department replies that recently each year there has been an appropriation of 1,000,000 and more taels for the Board of Works for the Imperial Household, or it may have been several hundred thousand taels. What we propose is that the Household Department omit calling on Fukien for payment.

Fukien owes Taels 180,000 to 190,000 grain tax, not yet paid for each of several years past. The payment may be claimed and a limit of time fixed.

Jehol.—In the hunting park near Jehol the people owe for personal service and grain tax one million and several hundred thousand taels. Excepting the amount from which the tax payers have been exempted by edict, we propose that to help the present need of the government the sum due be paid within a certain limit of time.

The Peace Protocol.

Indemnity of Taels 450,000,000.

News was, early in 1901, received by telegraph from Peking that the Peace Protocol had been signed by the Plenipotentiaries of the Powers and of China. The following is a translation of the French text:—

Final Protocol.

The Plenipotentiaries:—

Of Germany:	His Ex.	A. Mumm de Schwarzenstein.
Of Austro Hungary:	„	Czikann de Wahlborn.
Of Belgium:	„	Mr. Joostens.
Of Spain:	„	Mr. B. J. de Cologan.
Of U. S. of America:	„	Mr. W. W. Rockhill.
Of France:	„	Mr. P. Bean.
Of Great Britain:	„	Sir Ernest Satow.
Of Italy:	„	Marquis Salvago Raggi.
Of Japan:	„	Mr. Jutaro Komura.
Of Holland:	„	Mr. F. M. Knobel.
Of Russia:	„	Mr. de Giers.

and

Of China: His Highness I Kuang, Prince of the first rank; Ching, President of the Ministry of Foreign Affairs; and His Excellency Li Hung-chang, Count of the first rank, Tutor of the Heir Presumptive, Grand Secretary of the Shun-ho-tien Hall, Minister of Commerce, Superintendent of Northern Ports, Governor-General of Chihli, have met in order to establish that China has announced her agreement to the satisfaction of the Powers, with the condition which are set forth in the note of 22nd December, 1900, which were accepted as a whole by His Majesty the Emperor of China by an Edict of 27th December, 1900 (annex 1).

Article 1a.

By an Imperial Edict of 9th June of this year (annex 2) Tsai Feng, Prince of first rank, Chun, was appointed Ambassador of H. M. the Emperor of China, and in this capacity was commanded to express to H. M. the German Emperor the regret of H. M. the Emperor of China and the Chinese

Government for the death of the German Ambassador, His Excellency Baron von Ketteler.

Prince Chun left Peking on the 13th July of this year to carry out the commission entrusted to him.

Article 1b.

The Chinese Government has announced that it will erect, on the spot of the murder of His Excellency Baron von Ketteler, a memorial monument corresponding to the rank of the deceased, with an inscription in Latin, German, and Chinese, which shall express the regret of H. M. the Emperor of China for the murder done.

Their Excellencies the Chinese Plenipotentiaries have informed their Excellencies the German plenipotentiaries by a letter of 22nd July of this year (annex 3) that an arch will be erected across the entire breadth of the street on the spot mentioned and that the work was begun on the 25th June of this year.

Article 2a.

Imperial Edicts of the 13th and 21st February, 1901 (annexes 4, 5, and 6) pronounce the following punishments upon the chief culprits for the attacks upon, and crimes against, the friendly governments and their subjects :—

Tsai Yi, Prince Tuan, and Tsai San, Duke Fu Koo, were condemned to death at the autumn session, and it is further determined that if the Emperor thinks their lives should be spared, they shall be banished to Turkestan and there shall be imprisoned for life, with no possibility that the punishment will ever be revoked.

Tsai Kin, Prince Chuan, Ying Min, President of the Censorate, and Chao Shu-chiao, President of the Ministry of Justice, shall be condemned to commit suicide; Yü Hsien, Governor of Shansi; Chi Hsien, President of the Court of Ceremony; Hsu Chien-yu, formerly Director in the Ministry of Justice, shall be condemned to death.

Degradation after death was pronounced against Kang Yi, assistant member of the Grand Secretariat and President of the Ministry of the Interior; Hsü Tung, member of the Grand Secretariat; and Li Ping-hêng, formerly Governor-General of Szechuan.

An Imperial Edict of 13th February, 1901 (annex 7), re-instated, after death, in their titles and offices of honor the

President of the War Office, Hsu Yung-yi; the President of the Ministry of Finance, Li Shan; the Director of the Ministry of the Interior, Hsü Ching-cheng; the Vice-Chancellor in the Grand Secretariat at Hien-yuan; and the Director in the Court of Sacrifices, Yuan Chang, who were executed because they protested against the hitherto unheard of offences against international right which took place during the last year.

Prince Chuan committed suicide on the 21st February, 1901; Ying Min and Chao Shu-chiao on the 24th; Yü Hsien was executed on the 22nd February, 1901; Ch'i Hsien and Hsü Chien-yü on the 26th.

The General of Kansu, Tung Fu-hsiang, was deprived of his office by Imperial Edict of 13th February, 1901, until it shall be decided what final punishment shall be pronounced against him. Imperial Edicts of 29th April, 1901, and of later date have pronounced suitable punishments against provincial authorities who confessedly were guilty of crimes or murder during the course of last summer.

Article 2b.

An Imperial edict (annex 8) has ordered the suspension of the official examinations during five years in all provinces where foreigners have been murdered or subjected to harsh treatment.

Article 3.

In order to make suitable amends for the murder of Mr. Sugiyama, Chancellor of the Japanese Legation, H. M. the Emperor of China, by an Imperial Edict of 18th June, 1901 (annex 9), appointed the Vice-President of the Ministry of Finance, Na Tung, an Extraordinary Ambassador, and commanded him in particular to convey to H. M. the Emperor of Japan the regret of H. M. the Emperor of China and his government for the murder of Mr. Sugiyama.

Article 4.

The Chinese government has undertaken to erect an expiatory monument in each of the international cemeteries which have been desecrated, or in which monuments have been destroyed. To this end it has been arranged with the representatives of the Powers that the Legations concerned will indicate what is necessary for the erection of these monuments, with the undertaking on the part of China to bear all the costs, which are fixed at 10,000 taels for the cemeteries in Peking and its neighbourhood, and 5,000 in the provinces. These sums have been paid, and the receipt is herewith acknowledged (Appendix 10).

Article 5.

China has agreed to forbid temporarily the importation of arms and ammunition, as well as of all material exclusively employed for the manufacture of arms. An Imperial Edict was published on 27th August, 1901 (Appendix 11), which forbids such importations for two years.

Further Edicts can be promulgated in future, in order to extend this period every two years, in case the Powers, deem it necessary.

Article 6.

In an Imperial Edict of 29th May, 1901, H. M. the Emperor of China has undertaken to pay the Powers an indemnity of 450 million Haikwan taels.

This sum represents the total of the indemnity for the States, societies, individuals, foreigners, and Chinese which are mentioned in Article 6 of the note of 22nd December.

(*a.*) These 450 million taels form a debt in gold in which the rate of the Haikwan tael is calculated in the gold currency of each country in the following manner:—

1 Haikwan Tael=	Mark	3.055
	Austro-Hungarian Krone	3.595
	Gold Dollar	0.742
	Francs	3.750
	Pound Sterling, Shanghai	0.3.0
	Yen	1.407
	Dutch Gulden	1.796
	Gold Rouble	1.412

This sum in gold shall bear interest at the rate of 4 per cent. per annum and the principal is to be reimbursed by China in thirty-nine years on the conditions indicated in the plan of amortisation annexed hereto (Appendix 13). The capital and interest will be payable in gold or at the rate of exchange corresponding to the dates of the different payments.

The operation of the amortisation will commence on the 1st January, 1902, in order to end at the expiration of the year 1940. The amortisations will be payable annually; the first date of maturity being fixed as the 1st January, 1903.

The interest will be calculated to begin from the 1st July, 1901, but the Chinese government will have the privilege of freeing itself in a period of three years, commencing on 1st January, 1902, of the arrears of the first half-year ending 31st December, 1901, on the condition, however, of paying interest at four per cent. per annum on the sums of which the payment will have been thus deferred.

The interest will be payable half-yearly; the first maturity being fixed for the 1st July, 1902.

(*b.*) The service of the debt will be effected at Shanghai in the following manner:—

Each Power will be represented by a delegate in a commission of bankers, which will be charged with the collection of the amount of the interest and the amortisations, which will be paid by the Chinese authorities designated for that purpose. The delegates will divide this among those interested and give receipts for it.

(*c.*) The Chinese government will remit to the doyen of the Diplomatic Corps at Peking a lump coupon, which will be subsequently exchanged for notes provided with the signatures of the delegates of the Chinese government designated for that purpose. Each operation, and all those which are connected with the establishment of the titles, will be effected by the aforesaid commission conformably to the instructions which the Powers will send to their delegates.

(*d.*) The product of the sources of revenue applied to the payment of the coupons will be paid monthly into the hands of the commission.

(*e.*) The sources of revenue applied to the guarantee of the coupons are enumerated herewith:—

1. The balance of revenues of the Imperial Maritime Customs after payment of the interest and the amortisation of the previous loans pledged on these revenues, augmented by the product of the raising to an effective five per cent. of the actual tariff on maritime imports, including articles which have hitherto entered free, with the exception of foreign rice, cereals, and flour, as well as gold and silver, coined or uncoined.

2. The revenues of the native Customs administered in the open ports by the Imperial Maritime Customs.

3. The total of the revenue of the salt gabelle, excepting the fraction previously guaranteed to other foreign loans.

The raising of the actual tariff on imports to an effective five per cent. is consented to on the following conditions :—

The putting in operation of that increase will commence two months after the date of the signature of the present protocol, and there will be only exceptions for merchandise *en route*, at the latest six days after that date.

1. All the duties on importations levied *ad valorem* will be converted into specific duties as far as it is possible to do so and with the least delay. This conversion will be established as follows: The average value at the time of their disembarkation during the three years—1897, 1898, 1899—will be taken as the basis of the valuation, that is to say, the value on the market, deduction being made of the import duties and the accessory expenses. Until the result of that conversion is known, the duties will be imposed *ad valorem.*

2. The course of the Peiho and the Whangpoo will be improved with the financial participation of China in the expense incurred.

Article 7.

The Chinese government has agreed that the quarter occupied by the Legations shall be considered as a quarter specially reserved to their usage and placed under their exclusive police, where the Chinese shall not have the right to reside, and which may be put into a state of defence. The limits of the quarter have been drawn on a plan as in Appendix 14 :—

I.—To the west, lines 1, 2, 3, 4, 5 ;
II.—To the north, lines 5, 6, 7, 8, 9, 10 ;
III.—To the east, Ketteler Street, lines 10, 11, 12 ;
IV.—To the south, lines 12—1 ; drawn along the foot of the exterior of the Tartar wall, in following the bastion.

By the protocol annexed to the letter of 16th January, 1901, China has recognised that each Power has the right to retain a permanent guard in the said quarter for the defence of its Legation.

Article 8.

The Chinese government has consented to have the Taku forts razed, and those which could prevent free communication between Peking and the sea. Arrangements have been already made to raze the forts.

Article 9.

The Chinese government has recognised that the Powers, by the protocol annexed to the letter of the 16th January, 1901, have the right to occupy certain points to be determined by agreement between them, in order to maintain free communication between the capital and the sea. The points occupied by the Powers are: Whang-ts'un, Lang-fang, Yang-ts'un, Tientsin, Kiün-liang-c'heng, T'ang-ku, Lu-t'ai, T'ang-shan, Lan-chow, Chang-li, Chin-wang-tao, Shan-hai-kuan.

Article 10.

The Chinese government has engaged to post and publish during two years in all the towns of the district concerned the following Imperial Edicts (Appendix 15):—

(*a.*) Edict of the 1st February, 1901, perpetually forbidding, under pain of death, membership in any anti-foreign society.

(*b.*) Edict of July 31, 1901, containing the enumeration of the punishments which have been inflicted on the guilty.

(*c.*) Edict suppressing the examinations in all the towns where foreigners have been massacred or have been subjected to harsh treatment.

(*d.*) Edict of 1st February, 1901 (Appendix 16), declaring that all the Governors-General, Governors and functionaries, provincial or local, are responsible for order in their districts, and that in case of new anti-foreign troubles, or even of other infractions of the treaties, which are not immediately repressed, and of which those guilty shall not have been punished, these functionaries will be immediately removed, and shall not be called to new functions nor receive new honours.

Later the posting of these Edicts is to be extended progressively through the whole empire.

Article 11.

The Chinese government engages to negotiate amendments judged useful by the foreign governments in the treaties of commerce and navigation, and other subjects touching commercial relations, with the view of facilitating these commercial relations with foreign countries.

From this time and in consequence of the stipulations included in Article VI on the subject of the indemnities, the

Chinese government has engaged to co-operate in the amelioration of the course of the rivers Peiho and Whangpoo, as set out below :—

(*a.*) The works of amelioration and of the navigability of the Whangpoo, commenced in 1898, with the co-operation of the Chinese government, have been recommenced under the direction of an international commission. As soon as the administration of Tientsin shall have been remitted to the Chinese government, that government may be represented in that commission, and shall pay each year a sum of sixty thousand Haikwan taels for the maintenance of the works.

(*b.*) A River Council is now created, charged with the direction and control of the works of the Whangpoo and of the amelioration of the course of the river.

This Council is composed of members representing the interests of the Chinese government and those of foreigners in the maritime commerce of Shanghai. The expense necessitated by the works and the general administration of the enterprise has been estimated at the sum of 460,000 Haikwan taels during the first twenty years. This sum will be furnished, half by the Chinese government and half by the foreigners interested. The details of the stipulations in connection with the composition, the attributions, and the revenues of the River Council are the subject of Appendix 17.

Article 12.

An Imperial Edict of 24th July, 1901 (Appendix 18) has reconstructed the Office of Foreign Affairs (Tsung-li Yamen) in the direction indicated by the Powers, that is to say, has transformed it into a Ministry of Foreign Affairs (Wai-wu-pu), which takes rank before the other six Ministries of State; the same edict has named the principal members of this office.

An accord is also established on the subject of the modification of the ceremonial of the Court relative to the reception of the foreign representatives, and has been the subject of several notes from the Chinese Plenipotentiaries named in a memorandum herewith annexed (Appendix 19).

Finally, it is expressly understood that, for the declarations above named and the documents attached emanating from the Foreign Plenipotentiaries, the French text is alone to be taken as authentic.

The Chinese government having thus conformed to the satisfaction of the Powers, to the conditions enumerated in the aforesaid note of 22nd December, 1900, the Powers have acceded to the desire of China to see the situation created by the disorders of the summer of 1900 come to an end. In consequence the Foreign Plenipotentiaries have authorised the declaration, in the name of their governments, that, with the exception of the Legation guards mentioned in Article VII, the international troops will completely evacuate the city of Peking, the 1901, and, with the exception of the places mentioned in Article IX, will retire from the province of Chihli.

The present final protocol has been written out in twelve identical copies and signed by all the Plenipotentiaries of the contracting countries. A copy will be remitted to each of the foreign Plenipotentiaries and a copy will be remitted to the Chinese Plenipotentiaries.

Peking, the
certified copy.

(Signed) A. von Mumm.
M. Czikann.
Joostens.
B. J. Cologan.
W. W. Rockhill.
Beau.
Ernest Satow.
Salvago Räggi.
Tintaro Komura.
F. M. Knobell.
M. de Giers.

Secretaries : A. d'Anthouard.
B. Pronosensky.
Reginald Tower.
G. Bohlen Halbard.

Peace Protocol and Indemnity.

The foreign indemnity requires the payment of Taels 25,000,000 annually, and in addition the new indemnity of 450,000,000 taels involves also the need of paying Taels 18,000,000 each year. To meet this indebtedness it has been agreed that the salt revenue shall pay yearly Taels 11,000,000. By the effective *ad valorem* five per cent. duties there will be available Taels 2,000,000 to 3,000,000. Also the native customs will yield Taels 4,000,000 to 5,000,000. The foreign customs establishment has no control over the salt department. If, however, the Emperor were asked to order the governors of the provinces producing salt from October 11th onward to transmit the amount agreed upon to the Shanghai Taotai for payment by him to the various banks which receive money for the foreign powers this would be more satisfactory.

Remarks upon the Indemnity of 1901.

On June 22nd at Tungchow the prefect paid to Dr. D. Z. Sheffield Taels 16,000, and Taels 10,000 had been already paid. This amount, Taels 26,000, is an indemnity for destroyed property belonging to native Christians. It is assessed on certain villages which actively supported the Boxers in the spring of 1900. This indemnity does not cover any destroyed property of non-Christian owners, and they have no prospect of securing an indemnity.

Chung-wai-pau, July 12th, 1901.—The indemnity, the promise to pay which secures the departure of the foreign troops from Peking, is Taels 450,000,000. It will be paid in full in forty-four years. The signatures are not yet affixed, but an understanding has been arrived at between the Plenipotentiaries and the foreign Ministers. Half the Chinese revenue, or forty million taels, will be required annually to pay all foreign debts.

Sin-wen, August 2nd, 1901.—Extract from the memorial of the Plenipotentiaries regarding indemnities in Peking to French, American, British, and Russian claimants. Taels 10,000 is allowed to each of seven cemeteries desecrated by the Boxers. The tombs of Schaal and Verbiest, who were in office as Imperial astronomers, are among the desecrated monuments.

We request an edict to grant Taels 70,000 to be given into the hands of the respective foreign Ministers. Each nation will repair the monuments as they desire to do. This item of expenditure should not be charged to the public indemnity, but should be paid at once. The French ask to be paid at once for Roman Catholic losses and for losses of native Christians, Taels 500,000. A similar claim for the American Methodists, the American Congregationalists, the American Presbyterians, and the London Missionary Society amounts to Taels 1,105,009. The claim was urged that payment in part should be made to enable the distressed Christians to find homes for themselves. In all Taels 2,000,000 are required, which the memorialists earnestly request may be sent soon. Beside this sum the amount of Taels 48,000 and Taels 25,600 is required for the American Mission at Pau-ting-fu for buildings and indemnity to native Christians. The memorialists recognize that at Tientsin and in various localities in the province of Chihli the same principle of indemnity for losses should be carried out loyally.

Shen-pau, August 2nd, 1901.—Tientsin indemnity to mission property destroyed and to native Christians, Taels 250,000.

The amount of indemnity to missions in Peking to be charged to the 450 million taels indemnity is Taels 1,981,478.

Mode of Payment.

The payment of the indemnity of 450 million taels of silver has been arranged by the Plenipotentiaries with the foreign Ministers :—

1901 to 1910 inclusive the yearly payment shall be Taels 18,829,500. The total for nine years will be Taels 109,465,500.

1910 to 1914 inclusive the yearly payment will be Taels 19,899,300.

The total for four years will be Taels 79,597,200.

1915.—For this year the interest and principal will be Taels 23,283,300.

1916 to 1931, in all sixteen years, the yearly payment will be Taels 24,483,800. Total for sixteen years, Taels 391,740,800.

1932 to 1940, in all nine years, Taels 35,350,150. Total Taels 318,151,350.

Grand Total during thirty-nine years, principal and interest, Taels 982,238,150.

The Spanish Consul being doyen, has sent this statement in a despatch to the two plenipotentiaries. The interest is four per cent., and it is to be counted as due from April 1st, 1901, and the silver is to be of the Haikwan scale. The value of silver on April 1st, 1901, is to be taken as the standard value. The payments are to commence with January 1st, 1902, and to terminate in 1940. On January 1st, 1902, it will be only necessary for China to pay the interest for six months of 450,000,000 taels. This reduction of three months is made out of consideration for the low state of Chinese finances at present. See *Shen-pao*, August 22nd, 1901.

Indemnity in Shansi.—The *Chung-wai-pao*, September 12th, says the combined rich men of Shansi province pay Taels 1,700,000 for the Roman Catholic and Protestant indemnities. Out of this amount Tai-ku, hitherto reported a rich city, pays Taels 170,000.

The indemnity for burned buildings belonging to the China Inland Mission is not asked for. *Chung-wai-pao*, September 13th:—Mr. Hoste has made an agreement with the Shansi Board of Foreign Affairs. Three copies of the agreement are made; one for the governor, one for the Foreign Board, and one for the mission.

Chung-wai-pao, October 3rd, 1901, states that the Roman Catholic claim for Taels 2,500,000 has been agreed to in Peking by Viceroy Li. The Protestant claim for Taels 200,000 has been agreed upon in Shansi.

The Term of Forty-four Years.

In 1901 the indemnity for the siege of Peking was fixed by the foreign ministers at Taels 450,000,000. The whole is to be paid in forty-four years. Each year 22,000,000 will be paid. This is not exactly what is required. In fact if the whole, including interest, were paid in thirty-nine years, Taels 23,000,000 would need to be paid each year. This would yield a total of Taels 894,950,000. The indemnity is doubled by the interest at 4 per cent. to be paid each year.

The *Shen-pao* of July 22nd, 1901, says that China will from 1902 to 1905 inclusive pay 18,000,000 a year on indemnity account. From 1906 to 1909 inclusive China will pay each year Taels 18,750,000 on the same account. In forty-four years she will pay altogether Taels 1,075,000,000.

The *Chung-wai-pao* of July 12th, 1901, says the plenipotentiaries have arranged with the foreign ministers that in forty-four years the indemnity and other foreign debts will all be paid in full. Half the revenue of China will be needed to pay this sum each year. The entire revenue is about Taels 80,000,000.

The *Chung-wai-pao*, July 9th, 1901, says the plan proposed by England for paying Taels 450,000,000 has been adopted.

Plan for Payment in Seventy Years.

The *Chung-wai-pao* of June 27th, 1901, gives details of a plan for paying the indemnity in seventy years. Taels 22,000,000 is as much as China can pay in a year. The guarantees are the foreign and native customs' collections, with the salt and lekin. If required, the lekin tax can be increased. Many countries increase import and export duties. In the proposed remodelling of the customs' tariff in China it will be necessary to make five per cent. *ad valorem* the standard in all cases of imports. But this is not yet settled. The salt and lekin will yield 10,000,000, the native customs 3,000,000 taels. These may be depended on.

The same journal, of June 17th, says China is now paying to Western countries every year Taels 24,000,000. By the addition of this indemnity 18,000,000 a year are needed. The amount required will be 42,000,000 taels. The whole may be paid in forty-five years. In order that this may be done the native customs should be under foreigners. It would then be possible to raise Taels 5,000,000. If five per cent. *ad valorem* were made uniform for all imports and if lekin were made free, Taels 6,000,000 could be raised. Salt and lekin might amount to 10,000,000. The remaining 8,000,000 might be raised through the lekin.

Reduction of Army Expenditure.

Sin-wen-pao, September 21st, 1901. The viceroy and governor of Hupei have ordered the Taotais in charge of the lekin, the licensed brokers, the Shanhow and other collectors of taxes to meet them at the viceroy's yamên to take into consideration the payment of one million taels towards the foreign debt. The Taotais said that they had collected all they could in the form of taxes on sugar, wine, houses, shops, tobacco, deeds of sale, opium. No more could be collected. The viceroy saw that it was really so. He then decided to dismiss two-thirds of the troops at Ichang, Sha-shi, and Siang-yang. Also he decided to reduce the monthly allowance of ammunition and arms to the navy in the province by one-half. The Taotais present undertook to carry out his instructions. The viceroy is anxious to save the people from further exactions and to reduce the expenditure on the army and navy. In this he is greatly to be admired.

Chihli Payment of Foreign Loans.

On December 9th, 1898, appeared in the *Gazette* a memorial from Yu Li, Viceroy of Chihli, reporting the native opium collection to October 6th, 1896. The former Treasurer Yu Ch'ang and the Acting Judge T'ing Yung have presented a return of the collection from October 7th, 1896, to September 29th, 1897. The port dues, or *lo-ti* duty, on native opium amounted to Taels 25,294, with a remainder. The treasurer and judge asked leave to retain 15 per cent. for expenses, that is to say, Taels 3,794 which has been used in the management. The remainder, Taels 21,500, has been forwarded to the Board. On the occasion of the fifth time of making a return the amount was Taels 19,118. On occasion of the fourth return it was Taels 8,229.

	21,500
	19,118
	8,229
Taels	48,847

This amount was forwarded to the Board in April, 1898. Fifty thousand taels were credited to the customs at Shanghai to pay back the amount due to Russia, France, and Germany from Chihli province. This amount had not been made up by the former acting Viceroy Yuen Shih-kai while he was in charge here.

Kiangsu Payment.

The *Chung-wai-pao*, July 8th, 1899, states that the Kiangnan Viceroy reported payment of Russian and French loan for 1898, amounting to Taels 5,001,143.

Proportional Payments to Loan of 1898.

The following example may be adduced of provincial payments to the native loan of 1898: The Hwai-pei salt merchants have recently contributed Taels 200,000. The Hwai-nan contribution was Taels 680,000. The sellers' (塲商) Ch'ang-shang contribution was Taels 100,000. The merchants at the ports of consumption contribute Taels 200,000. The Ch'ang-shang are engaged in salt business at the place of production. This money was to be paid in the 6th, 9th, and 12th months of the 24th year of Kwang Hsü.

Military Expenditure in West China.

In the year 1826 the Hwai-an salt farmers were called on to contribute two million taels. It was applied to use in quelling a Mahommedan rebellion in Western China. The subscription would be levied on a similar principle at that time as now. A large number of merchants, great and small, pay each the amount fixed in Peking by the Board of Revenue.

Detailed Statement of Foreign Loans.

In the *Sin-wen-pao*, February 23rd, 1900, there is a memorial of the Hupu giving details regarding payment of foreign loans. Through a rise in the value of gold the amounts contributed by the provinces need to be increased. Otherwise the amounts before arranged for will be insufficient.

The Russian and French loan requires each year, 21,154,752 francs, or Taels 5,000,000, as it was at first calculated.

The English and German loan requires each year £966,952, or Taels 6,000,000.

Since the memorial of the Board of Revenue in June, 1896, containing these data the various custom houses in the provinces have forwarded their respective amounts accordingly and reported that they had done so. In 1896 one tael of silver was equal to four francs, but now it is necessary to pay one tael two mace for four francs. In paying the English and German loan in 1896 six taels were equal to one pound gold, but at present seven taels and six or seven mace are equal to a pound. The deficit each year amounts to Taels 2,400,000 or Taels 2,500,000.

The additional amounts which need to be forwarded by the provinces are calculated in the following table at 2½-tenths in each instance.

Russian and French Loan.	Amount to be paid as fixed in 1896.	Additional amount to be paid as fixed in 1900.	Russian and French Loan.	Amount fixed in 1896.	Additional amount fixed in 1900.
	Taels.	Taels.		Taels.	Taels.
Canton	240,000	60,000	Shanghai customs	400,000	100,000
Kiangsu	200,000	50,000	Canton ,,	360,000	90,000
Szchwen	200,000	50,000	Foochow ,,	160,000	40,000
Chekiang	160,000	40,000	Ningpo	160,000	40,000
Hupei	160,000	40,000	Chinkiang* ...	220,000	55,000
Honan	140,000	35,000	Kiukiang ...	180,000	45,000
Chihli	120,000	30,000	Hankow	160,000	40,000
Shantung	120,000	30,000	Ichang	80,000	20,000
Shansi	120,000	30,000	Chungking ...	40,000	10,000
Anhwei	120,000	30,000	Mengtsz	40,000	10,000
Kiangsi	100,000	25,000	Wenchow ...	40,000	10,000
Hunan	100,000	25,000	Tientsin	120,000	30,000
Fukien	100,000	25,000	Chefoo	30,000	7,500
Shensi	100,000	25,000	Newchwang ...	40,000	10,000
Kwangsi	70,000	17,500	Wuhu†	20,000	5,000

* Including Taels 160,000 from Wuhu.

† This is additional to Taels 160,000 of the Chinkiang amount.

English and German Loan.	Amount fixed in 1896.	Additional amount fixed in 1900.	English and German Loan.	Amount fixed in 1896.	Additional amount fixed in 1900.
	Taels.	Taels.		Taels.	Taels.
Canton	380,000	95,000	Shanghai customs	600,000	150,000
Kiangsu	320,000	80,000	Canton ,,	520,000	130,000
Szechuen	320,000	80,000	Foochow... ...	240,000	60,000
Chekiang	220,000	55,000	Ningpo	240,000	60,000
Hupei	220,000	55,000	Chinkiang ...	320,000	80,000
Honan	190,000	47,500	Kiukiang ...	260,000	60,000
Chihli	170,000	42,500	Hankow	240,000	60,000
Shantung	170,000	42,500	Ichang	120,000	30,000
Shansi	170,000	42,500			
Anhwei	170,000	42,500			
Kiangsi	140,000	35,000	Wuhu*	40,000	10,000
Hunan	140,000	35,000	Chungking ...	80,000	20,000
Fukien	140,000	35,000	Tientsin	180,000	45,000
Shensi	120,000	30,000	Chefoo	50,000	12,500
Kwangsi	100,000	20,000	Newchwang ...	60,000	15,000

* This is additional to Taels 240,000 to the account of Chinkiang.

The English and German, and Russian and French loans require payment each year amounting to Taels 12,000,000. This is met by Taels 2,000,000 derived from additions to the salt tax, to the pension tax, and the Canton lottery. The foreign customs contributes Taels 10,000,000. Together these sums make up the necessary annual payment. The addition now needed to meet the increased value of gold is Taels 2,500,000, and this is taken from the foreign customs only. No addition is made to the contributions of the native customs' collections, the salt tax, the official pension tax, or the Canton lottery.

The payments for loans are made quarterly. For example, Wuhu pays Taels 240,000 in a year in quarterly instalments of Taels 60,000. *Sin-wen-pao*, January 14th, 1901:—Wuhu has forwarded Taels 60,000 in payment of foreign loan. *Shen-pao*, February 14th, 1901:—Chekiang forwarded in the eighth month Taels 7,500, half being taken from the duty on foreign goods and half from the duty on goods of native origin. Chekiang pays in all each year 24,000 taels and 6,000 additional. This is levied upon the customs' revenue and the opium lekin, and is transmitted by the banking firm Yang-yuen-feng.

The *Shen-pao* of March 19th, 1901, has a memorial of the Chekiang governor Hwei, which contains a return of payments made by the Ningpo customs on account of the debt to France and Russia. The amount, Taels 100,000, has been paid—in April, Taels 96,000 and in October, Taels 64,000. By order from the Board of Revenue, from 1900 and onwards Taels 40,000 were to be paid in addition. In October, 1900, the sum of Taels 80,000 should be sent. The receipts in that custom house were deficient in the department of duties, opium lekin, etc. Forty thousand was all that could be paid. The former governor had arranged that the Hangchow customs should contribute Taels 40,000. In this way the required amount being raised, it was sent by transmission bankers to Shanghai and delivered to the customs there.

Chihli Payments by Cities and Districts.

Chung-wai-pao, August 20th, 1901.—Yung Lu was ordered to inquire what sums could be obtained from Chihli to meet the claims of the indemnity for the destruction of Christian churches. The viceroy stated the figures as under :—

The Province, Taels 2,900,000.

Siuen-hwa-fu, Taels 1,600,000. Of this amount upwards of 600,000 will be charged to the national indemnity fund. The remainder will be paid by the prefecture.

Ho-kien-fu.—The prefect states the sums due for seven districts and sub-prefectures.

Hien-hien, 200,000 strings of cash.

King-chou, 170,000 strings of cash, half to be paid by the foreign indemnity fund.

Tung-kwang-hien, 40,000 strings of cash, half to be paid by the foreign indemnity fund.

The other three cities will pay 2,000 or 3,000 strings or a few hundred strings according to their ability.

Payment by Each Province.

Chung-wai-pao, October 22nd, 1901.—The proportion to be paid annually by the various provinces towards the indemnity, principal and interest, is here given :—

Chihli	Taels 800,000
Kiangsu	2,500,000
Anhwei	1,000,000
Shantung	900,000
Shansi	900,000
Honan	900,000
Shensi	600,000
Kansu	300,000
Sinkiang	400,000
Fukien	800,000
Chekiang	1,400,000
Kiangsi	1,400,000
Hupei	1,200,000
Hunan	700,000

Szechwen	2,200,000
Canton	2,000,000
Kwangsi	300,000
Yunnan	300,000
Kweichow	200,000
Total, Taels	18,800,000

Arnhold and Karberg Loan.

In the *Chung-wai-pao*, January 6th, 1901, a Wuhu correspondent says, the date for payment of Arnhold and Karberg's loan is January 1st, 1901. The 11th payment of capital and interest together amounts to 960,134 marks. The viceroy has ordered the treasurer and superintendent to forward this sum in their several proportions to the Shanghai Superintendent of Customs, who will pay it to Arnhold and Company.

English and German Loan.

In the *Sin-wen-pao* of January 12th, 1901, it is stated that the Nanking viceroy has decided to pay the amount due on account of the English and German loan in part with Nanking customs' receipts. The customs' receipts at Hankow and Tientsin are less than usual on account of the troubles in the north. By applying the money in hand at Nanking the difficulty will be met and the amount paid will be sufficient.

Ewo Loan.

The Hupu has written to the Shantung governor, Yuen Shi-kai, that it is necessary to expend Taels 210,000 of Shantung funds towards the payment of the debt incurred by the Jardine and Matheson Loan. This sum is made up out of the customs' revenue, salt tax, and lekin 300,000.

Mode of Estimating Indemnity for Houses Destroyed.

The value of property destroyed is, in the claims of the Protestant missionaries, estimated on the principle that a kien or compartment of a house is worth fifty taels and the property in it another fifty taels.

Taels 26,000 have been paid for loss of property in houses and furniture by Christians in Tungchow. This was paid in June, 1900, and the amount was assessed on villages.

THE CHINA MASSACRES OF 1900.

The Rev. J. W. Stevenson, Director of the China Inland Mission, has compiled for the *North-China Daily News* the following complete list of the Protestant missionaries who were killed, or who died from injuries received, during the Boxer uprising of 1899 and 1900; the Societies with which they were connected, the provinces in which they were located, and their nationality.

Society.	Adults.	Children.	Total.
China Inland Mission	58	20	78
Christian and Missionary Alliance...	21	15	36
American Board of Commissioners for Foreign Missions	13	5	18
English Baptist Mission	13	3	16
Sheoyang Mission	11	2	13
American Presbyterian Mission (North)	5	3	8
Scandinavian Alliance Mongolian Mission	5	—	5
Swedish Mongolian Mission ...	3	1	4
Society for the Propagation of the Gospel	3	—	3
British and Foreign Bible Society ...	2	3	5
	134	52	186

Province.	Adults.	Children.	Total.
Shansi and over the Mongolian border	112	45	157
Chihli...	13	4	17
Chekiang	8	3	11
Shantung	1	—	1
	134	52	186

Nationality.			
British	70	28	98
Swedish	40	16	56
United States of America	24	8	32
	134	52	186

Origin of Indemnities and Loans.

Want of money is felt when the government pays indemnities arising out of foreign wars. Opium-smoking has led to depletion of the currency. From these causes foreign loans have originated. The provinces have to pay their proportion to loans contracted for by the central government. Such facts as have now been collected regarding loans are therefore placed here.

Famines and short harvests lead to local want of currency. There is no sale of food to attract money to the markets. One province when rich lends or gives money to another province which may be poor. The richest provinces are those which have plentiful harvests and export manufactured goods and all sorts of saleable articles. The treasurer of a rich province can lend money to poor provinces, and this he is required to do by order from Peking when occasion calls for such loans.

Poverty of Kansu.

The poverty of the province of Kansu is such that the expenditure exceeds the receipts. Assistance is afforded by Kiangsu, Chekiang, Anhwei, and Hupei. At present, said the *Hu-pao* of November 16th, 1898, the debt to Kansu amounts to Taels 300,000. These four provinces have to pay a share to the foreign debt and navy expenditure for drilled troops and for schools. The writer asks how they will meet the difficulty?

The Yellow River.

The repairs of the Yellow River need Taels 600,000 a year. This was fixed as the amount that must not be exceeded by advice of Hü Chen-wei a few years ago when he was chief manager of the Yellow River, Ho-tung-ho-tao Tsung-tu. 河東 refers to the province Honan. He became in 1893 governor of Canton and lost his post when the emperor abolished that and two other governorships. He is now no longer living. This sum is paid by the Board of Revenue.

In 1806, Taels 400,000 were needed for the river repairs. The Chihli viceroy asked the emperor to direct that one cash more on each catty should be levied on the Lu-t'ai salt merchants. The emperor refused this and said it had been levied for a brief period, but the Tientsin salt farmers could not bear the burden. Tung-hoa-lu, ch. 7, p 22. Among the salt farmers, who are at Tientsin very numerous, Hai-chang-wu is the richest. The emperor's reference is to the poorer salt merchants.

The chief manager of the Yellow River 河東河道總督 has charge of it in Honan and Shantung. His guard (piao) consists of eight regiments, that is to say, 4,000 or 5,000 soldiers. These soldiers, it is said, are merely for display. They do no real work. The Tsung-tu receives 8,000 taels salary, which is small compared with the Nanking viceroy, who has Taels 18,000 and with the governor of Kiangsu, who has Tls. 12,000.

The Indemnity in Canton Province.

Sin-wen-pao, 6th October, 1901.—A foreigner's letter from Swatow says the viceroy and governor of Canton having to meet calls for the foreign indemnity, have issued a proclamation saying that in both provinces five per cent. must be added to each class of taxes. At Tengchow the magistrate called a meeting at his yamên of headmen to consider the question of a house tax. Only six headmen responded. This was not a sufficient number. Later the magistrate went to a commercial meeting where they were discussing trade. They said, let us wait to see what the headmen at Canton will do in this matter. We will do as they do. We now hear that the magistrate is collecting the house tax, and in the case of prosperous householders he collects five per cent. more to meet the road and police expenditure. The gentry are not pleased, and there will probably be a change in the mode of procedure.

SHANSI INDEMNITY FOR CHRISTIANS MURDERED.

Shen-pao, 19th November, 1901.—Letter from Shansi. There are four sources of payment of the indemnity: 1. Addition of two candareens to each tael of land tax. 2. Loans from traders. 3. Addition to opium tax, salt tax, and salt tax in Mongolia. 4. The rich traders will be invited to subscribe.

PEKING PAYMENTS ON IDEMNITY ACCOUNT.

French eastern cathedral, Taels 500,000.

French cemeteries, five in all; Russian Cemetery; British cemetery. All these cemeteries are in and near Peking. Total for seven cemeteries, Taels 70,000.

French Roman Catholic murder of Christians in Peking.

American Congregationalist converts murdered.

American Presbyterian converts murdered.

British converts of London Mission murdered.

Russian Greek church converts murdered.

Total indemnity, Taels 1,097,009.

Plan for raising Taels 2,000,000 (*Sin-wen-pao*, October 24th, 1901) to pay this indemnity for destruction of Christian life and property in Peking:—Kiangsu, and Chekiang, Taels

1,360,000 silver saved by change of grain tribute to silver payment; Shantung, Taels 110,000 from funds saved by silver payment; Kiangsu diverted Taels 220,000 from army fund newly subscribed; Ichang custom house, Taels 100,000; Anhwei, Taels 110,000 diverted from the amount due for grain tax; the merchant's bank 通商銀行, due for military guard 武衞軍, Taels 10,000.

Loans for the Support of the Army.

Before 1895 no loans were required for the support of the army. The receipts and expenditure were sufficient to meet army expenses. In 1896 it was necessary to borrow; native capitalists contributed Taels 215,000. During five months of 1898 native capitalists had contributed only Taels 500,000, which was far short of the amount required. Each year Taels 2,000,000 are required for the army according to the rate fixed by the Board. The deficit in the amount forwarded is very large.

In 1897, Taels 1,300,000 were forwarded. This was less by 700,000 than the sum fixed at that time; a despatch stated that only Taels 440,000 could be forwarded. The deficit then amounted to Taels 800,000. When the amounts coming from the Coast Defence Subscriptions, the Hankow foreign customs, and the Hankow duties are received, the amount required for the army will still be far from sufficient.

Despatch of Yung Lu.

Yung Lu stated in his despatch (*Shen-pao*, August 13th, 1898) that for the brigade under the Chihli general-in-chief the annual amount of Taels 1,500,000 from the lekin collection is not now available. To meet the expense of supporting twenty regiments and the three armies of drilled troops special funds will be required. The lekin collection is set apart to pay the foreign loans and cannot be drawn upon for army pay.

Proportion of Provinces in Payment of Foreign Loans.

A foreign loan is paid for by dividing out certain amounts among the foreign custom houses. Thus in the *Sin-wen-pao*, October 15th, 1898, it is stated that the Wuhu superintendent sent 10,000 taels of silver to the Shanghai customs, being the share of Wuhu in payment for the English and German loans due in September. He also sent Taels 14,000 to Shanghai as the share of Wuhu towards the repayment of the French and Russian loan for 1897.

New Rule in Regard to Foreign Loans in the Provinces.

In the *Hu-pao*, October 15th, 1898, it is stated that Taels 2,000,000 silver had been received by the Board of Revenue as the result of subscriptions to the native loan. The amount still expected by the Board was Taels 1,100,000.

On November 25th, 1891, it was stated in the *Shen-pao* of November 4th, 1898, that it was decided by edict on the recommendation of the Hupu, conjointly with the Tsung-li Yamên, that when loans were negotiated with foreigners by Chinese officers of whatever rank, high or low, the foreigner who lends must first ask through the minister of his nation for permission. Such foreign minister will state the matter in a despatch to the Yamên. When permission is given by the Yamên the foreign capitalist can lend the money. If this mode of procedure is neglected the government is not bound to pay back the sum lent, whether the document is sealed or not sealed. The government must first have consented to the loan. The approval of this mode of procedure by the emperor was notified to the foreign ministers resident in Peking that they might communicate the new rule to their nationals.

New Coast Defence Subscriptions.

These subscriptions entitle the subscriber to enter the official class, the prizes consisting of rank and titles which are in some cases mere titles with *ting-tsz* (button) and *pu-kwa*, with civil or military heraldic breast plate. In other cases they give him a post as district magistrate or prefect. *Chung-wai-pao*, July 31st, August 1st, 1899. The Hupu statement of subscriptions from December, 1889, to June, 1899, is here appended :—

1899, May.	Taels.	Cash.
Subscriptions of fifty-five persons.	31,644	4,219,200
Fees paid by four persons for exemption from examination on appointment to office ...	990	132,000
Fines paid by eight persons for passing the limit of time ...	750	99,800
Purchase by twelve persons of higher rank	3,060	408,000
Purchase of office by thirty persons	1,334	177,400
	37,778	5,036,400

Thirty-two names, Total 10,769

Metropolitan new coast defence subscriptions... ... Taels 2,199,401

Provincial new coast defence subscriptions :—

Chihli	Taels 6,845,668. less $\frac{1}{100}$th,	Taels, 68,456.6.8
Shansi	102,737. less $\frac{1}{100}$th,	1,027.3.7
Kiangsi	371,412.8	
Kiangsu	135,535.7	
Shensi	180,540.	
Shantung... ...	3,300,557.9, less expenses	3,305.579
Honan	179,351.3	
Hupei	455,448.6.6	
Kwangtung ...	659,243.8	

Anhwei ...	...	Taels	274,960.3	less expenses	2,749.6.3
Chekiang...	...		274,686.4		
Szechuen ...	...		148,885.8		
Kansu ...	...		106,330.8		
Kiangning	...		191,709.1.3	less expenses	1,917.0.9
Hunan ...	...		280,763.4	less expenses	190.9.4
Fukien ...	...		678,911.3.6		
Yunnan ...	...		257,288.3.2		
Kweichow	...		97,268.4		
Kwangsi ...	...		208,752.1.4	less expenses	2,087.5.1
Heilungkiang	...		136.8		
Kirin ...	...		10,693.2	less expenses	76.5.6
Sinkiang ...	...		76,880.8.9.6		

Total from 1889, Dec., to May, 1899, Taels 16,042,791.0.0.6

Less expenses of subscription office, Taels 109,465.1.3.7.9

Securities on Loans.

The securities on foreign loans are, for example: 1. Requisite control of some part of the revenue. 2. Right conceded to make some railway, *e.g.*, British loan under discussion, December 30th, 1897, Railway from Burmese frontier to Yangtsz valley. 3. Guarantee in case of a British loan that no territory in the Yangtsz valley will be conceded to any other power. 4. Some treaty port to be newly opened. In the British negotiations Ta-lien-wan was mentioned. 5. Greater freedom of internal trade. 6. Freedom of foreign goods from lekin in the Treaty Ports.

Russian Four Per Cent. Loan at Ninety-three as the Price of Issue.

Russia offered China a four per cent. loan at ninety-three as the price of issue, guaranteed by the Russian government. The security demanded was Chinese land tax and lekin. The advantages claimed were the financing, construction, and control of all railways in Manchuria and North China and that a Russian should be made Inspector-General when the post became vacant. December 22nd, 1897. This loan was stated at the time by the British government to be commercially not likely to succeed and therefore not to be thought of.

British Loan at Four Per Cent.

The British loan of twelve million pounds sterling was offered January 8th, 1898, at four per cent., to be repaid in fifty years, principal and interest. The securities were to be the maritime and native customs, salt tax, and lekin. The ports were to be open to foreign salt. Lekin was understood to include all taxes paid on merchandise in transit from one place to another on arrival and at the place of production. The revenues named as securities were to be audited by an Englishman, and in case of default to be placed under English control. The securities agreed to by the Chinese government were the remainder of the maritime customs' revenue, lekin, salt, and native customs. They also agreed to the appointment of English inspectors to be probably taken from the foreign customs' staff. These inspectors were to examine accounts and prepare monthly reports or periodical statements of lekin and salt tax.

On January 21st, 1898, the Chinese government wished that the loan should be for £16,000,000. New advantages were asked for, that is to say, that Nan-ning and Siang-tan should be opened to trade. Any British Consul on application shall be supplied with information from the provincial authorities upon the imports levied on goods *en route* to any specified place in the interior.

On January 24th, the British government declined to increase the offered loan beyond twelve millions.

On January 28th, the Chinese government proposed to divide the loan between Russia and England.

Refusal of Loan by China.

February 4th —The loan was refused by China.

Hongkong and Shanghai Bank Loan at Four and a Half Per Cent.

The Hongkong and Shanghai Bank signed a loan for £16,000,000. The lekin was to be under Customs' control. Date of signature February 19th. The Bank was allowed ten days for definite acceptance. The interest was four and a half per cent.

The seven lekin offices which pay the English and German loan are Kien-kiang, Eastern Chekiang, Ichang, Soochow, Shanghai, Wuchang and Anhwei.

In the *Shen-pao* of August 8th, 1899, the Wuchang correspondent says that according to rule a million taels was due from the salt lekin collection to be sent to Peking under the heading 京餉 (king-hiang) and to other provinces under the heading (hiê-hiang) 協餉, but since the appointment to pay this amount to foreign loan account, it was not available. The Viceroy Chang Hiang-t'ao prayed the emperor to order the Board of Revenue to find the money elsewhere or diminish the demand from Hupei. But a telegram came from the Board saying that this year the whole million was indispensable. The Board prays the Emperor to order the viceroy to send the amount. The viceroy accordingly consulted with the acting treasurer and with the grain and salt Taotais as well as with the Customs' Taotai. The result of inquiry was that no more than 300,000 taels were obtainable. But the viceroy told them they must find some way to obtain the money required to complete the million.

COMMISSIONER HIPPISLEY'S STATEMENT OF THE ANNUAL PAYMENTS BY CHINA FOR FOREIGN LOANS, FROM 1901 TO 1943.

1901 to 1908	annual payment	...	... Taels	24,500,000
1909 to 1912	,, ,,	...	...	23,500,000
1913 to 1914	,, ,,	...	...	23,000,000
1915	,, ,,	...	...	20,500,000
1916 to 1931	,, ,,	...	...	19,200,000
1932	,, ,,	...	...	13,100,000
1933	,, ,,	...	...	6,000,000
1943	,, ,,	...	...	1,000,000

NATIONAL LOANS.

The Corean treasury is without funds. *Shen-pao*, December 11th, 1901. The treasurer has resigned on account of the want of money to pay demands. The new treasurer pays no salaries, nor does he give out money for the army. He has none to give. Many magistrates report that taxes are in arrears. A new law has been made that if arrears of taxes amount to Taels 10,000 in the accounts of any magistrate he is to be dismissed and punished. These facts show how a loan becomes necessary and a nation can borrow because the land belongs to the State and ultimately the loan can be repaid.

In the *Chung-wai-pao* of May 1st, 1899, and subsequent days, the loans of the present time and the payments which need to be made are stated as calculated by native bankers.

FRENCH FIVE PER CENT. LOAN.

The French five per cent. loan, dating from May 1st, 1899, was announced in the money article of the *Times* of the 12th of April, 1899, in the following manner:—

The Chinese Imperial government has arranged with the Banque de Paris et des Pays Bas and other French financial institutions for the issue of a Chinese five per cent. gold loan for 112,500,000f. (or about £4,500,000) in 225,000 bonds of 500f. each. The first issue consists of 133,000 obligations, and the price of issue is 96½, or 482·50f. for each bond of 500f. Interest will be payable as from May 1st, 1899. The subscription will be opened in Paris, Brussels, Amsterdam, and Geneva on Wednesday, April 19th. The loan is issued in virtue of an Edict of his Majesty the Emperor of China signed on August 11th, 1898, and the loan, we observe, is expressly described as the "Chinese Five per Cent. Gold Loan of 1898." The loan will be repaid at par in twenty years by drawings to commence in 1909. The Chinese government undertakes not to increase the sinking fund, to repay the loan, or to convert it before September 1st, 1907. The bonds are exempted for ever *(à tout jamais)* from all Chinese taxes, present or future, as well as from any other exaction on the part of China. The money is to be employed in building a railway from Lukouchiao, near Peking, to Hankow, in the province of Hupeh, on the Yangtzekiang. The Franco-Belgian syndicate known as the Société d'Etudes de Chemins de fer en Chine will have full control over the construction and working of this line, which is nominally in the hands of a company called the Compagnie des Chemins de fer Chinois.

Native Subscription Loan of 1898.

The native subscription loan known under the name 昭信 will be fully repaid, principal and interest, in twenty years. The certificate has on it the dragon border. There are upon it twenty divisions, one of which is torn off each year when the principal and interest for that year are paid. This loan was settled by an edict of February 4th, 1898. The interest is five per cent. The certificates can be sold. It can be used in payment of taxes and salt dues. One million copies were issued and offered to the patriotic feeling of the country. Viceroys and governors are urged in the edict to be prominent in purchasing certificates as an example to the monied classes. Those who subscribe liberally will be rewarded with honorary titles.

Payment of Interest on Loans.

Shen-pao, January 5th, 1901.—Prince Ching telegraphed to Viceroy Liu at Nanking saying that the interest for the British and German loan of £900,000 must soon be paid, and asked him to make the necessary preparations. Also the Director-General of Railways, Sheng Hang-sun, telegraphed saying that by December 11th, the interest due to the Hongkong and Shanghai Bank, with the capital, amount to £290,000. This is in silver, Taels 2,030,000. In May, the Board of Revenue arranged payment in the following manner: Canton lekin and salt gabelle remainders, Taels 1,600,000; Anhwei remainder of the province expenditure fund, Taels 70,000; Kwangsi remainder from the province expenditure fund with the payment to be made from the external expenditure board in the prefectures and districts, Taels 40,000; Kiangsi duties and lekin, together with the addition made in Hupei, Anhwei, and Hwaian to the lekin, Taels 213,000; remainder from Chekiang duties—lekin and salt revenue—Taels 105,000. Also, December 19th, the interest due on Jardine and Matheson's loan (克 薩), £30,000. This is in silver, Taels 210,000.

Indemnity to the Peking Missions.

The mission houses and other property of Roman Catholic and Protestant societies in Peking were destroyed by the Boxers, except the cathedral, protected by Bishop Favier and the native Christians. The Chinese government agreed to pay an indemnity of two million taels. This amount was assessed on certain provinces, ports, and commercial companies.

Kiangsu and Chekiang grain tribute commuted	Taels	1,360,000
Shantung grain tribute commuted ...		110,000

Kiangsu new contribution for the army...	220,000
Ichang customs' collection	100,000
Anhwei grain tribute, amount due and still unpaid	110,000
International Bank, amount due for the Wu-wei army	100,000
Taels	2,000,000

In 1899 it was decided on the recommendation of Kang Yi that the International Bank conducted on foreign principles, the China Merchants' Navigation Company, and the Telegraph Company should pay annually a contribution to the revenue. —*Sin-wen-pao*, October 24th, 1901.

RETURN OF CHINESE LOANS, 1887 TO 1898.

This return of money due by China on account of foreign loans was prepared by the Customs' Bank and was printed in Chinese in the *Chung-wai-pao* newspaper, May, 1899.

The amounts are in Hai-kwan taels. Taels 100 are equivalent to Shanghai taels 106.6.

[See Table next page.]

RETURN OF CHINESE

Year of the reign of Kwang Sü.	Year Anno Domini.	1887 German loan, five million marks, 5½ per cent.	1894 Hongkong and Shanghai Bank, Taels 10,900,000, 7 per cent.	1895 Jardine and Matheson, one million pounds sterling, 6 per cent.	1895 Arnhold, Karberg and Co., one million pounds sterling, 6 per cent.
25	1899	213,000	689,800	436,400	436,000
26	1900	203,100	do.	do.	do.
27	1901	193,300	do.	906,900	906,900
28	1902	183,500	do.	877,100	877,100
29	1903	*Paid in full.*	do.	848,700	848,700
30	1904		do.	819,600	819,600
31	1905		1,675,100	789,200	789,200
32	1906		1,606,100	761,500	761,500
33	1907		1,537,200	732,400	732,400
34	1908		1,468,200	702,500	702,500
35	1909		1,399,200	675,400	675,400
36	1910		1,330,200	646,000	646,000
37	1911		1,261,300	615,300	615,300
38	1912		1,192,300	586,900	586,900
39	1913		1,123,300	557,800	557,800
40	1914		1,054,300	528,000	528,000
41	1915		*Paid in full.*	499,600	514,200
42	1916			*Paid in full.*	*Paid in full.*
43	1917				
44	1918				
45	1919				
46	1920				
47	1921				
48	1922				
49	1923				
50	1924				
51	1925				
52	1926				
53	1927				
54	1928				
55	1929				
56	1930				
57	1931				
58	1932				
59	1933				
60	1934				
61	1935				
62	1936				
63	1937				
64	1938				
65	1939				
66	1940				
67	1941				
68	1942				
69	1943				

LOANS, 1887 TO 1898.

1895 Hongkong and Shanghai Bank, three million pounds sterling, 6 per cent.	1895 Russia and France, 400 million Francs loan, 4 per cent.	1896 English and German loan, sixteen million pounds sterling, 5 per cent.	1898 English and German later loan, sixteen million pounds sterling, $4\frac{1}{2}$ per cent.	Total. Amount due in each year from 1899 to 1943 in Haikwan Taels.	Deficit and Surplus.
1,309,100		19,191,700		22,276,200	Deficit. 1,808,300
2,763,600		do.		23,720,900	3,253,000
2,676,400		do.		24,564,900	4,097,000
2,589,100		do.		24,408,200	3,940,300
2,501,800		do.		24,080,700	3,612,800
2,414,500		do.		23,935,200	3,467,300
2,327,300		do.		24,772,500	4,304,600
2,240,000		do.		24,560,700	4,092,800
2,152,700		do.		24,346,300	3,878,400
2,065,500		do.		24,130,400	3,662,500
1,966,700		do.		23,908,300	3,440,400
1,890,900		do.		23,704,800	3,236,900
1,803,600		do.		23,487,100	3,019,200
1,716,700		do.		23,274,400	2,806,500
1,626,100		do.		23,056,700	2,588,800
1,541,800		do.		22,843,800	2,375,900
Paid in full.		do.		20,205,500	Surplus. 262,400
		do.		19,191,700	1,276,200
		do.		do.	do.
		do.		do.	do.
		do.		do.	do.
		do.		do.	do.
		do.		do.	do.
		do.		do.	do.
		do.		do.	do.
		do.		do.	do.
		do.		do.	do.
		do.		do.	do.
		do.		do.	do.
		do.		do.	do.
		do.		do.	do.
		do.		do.	do.
		do.		do.	do.
		Paid in full.			
		7,032,400	6,074,400	13,106,800	7,361,100
		Paid in full.	do.	6,074,400	14,393,500
			do.	do.	do.
			do.	do.	do.
			do.	do.	do.
			do.	do.	do.
			do.	do.	do.
			do.	do.	do.
			do.	do.	do.
			do.	do.	do.
			do.	do.	do.
			1,012,400	1,012,400	19,455,500
			Paid in full.		

Indemnities, Old and New.

Sin-wen-pao, January 8th, 1902.

The total amount, Taels 450,000,000, is divided into five sections :—

§ 1. Taels 75,000,000, to be paid from 1902 to 1940, in thirty-nine years. This amounts each year to $\frac{100}{1\cdot106}$th of seventy-five millions.

§ 2. Taels 60,000,000, beginning from 1911; in all thirty years. Each year $\frac{100}{1\cdot783}$. Before 1911 only interest will be paid.

§ 3. Taels 150,000,000, beginning from 1915; in all twenty-six years. Each year the payment is $\frac{100}{2\cdot256}$. Before 1915 interest only will be paid.

§ 4. Taels 50,000,000, beginning from 1916; in all twenty-five years. Each year $\frac{100}{2\cdot401}$. Before 1916 interest only will be paid.

§ 5. Taels 115,000,000, beginning with 1932; to be fully paid in nine years. Each year $\frac{100}{6\cdot446}$. Before 1932 interest only will be paid.

Payments in Successive Years, 1902 to 1940.

A.D. 1902. § 1. Principal and interest, Taels 3,829,500. § 2. Interest, Taels 2,400,000. § 3. Interest, Taels 6,000,000. § 4. Interest, Taels 2,000,000. § 5. Interest, Taels 4,600,000. Total, Taels 18,829,500.

A.D. 1903 to 1910. § 1. Principal and interest, Taels 3,829,500. § 2. Interest, Taels 2,400,000. § 3. Interest, Taels 6,000,000. § 4. Taels 2,000,000. § 5. Taels 4,600,000. During each of these eight years the total payments are Taels 18,829,500.

A.D. 1911. § 1. As above. § 2. Principal and interest, Taels 3,469,800. §§ 3, 4 and 5. As above. Total payments, Taels 19,899,300.

A.D. 1912 to 1914. § 1. Principal and interest, Taels 3,829,500 each year. § 2. Principal and interest, Taels 3,469,800. § 3. Interest, Taels 6,000,000. § 4. Interest, Taels 2,000,000. § 5. Interest, Taels 4,600,000. During each of these three years, total Taels 19,899,300.

A.D. 1915. §§ 1 and 2. As above. § 3. Principal and interest, Taels 9,384,000. §§ 4 and 5. As above. Total, Taels 23,283,300.

A.D. 1916. §§ 1, 2 and 3. As above. § 4. Principal and interest, Taels 3,200,500. § 5. As above. Total, Taels 24,483,800.

A.D. 1917 to 1931. During each of these fifteen years: § 1. Principal and interest, Taels 3,829,500. § 2. Principal and interest, Taels 3,469,800. § 3. Principal and interest, Taels 9,384,000. § 4. Taels 3,200,500. § 5. Interest only, Taels 4,600,000. Total during each of these fifteen years, Taels 24,483,800.

A.D. 1932. § 1, 2, 3 and 4. As before. § 5. Principal and interest, Taels 15,366,350. Total, Taels 35,350,150.

A.D. 1933 to 1940. § 1. During each of these eight years China will need to pay principal and interest, Taels 3,829,500. § 2. Taels 3,469,800 in each of eight years, principal and interest. § 3. Taels 9,384,000; conditions as under §§ 1 and 2. § 4. Taels 3,205,000. § 5. Taels 15,366,350. In these two sections conditions as above, principal and interest. Total in each of the eight years, Taels 35,350,150.

Grand Total in 1940, Taels 982,238,450.

The payments on account of the old and new indemnities will be found in the following table :—

	New indemnity, principal and interest.	Outstanding loans, principal and interest.	Total debt.
A.D. 1902	Taels 18,829,500	Taels 23,600,000	Taels 42,429,500
1903	18,829,500	23,300,000	42,129,500
1904	18,829,500	23,300,000	42,129,500
1905	18,829,500	24,100,000	42,929,500
1906	18,829,500	23,900,000	42,729,500
1907	18,829,500	23,700,000	42,529,500
1908	18,829,500	23,400,000	42,229,500
1909	18,829,500	23,400,000	42,229,500
1910	18,829,500	23,200,000	42,029,500
1911	18,899,300	22,800,000	42,699,300
1912	18,899,300	22,600,000	42,499,300
1913	18,899,300	22,400,000	42,499,300
1914	18,899,300	22,100,000	41,999,300
1915	23,283,300	19,400,000	42,683,300
1916 to 1930 each year	24,483,800	18,500,000	42,983,800
1931	24,483,800	18,400,000	42,883,800
1932	35,350,150	7,500,000	42,850,150
1933	35,350,150	6,800,000	42,150,150
1934 to 1940 each year	35,350,150	5,900,000	41,250,150

The new indemnity amounts, as stated above, to	Taels 982,238,450
The old loans constitute a debt amounting to	672,700,000
Taken together in January, 1902, the debt of China amounts to ...	Taels 1,654,938,450

This debt of about £230,000,000 China has the prospect of paying off in forty years, or she may borrow again from new creditors in order to discharge the obligations she is under to creditors who have already lent her money during the last twenty years.

Hunan Share of Indemnity.

Chung-wai-pao, January 12th, 1902.—Hunan share of indemnity.—Hunan has to pay Taels 700,000. To raise this amount four cash a catty will be charged on Hwai-an salt. The gentry say in their petition to the governor, who in Honan manages the salt tax, that by adding four cash a catty from January 24th, 1902, onward they can raise Taels 500,000.

KIANGSU ADDITIONAL INDEMNITY PAYMENTS FOR 1902.

The salt of Hwai-an is taken to four provinces. Under the new arrangement the salt merchants contribute annually a certain sum. The Yangchow granaries will now add to the price. This is collected by the Hwai-an salt commissioner. Yearly collection ...	Taels 230,000
By the new lekin the officers, on account of increase in the salt tax, will collect in Hupei	210,000
Hunan	230,000
Kiangsi	140,000
Anhwei	110,000
Annual collection at Cheng-yang-kwan ...	70,000
The salt Taotai at Nanking will collect annually additional salt duties from granaries under his jurisdiction ...	8,000
The salt board of Hwai-pe has four granaries under its control, and will collect each year	10,000
The deputy salt commissioner at Hai-chow will collect additional duties each year amounting to	192,000
Total	1,200,000

This amount will be sent by monthly installments to the Shanghai Taotai.—*Chung-wai-pao*, January 16th, 1902.

KIANGSU PROPER SHARE OF INDEMNITY PAYMENTS, 1902.

The Viceroy (*Chung-wai-pao*, January 16th, 1902) has stated that Kiangsu will pay each year	Taels 2,500,000

Salt, increase in price	Taels 700,000
Chekiang salt joined with Hwai-an salt will, by the increased price, yield to the Soochow treasurer	800,000
The Nanking treasurer will receive from salt through the increase in price ...	400,000
The Nanking custom house will supply ...	100,000
The salt merchants will, from the increase in the salt tax and special contributions, supply	200,000
The lekin salt administration will furnish	300,000
Total, Taels	2,500,000

These amounts are transmitted to the Shanghai Taotai from a new board of management in Nanking, which is directly subject to the viceroy and is named 派辦處 p'ai-pan-ch'u. The treasurer at Nanking does not manage the salt revenue.

First Indemnity Payment in 1902.

The disposition of the first indemnity payment is arranged by the international commission of bankers, but this arrangement is only temporary; the commission being not yet definitely constituted or instructed: Russia, 29 per cent.; Germany, 20 ; France, 15.7 ; Great Britain, 11 ; Japan, 8 ; United States, 7; Italy, 6; Belgium, 2; Austria Hungary, 1 ; Holland, 0.2; Spain, 0.1. Total, 100.—*North-China Daily News*, January 23rd, 1902.

Honan share of the indemnity.—A sum of Taels 300,000 will result from an increase of one mace to each tael in the land and personal service tax and by adding one-tenth to the deed tax.—*Chung-wai-pao*, January, 1902. This will enable the treasurer of Honan province to discharge his debt to the indemnity for a year.

Translation of Proclamation

Issued by Ts'en, Governor of Shan-si, on the 29th day of the 8th moon, 27th year of Kuang-hsü (11th October, 1901).

The Governor hereby notifies by proclamation that, in the second paragraph of the agreement made by Mr. Hoste with the Foreign Office at T'ai-yuen Fu, it is stated that the China Inland Mission wishes no indemnity for the chapels and dwelling houses that had been erected or bought in the following fifteen cities, viz., P'ing-iao, Kiai-hsiu, Hsiao-i, Sih-cheo, Ta-ning, Kih-cheo, Ho-tsin, K'üh-u, Lin-fen (P'ing-iang Fu), Hong-tong, Ioh-iang, Ch'ang-chï (Lu-an Fu), T'un-liu (Ü-u), and Lu-ch'eng; also the city of Ta-t'ong, to the north of the province, all in Shan-si, whether they have been burned, destroyed, or partly destroyed, and the same applies to the articles of furniture, miscellaneous goods, books, etc.; it being already agreed by the said Mission that they will themselves effect repairs and replace lost property.

In the 6th article it is stated that the Mission requests the Governor to issue a proclamation to be hung up in each of the church buildings for the erection of which no indemnity has been asked, stating that the Mission in rebuilding these churches with its own funds aims in so doing to fulfil the command of the Saviour of the world that all men should love their neighbour as themselves, and is unwilling to lay any heavy pecuniary burden on the traders or on the poor. In this the object of the Mission is not in any way to seek the praise of men. The Mission asks that the proclamation stating these things may be pasted on a wooden board, varnished and hung up in each building for worship, in order that henceforth there may be perpetual peace in its vicinity. These statements are supported by the despatch of the Foreign Office enclosing the agreement.

I, the Governor, find then, having made myself acquainted with the facts, that the chief work of the Christian religion is in all places to exhort men to live virtuously. From the time of their entrance into China, Christian missionaries have given medicine gratuitously to the sick and distributed money in times of famine. They expend large sums in charity and diligently superintend its distribution. They regard other men as they do themselves, and make no difference between this country and that. Yet we Chinese, whether people or scholars, constantly look askance on them as professing a foreign religion, and have treated them not with generous kindness, but with injustice and contempt, for which we ought to feel ashamed. Last year the Boxer robbers practiced deception and wrought disturbance. Ignorant people followed them spreading everywhere riot and uproar. They did not distinguish country, or nation, or Mission, and they, at the will of these men, burned or killed by sword or spear with unreasoning and extreme cruelty, as if our people were wild savages. Contrasting the way in which we have been treated by the missionaries with our treatment of them, how can anyone who has the least regard for right and reason not feel ashamed of this behaviour?

Mr. Hoste has arrived in Shan-si to arrange Mission affairs. He has come with no spirit of doubtful suspicion, hatred, or revenge; nor does he desire to exercise strong pressure to obtain anything from us. For the churches destroyed in fifteen sub-prefectures and districts he asks no indemnity. Jesus, in His instructions, inculcates forbearance and forgiveness, and all desire for revenge is discouraged. Mr. Hoste is able to carry out these principles to the full; this mode of action deserves the fullest approval. How strangely singular it is that we Chinese, followers of the Confucian religion, should not appreciate right actions, which recall the words and the Discourses of Confucius, where he says, "Men should respond with kindness to another's kind actions." By so doing we allow those who follow the Christian religion to stand alone in showing what is true goodness in our time. Is not this most dishonourable on our part?

On the whole it appears that while the Chinese and foreign religions have different names, they are at one in exhorting men to be virtuous. The Chinese and the foreigner are of different races, but they are the same as to moral aims and principles.

From this time forward I charge you all, gentry, scholars, army, and people, those of you who are fathers to exhort your sons, and those who are elder sons to exhort younger brothers, to bear in mind the example of Pastor Hoste, who is able to forbear and to forgive as taught by Jesus to do, and at the same time, to exemplify the words of Confucius to treat with kindness the kind acts of others.—以德報德.

Let us never again see the fierce contention of last year. Then not only will our country be tranquil and happy, but China and the foreigner will be united and enjoy together a prosperity which will, by this behaviour on the part of the peopie, be more abundantly displayed.

To enforce this on all persons, soldiers, or people, is the aim of this special proclamation, which let all take knowledge of and obey.

To be posted up in the preaching halls of the above mentioned places.

The Governor is a native of Kiang-si and son of the former Viceroy of Yunnan and Kuei-cheo. His name is Tsen Chun-ts'iuen.

欽命頭品頂戴兵部尚書都察院右都御史巡撫山西等處地方兼提督軍務節制各鎮管理驛政節制太原城守尉岑 為

出示曉諭事照得

耶穌教內地會何牧師斯德現與洋務局司道訂立合同內第二條稱內地會在山西平遙介休孝義隰州大寧吉州河津曲沃臨汾洪洞岳陽長治屯留潞城十四州縣又北路大同一縣所有教會建置之教堂並住房或焚毀或拆毀或未全毀以及會中公置之器具什物書籍等均不議賠現擬由本會自行修復購辦又第六條稱各處不議賠償之禮拜堂應請撫台出一告示聲明教會自行修復乃仰體

救世主愛人如己之意不忍令攤派商民竭小民之脂膏並非欲求商民見好也將原委一一敘明告示粘貼木板加蓋桐油懸掛教堂以期此後永遠相安各等情並據洋務局詳請前來本部院查

耶穌教會處處以勸人行善為宗旨自入中國以來如施藥放賑等事無不自捐鉅欵竭力經營視人如己彼教士等能悉除畛域吾華人士猶時時以為異教獨不能一視同仁褊狹已甚自愧迺上年拳匪煽亂無知愚民更復譁然風靡不問何國何教何會之人概曰洋人概曰教民盡情焚殺慘酷無理直同野蠻夫教士之待吾華也如彼而華人之待教士也如此稍明情理者又能無自愧乎此次何牧師來晉辦理教案不但不存猜忌報復分外要挾之心且又將十五州縣所毀教堂一律不索賠欵在

耶穌教以忍讓為宗旨本無報復之心何牧師能實踐是言極堪欽佩獨怪吾華服習儒教者何以不能體會以德報德之言致使能實行耶教者遂獨擅美於時不又重可恥乎要知中西教名雖有不同而勸人行善之心則同中外種族雖有不同而此心此理則無不同嗣後爾紳士軍民人等務當父詔其子兄勉其弟念何牧師之能力踐

耶穌忍讓之旨遂亦力踐以德報德之言萬勿再有齟齬則非但地方蒙福抑且中外一家大同之盛豈不於此益昭哉為此示仰軍民人等一體知悉毋違特示 遵

右仰通知

光緒二十七年八月 廿九 日

告示 押

實貼大同縣教堂

TAXATION IN THE CHINESE EMPIRE.

REVENUE OF 1899.

Peking Gazette, May 12th, 1901.

	Land tax.	Grain Tribute.	Foreign Customs.	Native Customs.
Shengking	Taels 31,500	Taels 8,200		
Fengtien	75,500	1,000	499,500	118,900
Chihli	2,151,000	18,600	632,500	351,100
Shantung	2,987,000	87,200	405,400	119,800
Honan	2,813,500	439,900		
Shansi	2,752,000	6,000	1,100	26,000
Shensi	1,315,000	15,900		80,500
Kansu	204,000		300	231,300
Anhwei	985,000	517,600	680,600	231,300
Kiangsu	1,700,000	786,800	7,294,800	111,300
Kiangsi	1,300,000	880,500	1,136,200	348,600
Chekiang	1,959,000	743,900	1,416,100	33,500
Fukien	1,010,000		1,625,000	192,800
Amoy			984,300	
Hupei	863,000	512,300	1,803,800	303,100
Hunan	1,065,000	286,200	114,200	16,100
Canton	917,000		3,856,200	523,500
Swatow			1,405,100	
Kwangsi	335,000	33,000	10,100	175,600
Szchwen	670,000	800	99,800	72,000
Yunnan			70,400	89,500
Kweichow	500,000	28,100		
Kirin	128,000	1,000		81,000
Heilungkiang		75,300		
Suiyuench'eng	36,000	5,300		21,600
Total,	23,797,500	4,447,600	22,035,400	2,906,400
			Including opium lekin, 4,965,300	

RIGHT OF TAXATION.

The right to tax is solely vested in the Emperor, and under the Emperor the Board of Revenue exercises supreme authority. The viceroys and governors, powerful as they are, cannot impose legally any tax. But they can petition the Emperor to make additions or diminish taxes, and their advice may be followed.

The taxes are the land and personal service tax, the miscellaneous taxes, the grain tribute, the waste and surplus tax, the salt tax, the native customs' duties, the lekin, the foreign customs' duties, and the subscriptions occasionally levied. There is a tax on land where reeds grow, a tax on wine and on lime, on opium, on silk, and on various other products. The 落地稅 *Lo-ti-shui* is a sort of equivalent to our port or wharfage dues.

Six Canons of Taxation.

The four canons of taxation, according to Adam Smith, are: economy, equality, certainty, and convenience. To these may be added ability to bear the burden on the part of the people and also their willingness.

In Adam Smith's time there was a duty of five shillings a ton on the export of coal from England or fifteen shillings a Newcastle chaldron. This coal duty was repealed in 1834. In 1845 Sir R. Peel imposed an export duty of four shillings a ton. The dissatisfaction expressed was so strong that it was repealed the same year. Since then in England there have been no export duties on coal. Hence it is plain that one canon of taxation is the willingness of the people to be taxed.

Taxation Forms.

A taxation form is sent to ratepayers in which the amount of the tax is written in a blank space.

Hu-pao, October 9th, 1901.—A Peking letter says the Hatamen custom house has hitherto collected the tax and impressed a stamp on the goods or upon the invoice if there was one. The trader did not know how much of what he paid was the tax. No taxation form was given him. Lately we hear that a printer has received orders to prepare a blank form of a duty receipt to the extent of several ten thousands of copies. This tax paper, after payment of duty, will be stamped. It states the amount of tax, so that the trader is in no danger of being asked to pay too much. [*N.B.*—This custom house is now ruled by Su Ts'in-wang as chief superintendent and by the President of the Board of Punishments, King Sin, as second superintendent. Blank forms were originally invented in China for collectors of taxes and for bankers, and probably date from the Tang dynasty.]

Revision of Taxes.

The result of Kang Chung-t'ang's revision of the Kiangsu taxes may be seen in the following statement in the *Peking Gazette* (*Chung-wai-pao*, February 22nd, 1900). Viceroy Liu in a memorial says the taxes on grain and land for the prefectures of Soochow and Chinkiang in thirteen districts (cities) amount to Taels 211,740, after correction for the land tax, and 149,420 piculs of grain tribute.

Offices for Collection of Taxes at and near Shanghai.

When a new office for tax collection is established by any governor it is placed under the control of the treasurer. In Shantung to raise more money for the public service a 籌款局 Ch'en-kw'an-chü was instituted. In 1901 this office collected duties on wine dealers, on opium shops, on opium lamps, and on shop signs. By these four kinds of taxes it was possible to raise in one year Taels 500,000.—*Chung-wai-pao*, July 29th, 1901.

In 1901 there were eight tax collecting offices in Shanghai and Woosung. They were :—

1. Shanghai tax office, 上海貨捐局 Hwo-kiuen-chü.

2. Shanghai tax office for cotton cloth and grass cloth, 上海布捐局 Pu-kiuen-chü.

3. Woosung tax office, 吳淞貨捐局 Hwo-kiuen-chü.

4. Woosung office for collecting taxes from junks trading to the northern ports and also from fishing junks, 吳淞沙釣船局 Sha-tiau-ch'iuen-chü.

5. Shanghai sugar tax office, 上海糖捐局 Tang-kiuen-chü.

6. Shanghai northern office for collecting silk and tea taxes, 上海絲茶北卡 Sz-ch'a-pei-ch'ia.

7. Shanghai office for managing grain transport by sea 海運滬局, Hai-yün-hu-chü.

8. Lekin office for Sungkiang and Shanghai, 淞滬厘捐局 Li-kiuen-chü.

Amount of Taxes in China.

In the reign of Kang Hi the revenue was Taels 36,000,000, the expenditure was also the same. Memorial of Yuen Ch'ang, *Shen-pao*, August 10th, 1899 :—In the reign of Chien Lung, 1745, the expenditure for troops was 24,000,000. In 1711 the remainder in the treasury was Taels 70,000,000.

In the year 1881 the revenue amounted to Taels 42,486,028. This amount included land and personal service, surplus, grain commutation, other grain taxes, miscellaneous taxes, customs, salt, land—in all nine sorts of taxes. The lekin in that year was Taels 18,580,444. This includes a remainder from the preceding year. The foreign customs revenue was Taels 14,990,276. In 1887 the opium tax yielded Taels 6,000,000.

Remission of Taxes.

During the present dynasty, because the population has increased enormously, the distress in times of famine is proportionately greater than in earlier times. The greater the number of people the greater the difficulty of providing food in famine years. There were no taxes remitted at the beginning of the Chow dynasty. In the Chow-kwan, an ancient manual of laws and administration, nothing is said of the remission of taxes. The people gave labour and were fed only. There was occasional relief from labour. To labour for the prince was then common, and to be relieved from it was an acceptable act of grace on the part of the sovereign. Persons were excused when old or maimed or otherwise invalided. In the Han dynasty the favour of the sovereign was shown in remission of taxes, and this act of grace has been granted since and has come to be a regular principle in times of drought and flood. Remission of taxes in these circumstances has been a marked feature in the Chinese system of government under the present dynasty. The oppressive weight of taxation on the poor is felt more acutely now when the population is large than in former ages, when the people were scattered thinly over the land. The common people had more land then than now and needed hired labour to a larger extent, because each farmer would possess more land than one man could cultivate.

Principle Adopted in the Levy of Land Tax.

Chinese taxes on land and grain are estimated on the principle that seven mow of land, or an acre and one-sixth, will support a man with his family. Many persons have less land than this and some have none. Still the normal quantity is in the eye of the law as here stated.

Land Taxation at Different Periods.

The gross amount of land tax in 1893 was Taels 23,329,533. This is distributed unequally in the provinces. The taxes are all decided upon in Peking. The viceroy and governor carry out the rule which is sent them in the form of an edict or of an order from the Wai-wu-pu, or Cheng-wu-ch'u.

In the feudal period, the Tsing-t'ien 井 田 or well arrangement was adopted. A square piece of land was divided into nine equal parts, each containing 100 mow. The central square of 100 mow belonged to the government. Eight families cultivated each their own square. The government square was cultivated by all. In the spring and autumn annals of Confucius it is said, under the year B. C. 592, that a land tax was then for the first time levied on the mow of land. This probably means that the old practice went out of use and was replaced by a regular annual tax on the land. See Legge Chun-tsien, p. 329. But Legge thought that in Confucius' time two-tenths of the produce went to the State. See the Lun-yü 12, 9, 3. Père Zottoli says there were two taxes—that of the Tsing-t'ien and that of the emperor's inherited land. In both, a tenth fell to the State.

The fact is worthy of note that in Corea the establishment of the Tsing-t'ien taxation is ascribed to Ki-tsï, who went over in the twelfth century before Christ and founded the Corean civilization. The preference of the Coreans for white clothing is referred to the origin of their civilization in the Shang dynasty, which honoured white colour. In those days the Babylonian colour philosophy was strongly held in China. The white, red, black, and yellow colours were adopted by the Yin, the Chow, the Ts'in, and the Han dynasties respectively.

Under the Han dynasty the payment to the government was one-fifteenth of the produce. Later it was made one-thirtieth. In the Sung dynasty one-tenth of a picul was required on each mow, which is about the twentieth. In the 14th century four *teu*, four *sheng* were collected on each mow. It amounted to twenty-two hundredths of the produce. At present, in the prefectures of Chinkiang and Ch'ang-chow, the tax is fifteen or sixteen hundredths of the produce of a mow. In the prefectures of Soochow and Sungkiang the land tax amounts to thirty-six or thirty-seven hundredths of the produce. The Wu district of Soochow prefecture contains 646,100 mow. See Soochow Fu-chï 14·44. It is divided for taxation into twenty-one portions called 則 tsê, a word which has here the sense of kind or type. Three portions are rice land cultivated by irrigation. Here the tax is $\frac{344}{1000}$ths of the produce of each mow. The land which is irrigated and bears this taxation amounts to 402,207 mow. A tax of $\frac{172}{1000}$ths of the produce is levied on 1,072 mow. A tax of one-tenth of a picul is levied on 4,570 mow.

In the case of land not irrigated, eighty-five hundredths of a picul are levied on 4·58 mow; thirty hundredths are levied on 2,573 mow; twenty-eight hundredths are levied on 15·73 mow; twenty-five hundredths are levied on 1,699 mow; twenty-three hundredths are levied on a lot somewhat less than a mow; two hundredths are levied on 2,245 mow; six hundredths of a picul are levied on 56,465 mow; five hundredths of a picul are levied on thirty-eight mow; one and a half per cent. of a picul are levied on fourteen mow.

In the case of hilly land 5·3 per cent. of a picul are levied on 31,059 mow, while 32 per cent. of a picul are levied on 22,735 mow and 1·5 per cent. of a picul on 4,704 mow.

In the case of marshy land $\frac{20}{100}$ths of the reeds produced on it are levied on 1,066 mow. On one mow and a third, one-tenth of the reeds is required. On ninety-seven mow 5 per cent. of the reeds are required. On 257 mow 3 per cent. of the reeds are required. On 21,705 mow 3 per cent. of the reeds are expected. These numbers are taken from the last edition of the Soochow History, A.D. 1877.

The amount of rice levied on the Wu district is 149,155 piculs. How is this made up? There are of rice and beans 74,182 piculs. The amount in the intercalary month is 236 piculs. Changed for silver the amount is Taels 56,365.

Waste and surplus tax, Taels 2,818 ; intercalary addition, Taels 784 ; duty on lime and for conveyance, etc., Taels 193.

The public accounts state the whole amount of the produce of the land in this district in rice. Whatever else is produced there it is so much rice *ad valorem.* The whole is labelled taxes on land. Rice is the basis of taxation.

If we reckon one picul of rice a mow as the amount of produce in the country round Soochow the land tax amounts to three *tou*, four *sheng*, or stated in silver $2·064. This is the tax if we take the rice to be worth three taels, six mace, or $6. To this is to be added one-fourth as waste tax. But the produce may be two or three piculs. The tax will be one-ninth if the produce be three piculs.

If the land yields two piculs the tax amounts to one-sixth. The amount of taxation is greatest in those years that are distinguished by unfavourable harvests. The amount of taxation varies according to the nature of the soil and the crops. The amounts are all fixed in Peking. The governor merely carries out the Peking decisions. A new edition of the topography of any city contains the latest corrected statement of the land taxes.

At Shanghai the tax at present is 29½ hundredths of a picul on each mow of good land. Since a picul of rice is worth about $5 and the harvest may be two piculs, the tax on one mow is about $1.50. On inferior land the tax $\frac{23·5}{100}$ths, is $1.25. Land outside of marshes is liable to a tax of $1, being $\frac{20·5}{100}$ths of a picul.

From these statements which occur in the most recent Shanghai topography, it appears that the land tax varies in each locality according to the productiveness of land. The magistrate states the circumstances. The prefect and superintendent report to the governor, who decides what tax the land should bear. For this he asks sanction from Peking. The origin of financial legislation in each district is local.

It must be authorized by the central government before it is adopted and made the rule in collecting the revenue in the spring and autumn of each year.

Land tax in the third century before Christ was fifteen per cent., or one fen wu li per tael per cent. It was made ten per cent. in A.D. 330. Three pints of rice were levied on each mow.

In the Tang dynasty grain was preferred to money. Under the Southern Tang efforts were made to have the poll tax changed to taxes on produce. Silk fabrics were taxed three per cent. *ad valorem.*

In the year A.D. 763 there was an edict stating that when there were three in a family only two should be taxed.

A tax on cultivated fields is called liang 量. A tax for personal service or capitation tax is called ting 丁. Land and personal service tax are called ti-ting 地 丁. Taxes differ in the north and south provinces. In Chihli and Shantung the tax on land is called keng 糠. It is included in ti-ting. In Kiangnan and Chekiang the grain tax is 賦 fu. The land tax is paid in silver. The names of other taxes are 漕項 t'sao-hiang, hau-tseng, the fisherman's tax, the reed tax, the appraiser's and broker's license tax. Miscellaneous taxes are also levied, such as the house, ox, and donkey taxes. The name pê-liang 白 糧 began to be used in the Ming dynasty. It was intended to afford additional maintenance to the Kwang-lu-sz Court of Banquets, the six Boards, the five Offices (Fu), the Censorate, the Imperial Academy, and the Inspectorates. Afterwards the maintenance of metropolitan offices, both in Peking and Nanking, was required. The prefectures which supplied these funds were Suchow, Sung-kiang, Ch'ang-chow, Kia-hing, and Huchow. The total amount was 217,410 piculs. Surplus tax, 166,140 piculs. Conveyance by boat, 293,940 taels.

The Manchu dynasty made a change, and the conveyance of grain tribute instead of being undertaken by traders was conducted officially. Soon the grain tribute was, to a large extent, commuted for silver, which was paid instead of so much rice at a fixed rate in order to save expense in conveyance. The saving amounted to several ten thousands of taels. In the reign of Shun Chih the rice of Kiangsu and Chekiang was valued at two taels a picul, and this was the amount of the tax in silver. When rice fell in value the tax became five or six mace for inferior rice. The best 白糧 pĕ-liang was two taels.

In 1736 the history mentions, Tung-hwa, ch. 1, p, 54, col. 13, that in Kuangsi in that year by edict the land tax on each mow in Wu-yuen district was made one mace. Before this edict two mace two candareens had been levied in silver. On soldiers' land in Wu-yuen district the levy amounted to a larger sum than that levied on the land of ordinary farmers.

In 1737 the soldiers' land at Wenchow and Taichow on the Chekiang coast had been taxed too heavily. Instead of the tax being Taels 0.1.7 and Tls. 0.1.4 *per mow* the emperor ordered that the same amount be levied as in the case of Hangchow soldiers' land, namely, Taels 0.1.2.8. The extent of land on which this levy was then made was 31,200 mow in Wenchow and 22,000 mow in Taichow.

In 1740 the emperor ordered that there should be no extra taxation under the heading Miscellaneous Imposts 雜辦. It was enough that there should be (1) the headings, land, and personal service 錢糧地丁, (2) 漕項 grain tribute, (3) reed land tax 蘆課, (4) 雜稅 miscellaneous taxes.

In the collection of official documents called 經世文 Ching-shih-wen, in the section on land tax, ch. 29, col. 5, an author, Chu-yün-chin, says that in the sixteenth century in the reign of Chia-ching there were 800,000 ch'ing of land on the registers. This was more than three times the number in the reign of Hung Wu, A.D. 1368 to A.D. 1399. In the reign of Wan Li, thirty years later, it was 950,000 ch'ing, or 15,833,333 acres. When the Manchus conquered China they retained the registers of the number of ch'ing fixed in the time of Wan Li. They only levied taxes on lands actually cultivated. Waste lands were stated to be 260,000 ch'ing. In A.D. 1810 a Land Tax Record 賦役全書 was published. The number of ch'ing is in this work stated at 1,074,805.93. Reckoning six mow to the acre this yields 17,913,432 acres. If we subtract land not productive through want of soil, diluvial action, and river encroachment, amounting to 324,579 ch'ing, ninety-four mow, the remainder 720,225 ch'ing, ninety-eight mow, is the amount of land now under grain cultivation. This is less than the amount under cultivation in the Ming dynasty in the sixteenth century. Probably cotton has taken its place to a large extent.

The phrase 錢糧 Ch'ien-liang means that cash are paid n place of grain tribute, and that grain is also paid. This phrase as describing soldiers' pay also has both meanings as in the colloquial sentence Chï-chien-liang-ti 吃錢糧的 one who lives on the amount of cash and grain allowed him by the government.

On September 9th, 1899, the *Shen-pao* stated that the contingent of grain for the province of Hupei is 30,000 piculs. The equivalent is Taels 70,000. There was a difficulty in obtaining the money. The treasurer had paid it to foreign loan account. The Board of Revenue insisted that it should be sent, and the treasurer of the province of Hupei was ordered to consult with the grain superintendent on the modes of obtaining this sum.

* T'sao is a boat or manger. T'sao-hsiang means conveyance tax. T'sao takes the sense of conveyance from the shape of the trough, of which it is the name as navigate is derived from navis. The city of T'sau-chow in Shantung is named from the grain passing it.

Sale of Titles to aid the Revenue.

To avoid raising money by direct taxation on the individual a method was thought of about B.C. 170 in the reign of Wen Ti. Money was then needed to defend the northern frontier. The Hiung-nu were troublesome. They had made several annoying incursions into North China and carried away much plunder. The troops at the passes needed to be doubled in number and must be fed, but the grain in the government granaries was insufficient. It was resolved to sell titles and badges of rank. Whoever gave money to the government or conveyed corn to the frontier for the use of the troops was rewarded with a certain rank. A gift of 600 to 400 piculs was rewarded by a low rank. The gift of 12,000 piculs secured a very high rank. To feed the soldiers in this inexpensive manner was a triumph of statesmanship.

This instance shows that the Chinese have sold titles to aid the revenue for more than two thousand years.

Twenty years later when there was dearth in Shansi and Chihli, titles were sold at a still cheaper rate than before. Also another measure was devised. Cavalry horses were needed. Officers who had committed faults in the discharge of their official duties were allowed to present horses to government. It became a common thing for such officers to have parks as breeding places for horses. Their chances of promotion would be in proportion to the number of horses they were able to furnish for the imperial stud.

Taxation of Waste Lands.

Common lands or waste lands in various parts of the Chinese empire, are gradually occupied by emigration. When Turkestan was reconquered from the Mahommedans the Manchu General Kin Shun in a memorial recommended the cultivation of new lands by emigrants brought to Ili for the purpose. This system is called 開墾屯田 k'ai-k'en-t'un-t'ien. Land was given them, with seeds and a cow. During three years no tax was levied. After this time the emigrants would be able to pay a tax 升課 and return the value of the seed and the cow.

Frequent wars cause lands to be deserted. After the passage of armies large tracts of land pass out of cultivation for want of owners. They revert to government and become soldiers' land. The Chinese army consists to a large extent of agriculturists who work in the fields when not required for military service. Formerly grain went to Peking from the five provinces—Kiang-su, Anhwei, Hupei, Kiang-si, Chekiang. It was guarded by soldiers on the way. These guards are paid by grants of land, 屯田 t'un-t'ien, which they cultivate. The land must revert to the government if the service the occupants render should cease. The grain junks are now no longer required and the Soochow authorities have announced that all lands so cultivated hitherto must be assigned to the authorities.

In the 安徽通志, Topography of the Province of Anhwei, the t'un-t'ien land is in amount 1,110,662 mow. In 1824, it was 1,183,977 mow. The fixed tax was Taels 40,526. The soldiers in occupation paid a proportional rate of Taels 2,404. But the real amount collected was Taels 42,930.

In the *Shen-pao*, December 14th, 1898, the governor of An-hwei says in a memorial that he has reported the amount of taxes collected in a year of deficient harvest and the measured area of new land cultivated. The waste land cultivated is of various quality. The result of taxation is therefore at present not known. He will report in the present year's account. The number of mow in the new land is 1,871,800.

Change of Grain to Silver.

The *Shen-pao* of October 20th, 1898, says on the grain tribute: Hu-pei, Hunan, and Anhwei, with some other provinces, have long since changed grain tribute to a silver tax. This has been found beneficial to the people. Opinions are divided as to the course that should be pursued in regard to Kiang-su. Some say a part should be changed for silver and the rest sent to the capital in kind. Others say the whole of the grain should be retained in the province and silver be substituted. There is the possibility to send grain by steamer from Chefoo to Tientsin in one day, from Shanghai in three days, from Fukien in five days, and from Canton in six days. From Newchwang two days would be required. But merchants, if conveyance of grain is left to them entirely, may raise prices, and this constitutes a difficulty.

The grain tribute of Kia-ting, near Shanghai, was in A.D. 1583 changed for silver by edict, and this change was made perpetual in A.D. 1596. A few years later an edict fixed five mace a picul as the commutation tax. In Kia-ting a tax of nine mace was required to be paid. After a few years seven mace was made the ordinary tax for grain tribute. Later on in the nineteenth century the change to silver was made final in Kia-ting and Pao-shan, both near Shanghai, because rice was not the produce of these districts.

In cases where cotton was the produce the farming people needed to labour hard, morning and evening, to make cloth and sell it for silver. To buy rice with silver and taxes afterwards was too great a strain upon the agriculturist, especially if rice should rise in price when the day of payment approached. He had also a melting tax and other charges to meet. Many farmers preferred to seek another home and escape these obligations. In such cases it was better to levy taxes in silver; on the other hand, if rice was the produce, and the former was obliged to pay taxes in silver, other difficulties arose. Silver may be lacking. The supply may be insufficient. To change grain taxes into silver payment requires a free circulation of silver. There are many dishonest servants of the Mandarins who cheat the people in exchanges. *Foreign trade, say the Chinese, carries money away from the country, and money as a means of purchasing articles becomes scarce.* The people find it hard to live. The change to silver payment becomes a hardship. If grain is conveyed to the north by traders it may rise in price. There may be a foreign war to interrupt navigation. Recently an edict directed Yi Kwang and Sun Kia-nai to consult and report on the feasibility of terminating grain tribute in kind. On October 2nd, 1898, the emperor in an edict ordered that grain tribute shall still be sent in kind. The reasons given are: the convenience in famines of retaining a part of the grain about to be transported; 2, the necessity that food in Peking shall not be insufficient; 3, the amount of silver available for currency could not be so much as five or six millions of taels as estimated by advocates of the change; 4, it is not right to give traders the liberty to raise prices for selfish reasons as they would do if all the buying and selling were in their hands.

The fear is felt by those who argue against silver payment that since rice must still be imported for the Peking population the common food of the country will be subject to the evil of high prices. Private importers will ask too much silver for their cargoes. These logicians forget that competition will reduce prices. Besides the government will keep the granary buildings occupied as of old. They will be filled when rice is cheap and the rice will be sold at a moderate price when the market value is high.

In the *Chung-wai-pao*, November 17th, 1898, it is stated that the Board of revenue has sent down an order to the Chekiang governor to the following effect: In future the waste tax 加耗, kia-hao will be one-fourth to every picul of rice, that is, 二斗五升, or twenty-five catties. This is estimated in silver at the market rate. If the tax payer delays payment to next year, he must, as is done in Kiangsu province, pay 300 cash in addition. The governor has announced this new rule for Chekiang province in a printed proclamation.

COMMUTATION TAX IN HONAN.

In 1898 the amount of commutation tax for grain tribute in Honan was made 2,800 to 3,000 cash or 4,000 cash. For a tael of silver 2,500 to 2,600 cash are levied. In some localities only 2,000 cash are claimed, and the same principle prevails in Kiangsi province. This want of uniformity leaves room for illegal increase in the levy made on the people and is a likely cause of disaffection and local riots.

In 1733 the governor of Honan reported that in his province the han-sien tax yielded, after deducting expense of administration 本地公事, the sum of 700,000 taels, together with millet and grain in store houses amounting to 280,000 piculs.

THE AVOIDANCE OF HEAVY TAXATION BY THE MANCHU DYNASTY.

Chang Chih-tung, viceroy of the Hu provinces, in his work 勸學篇 Ch'üen-hio-p'ien, states that a heavy tax known as Mien-fu-ch'ien 免夫錢 was by the Sung dynasty levied to supply funds to carry on war with the Liau dynasty, which lasted from A.D. 907 to A.D. 1125, and was brought to an end by the emperor Hwei Tsung. The tax realized 62,000,000 strings of cash. This is equivalent to £6,200,000 if the following data are correct. At that time ten ounces of silver were changed for one ounce of gold and 100 ounces of copper were one ounce of silver. If we take a cash for an ounce and calculate the amount in pounds sterling it will be £6,200,000, on the supposition that the string contained a thousand cash.

This would be the amount raised by taxation in A.D. 1125. But if the number of cash in a string was five hundred, which was possibly the case, the tax would raise £3,100,000. A few years afterwards the Golden Tartars conquered all North China. The unpopularity of the Sung dynasty, caused by severe taxation, would pave the way for the success of the Tartar invasion.

New Taxes under the Sung Emperors.

In the later Sung dynasty, when the capital was at Hang-chow, four new taxes were added to the former. They were called 經總制錢 King-tsung-chih-ts'ien, 月椿錢 Yue-ch'un-ts'ien, 板幔錢 Pan-man-ts'ien, 折帛錢 Che-pe-ts'ien. By these taxes several million strings were raised. They were retained till the time of the Mongols, A.D. 1260 to A.D. 1360.

New Taxes under the Ming Emperors.

In the Ming dynasty, A.D. 1360 to 1644, there was a tax levied, known as the Liau-hiang, for keeping in tranquillity the Manchurian province. Afterwards the tax called 勦餉 Ch'au-hiang and the 練餉 Lien-hiang, or army drill tax, were imposed. These in all amounted to twenty million strings. We must count a thousand cash to the string. The amount then becomes £2,000,000. This will be the total if we reckon the silver tael to have been ten times as cheap as gold. About A.D. 1520 silver began to arrive from Mexico. Between A.D. 1300 and A.D. 1770 silver fell from a value ten times less than gold to a value fifteen times less. Let us assume that through a plentiful supply from America it diminished in value until it was twelve and half times less in value than gold in the sixteenth century. The same number of cash would in the sixteenth century be worth £25,000,000.

In the eighteenth century they would be worth £30,000,000. The Ming dynasty sovereigns raised by taxation the former of these sums. The present Manchu dynasty has thought it more benevolent and more politic not to follow this example in levying the latter of these sums.

Causes of Light Taxation under the Manchus.

That the present dynasty has been able to avoid this heavy taxation is in part because able-bodied labourers have increased greatly in number and the personal service tax has continued to be collected. With the increased population the amount of grain tribute has become much more than formerly. Light taxation allows the people to develop various industries. Families increase when there is abundance in the means of living. Light taxation has been one of the characteristics of the legislation of the present dynasty.

In Northern Kiang-su and at Feng-yang prefecture in Anhui province many of the poor instead of cultivating good grain or hemp merely cut down grass for their living. They carry it to the nearest town and sell a thousand catties for five or six mace of silver. Deducting expense of conveyance they acquire a mace or two mace of silver. The tax on grass land is only one or two candareens. The very poor class can live without ploughing and weeding if they possess a mow or two of this land. This is the result of too light taxation. They need not buy a cow or seed or a plough. The writer in *Ching-shih-wen-pao* argues that it is not well to encourage idleness. Taxation should be heavy enough to lead to activity on the part of the poorer class.

Granary System.

There are two granaries at Tungchou and fifteen inside and outside of Peking.

In the Anhwei Tungchi, Vols. 2, 6, 23, A.D. 1748 there are remarks on the granary system, showing that the principle is to purchase grain when it is cheap, keep it in a granary under lock and key, and open it when the market price of grain is high. The magistrate orders the granary stores of rice and wheat to be sold under the market price to benefit the general population and ameliorate the evils of poverty.*

The granaries are under the superintendence of the grain Taotai, who has a treasury which is inspected at times by the Governor.

Faults in the Peking Seventeen Granaries.

The old rice is not removed to be replaced by the new rice which arrives from the south. The floors are damp and low, causing the rice to grow mouldy. Through the dampness the grain rots. The granaries are not swept and dust and refuse are mixed with the rice. In rainy weather the rice sprouts. Much of the rice remains for years in the granaries. It has no sun to shine upon and dry it, nor has it any wind to blow on it. Ants and other insects abound. The weevil appears and grows fat on the rice around him. The men in charge are careless and tread down the grain without thought. The earth and moisture on their shoes become mixed with the rice intended for the food of men.

Conveyance and Distribution of Tribute Grain.

The Peking distribution of grain is as here follows: Chekiang and Kiangsu send 220,000 piculs; of this the

* In an article in the *North American Review* June, 1897, Mr. H. Seton Karr recommends national granaries in England. England needs to secure the possession of food in case of war. There should be a small protective duty for the encouragement of wheat cultivation in England since only two million acres are sown at present. Four times this amount might be sown with wheat with a small protective duty. In addition to this there should be a granary system, so that England may not be entirely dependent on foreign countries for bread.

Tai-chang-sï and Kwang-lu-sï use for sacrifices, and for banquets, 2,000 piculs. The princes and high officers require 150,000 piculs to 160,000. The household, soldiers of the palace, and eunuchs receive 10,000 piculs. In the granaries there remain 50,000 piculs. The amount assigned to princes may be one-half white and one-half coarse rice, *keng-mi.* The remaining 12,000 can be changed for ts'ao-liang, that is, coarse grain. This will be a relief to the people, (Tunghwa, 2, 5), who will appreciate the privilege of contributing a less quantity of the better kinds of field produce.

The contribution of white rice from Kiangsu and Chekiang began in the Ming dynasty. At that time the Kuang-lu-sï, the Five Boards called Foo, the six Boards called Pu, and other establishments, had set apart for their use 217,410 piculs of white rice supplied from the prefectures of Soochow, Sung-kiang, Chia-hsing, Hu-chou, and Chang-chou. First the contribution was required at Nanking and afterwards both at Peking and Nanking. To the above amount must be added 166,140 piculs, and, in silver, Taels 293,940 for expense of conveyance. In the present dynasty the system of entrusting traders with the task of conveying rice to Peking was changed. It became the duty of special officers appointed for the purpose. This arrangement was made about A.D 1650. The price of rice was taken then at two taels a picul. When the Manchu conquest was completed the price fell to a tael and a half and to five or six mace only. If in commutation to silver payment the pressure was severe on the tax payer and rice was still counted at the price of two taels a picul, the people were overburdened *(Ching-shih-wen-pao).*

Kiangsu Grain Tribute.

In the Tung-hwa-hsü-lu, 1846, 12, 21, it is said in reference to Kiangsu that Sungkiang sends each year to Peking a diminished quantity of rice. It is now only 3,000,000 and a few hundred thousand piculs. It should by rule be neither short in quantity nor late in time of arrival. Next year, says the edict, it must be fully 4,000,000 piculs or 3,800,000 to 3,700,000 piculs at the least. A less quantity is not sufficient for distribution to princes, government officers, and soldiers. If this quantity is not sent, the high officers in Kiangsu will be severely punished. Whenever petitions are presented asking for delay or for complete exemption, the emperor says, he always grants the request or prayer of the petition because he trusts in the honesty of the petitioner. Fifty or sixty cities have been exempted during this year, says the edict. Is this because local expenditure has been heavy and can it be that pity for the victims of drought or flood is invented as a reason for exemption when the real cause is heavy local expenditure? The high officers in charge of that province ought not to forget the paramount need of the distribution of rice from the metropolitan granaries.

It should be noted that one Grain Taotai resides at Nanking, who is known as the 江安糧道 Kiang-an-liang-tao. He manages the rice tribute of Kiangsu in the north and west, as also that of Anhwei. The other is the 蘇松糧道 Su-sung-liang-tao, who controls the rice tribute of the prefectures of Soochow and Sung-kiang.

Quantity of Tribute Rice for Kiangsu in 1898.

In regard to the Shanghai Rice Tribute, the Board announced in February, 1898, that the China Merchants' steamers will convey to Tientsin 163,000 piculs. These are the amounts for three prefectures and a sub-prefecture. The amount for the district of Shanghai is 8,600 piculs. The other twenty-five districts contribute amounts in proportion to their size. The whole contribution, estimated at Taels 4.2.0 per picul, amounts to Taels 6,846,000 of silver, or nearly £1,000,000. The other provinces make up the revenue to more than three million pounds sterling.

The whole grain tribute for Kiangsu is in the Red Book fixed at 1,431,273 piculs. For Chekiang it is in the same work fixed at 612,720 piculs. These two totals make together about £3,000,000 in value.

In the spring of 1898, the Chekiang tribute grain sent to Tientsin was 430,000 piculs.

TAX ON TRIBUTE GRAIN JUNKS.

In the year 1897, the Tientsin superintendent collected from the tribute junks which came from Kiangsu and Chekiang from May 2nd, 1897, to April 13th, 1898, and from April 14th to May 19th of 1898, a tax called 海稅 hai-shui. The grain junks paying it were 212 in number. The goods they carried were, in accordance with a previous memorial, exempted from one-fifth of duty charged on other vessels. The amount, less one-fifth exempted, was Taels 8,462.6.9.8. The proportion exempted on China Merchants' steamers was also one-fifth, and the amount was Taels 4,286.5.2. The amount, less one-fifth exempted on grain junks from Kiangsu and Chekiang returning empty from Tientsin and Newchwang and carrying as freight peas and other articles, was Taels 1,263.2.7. The amount, less one-fifth exempted on vessels carrying rice and other grain, was Taels 17,039.3.7.2.

Total, less one-fifth exempted, Taels	31,051.8.6
Total collected from vessels not having exemption certificates,	9,015.4.6
Total	40,067.3.2

This total is in excess of the fixed amount by Taels 67.3.2. Subtracting this surplus from the amount on which there are exemptions, the remainder is Taels 30,984.5.4. The amount subtracting this from Taels 40,000 is Taels 9,015.4 6. Each 10,000 taels corresponds to Taels 2,253.8.6.5, and according to this rate the proportion in 26,000 taels due to the Board is Taels 5,860.0.4.9. Of this sum, writers' and servants' food and wages absorb one-tenth, Taels 586.0.0.4.9. The sum, less this amount sent to the Board, is Taels 5,274.0.4.4.1. The surplus, Taels 14,000, by calculating at the same rate, becomes Taels 3,155.4.1.1. This amount is sent to the treasurer. The Pei-yang superintendent adds that Wang Wen-shao, the former incumbent had not made this calculation. He has therefore done so and calls the amount hai-shui, a term which does not occur before. Yung Lu appears to be the first to make use of it. He adds the words of the edict as his authority.

Final Abandonment of Grain Conveyance by Sea and by Canal.

Chung-wai-pao, August 20th, 1901.—In an edict received in Shanghai August 29th and in Si-an on August 15th, it is announced that the conveyance of rice has long given rise to abuses. It has wasted imperial funds and increased the suffering of the people through additional taxation. It is necessary now to economise on account of increased demands on the treasury. All needless expenditure must be avoided. Henceforth beginning with the present year rice will cease to be sent to Peking on account of the government, either by sea or by canal. In all provinces tribute grain must be sold for silver and silver sent in place of it. Beside this every effort must be made to reduce expenses in Boards and in carriage of articles. All remainders must be kept to be applied as the Board of Revenue may indicate. The governors of provinces are directed to inquire into the expenditure in every district and sub-prefecture. Whatever remainders there are must all be faithfully added to the public fund and not wasted and misapplied as formerly. By this economy a large sum can be raised, and it will be the duty of viceroys and governors to state the amount in a memorial. As to the granaries, they will henceforth receive no tribute grain. Means must be found to keep them supplied. A new system to include purchase, conveyance, and storage, must be adopted and all abuses carefully avoided. The chief manager of grain conveyance, of Viceroy's rank, and the deputy manager of the rank of vice-president are hereby required within two months to formulate a new system of regulations and forward it in a memorial."

A writer in the *Sin-wen-pao*, August 20th, 1901, says that Feng Kwei-fen was the first to suggest that tribute grain in the south should be exchanged for silver. Many eminent statesmen adopted his opinion. The Board of Revenue rejected their proposals. From that time it has been commonly held that grain conveyance was a centre of corruption and abuse and that to change grain to silver was highly economical. The change is made by an edict of August 15th, which directs that government conveyance of grain by canal and by sea shall cease. The saving of expenditure thus secured will be not small, and it is reserved for the Board of Revenue to state to what use it shall be applied. Feng Kwei-fen says that each picul of grain conveyed to Peking costs eighteen taels. Two million piculs would cost six million taels. This seems a great saving, but times have changed. The passage by sea has only cost eight mace a picul.

The Relation of Copper and Silver in its Bearing on the Collection of Taxes.

In the year 1884, Tu Jên-shou, treasurer of the province of Hupei, addressed to the Emperor two memorials on the collection of grain tax. The abuses were great. They had been made the subject of memorials by Hu Lin-i in the reign of Hsien Feng. In 1884, the faults complained of were extortion on the part of the magistrate's messengers sent to farmers in the country to hasten payment of taxes, and overstatements at the magistrate's office when the farmers came to pay. The messengers on arriving at the farmer's home expect wine and food. When the assessment note of taxes due is presented several hundred cash more are demanded, and sometimes several thousand cash in excess of the amount actually due. If tax payers do not satisfy them, they threaten to bring a charge against them before the magistrate of obstructing the officer in collecting legal taxes 抗 糧 k'ang-liang. The country people are timid, and give them all they ask. The tax paper is called yü-t'iê 諭 帖. When the tax messenger comes on his rounds in the country with these papers, the amounts due are found to have been written by the magistrates' shoopans in large abbreviated script which the countryman is not qualified to decipher. This is commonly done by the shoopans also on tax receipts 糧 票 liang-p'iao. When written in this way the country farmer cannot at the time learn the real amount. He submits to extortionate charges the more readily on this account. In stating the quantity of grain, they substitute the *tow* for the *sheng;* in stating money, they substitute taels for mace. Countrymen who may come to the magistrate's office from places ten, twenty, or thirty miles' distance are at the mercy of the shoopans, who receive from them the amount of taxes. Unnecessary charges are added for travelling expenses and tax receipt expenses. The tax receipt is withheld till the shoopan is satisfied. Without it the country farmer is liable to ceaseless demands.

In accordance with the treasurer's advice the Empress-Dowager in 1884 ordered that the viceroy and governor should direct the sub-prefects and city magistrates of Hupei province to send a grain tax form with the amount due filled in. (易知由單.) This was to reach the farmer beforehand. He would bring it with him on going to the city to pay and exchange it for the tax receipt 糧票. No additional sum as a messenger tax was to be charged. If the sub-prefect or district magistrate should give unfair advantages to certain persons, they can be accused before the governor-general.

To assist the magistrate in collection of taxes there is a 縣丞 or deputy magistrate, a Siün-kien 巡檢 and a 典史 Tien-shï. The magistrate has a seal sent from Peking. The inferior collectors have only a wooden stamp made locally at their discretion.

In another memorial the same treasurer says that in carrying out the new edict of the empress the important point is to have the amount of tax distinctly written on the blank form. He had himself seen in forms the intentional filling in of large grass characters instead of plain numbers. It is to be feared that civil officers will still practise this deception. The overpayments in all the provinces due to the habit of indistinct filling in of money amounts reach a very large sum. The gain is that of civil officers. The ill repute of this practice falls on the government.

He proceeds to say that in 1799 the Emperor Jen Tsung-jui issued an edict to guide in collecting the grain tax. If the farmer brought copper cash in place of the silver required by law he ought not to be forbidden the exercise of this liberty, because being ignorant of the exact value of silver he would be the victim of extortionate charges on the part of the collecting officers. The emperor made it the duty of the viceroy and governor, when the time of collecting the half yearly tax was near, to find out by inquiry the market value of the tael of silver stated in copper cash of good size. The farmer, if he wishes to pay in silver, can do so. If he wishes to pay in large cash he can also do so, but the number of good cash that he pays must be regulated by the rate of exchange previously declared by the viceroy and governor. In the proclamation announcing that the farmer may pay in copper cash a warning is to be addressed to receivers of taxes never to ask too much from the ratepayer on pain of punishment.

From this edict of 1799 it is plain that at that time the Chinese government adopted the principle that silver payment of taxes is the rule; also that copper cash may be paid, but the cash must be good. The number of cash to the tael must be announced by the governor every half year, and it will vary according to the market rate as it existed in each city. The renowned governor of Hupei, Hu Lin-i, in his memorial on this subject in 1858 made a plain statement of the manner in which taxes of this kind ought to be collected. In every case the amount due should be stated distinctly on the assessment form. No special messenger should be sent to the country to hasten payment of taxes. The registration shoopans should themselves distribute the assessment forms, having the blanks filled in with the amount due from each farmer or taxpayer. If there is a mistake in the amount, the tax payer appeals to the shoopan to correct it. Should the shoopan be unfair or guilty of extortion or misstatement he should be liable to punishment such as the law directs. If there is any error in the tax receipt, or if there be delay in giving it to the tax payer, the shoopan who receives the tax may be charged with his fault before the magistrate.

The amount entered on the magistrate's register must agree exactly with the amount entered in the blank space on the assessment form. The tax must be paid in the magistrate's office. The tax payment counter must be spacious enough and the clerks employed numerous enough to prevent delays. There must be no calculation when the money is paid. It must be the amount stated on the assessment form. This must simply be compared with the register and no one must be kept waiting at the tax receiver's counter. Should the assessment form contain an error it is to be corrected by reference to the magistrates' register.

In this improved system the chief point is the abolition of the practice of sending special messengers to press for payment of taxes. The village constable is held responsible for the payment by the villagers for whom he acts and whose register he keeps.

When on account of drought or flood the Emperor remits taxes it is made the duty of the magistrate to have this fact entered in the assessment form. To secure exemption it is made necessary for the magistrate to submit to his superior officer a return of the localities suffering from drought or flood for the guidance of the viceroy and governor in their appeal to the Emperor to grant exemption.

If the Yamên servants and subordinate officials are just and upright in managing their affairs they are to be rewarded with presents of money for the better support of their families.

From a memorial of the Board of Revenue printed in Shanghai, September 5th, 1897, it appears that Pang Hung-shu had stated the taxation of Chekiang and Kiangsu more minutely than that of other provinces. The people were paying for the consolidated land and poll taxes two taels for one. They brought cash to the city magistrate, and he entered it in his books as silver. The treasurer decided all matters and fixed what sum should be levied on the tax-payer for expenses. This was a constant addition to the tax in each locality. In 1894, the sum levied was 2,200 cash. This was when silver was changed at 1,600 cash a tael or it might be 1,700. The addition was 400 or 500. In the year 1896 on account of the fall in silver the charge was made 2,000. This was in 1897 authorized from Peking. The silver value in cash had become 1,200 or 1,300 cash to the tael. The people were required to pay 700 or 800 cash more than the one silver tael.

On the whole, in Chekiang, Anhwei, and Kiang-su, three or four mace were added to the regulation tael in each case. The cash actually paid was 1,700 or 1,800. In 1897 a reduction of 100 cash was allowed. In all 2,200 cash are now being collected for each tael. When dollars are offered by the tax-payer, the tax-gatherer requires copper cash for every small defect in the coin. The tael tax becomes virtually two taels.

Grain Tax.—When the farmer brings his grain he is required to pay 1,000 cash in money for each picul. This is to meet the expense of conveyance, and it is more than the Treasurer's charge for meeting expenses and conveyance charges when silver is paid. This increase for grain conveyance is a burden on the farmer. The memorialist recommended that the Emperor should direct the Board of Revenue to consider the question and give him their opinion as to whether for the present not more than 400 or 500 cash for expenses should be added to the number of cash obtainable for one tael in the market and that when silver is paid not more than three-tenths or four-tenths of a tael be required in addition to each tael.

While silver by weight is legal payment the people are allowed to pay cash to the magistrate for their taxes because it is the dynastic coin. While cash were plentiful and exchange was high they did not suffer. The fall in the value of silver came and cash were scarce. The collectors still kept to the old system. Though they required less than before, the reduction they allowed was not equal to what it should be, and the burden is felt by the people to be heavy. The prices Pang Hung-shu recommended were as below :—

Kiangsu and Chekiang, 2,000 cash per tael; excess, 700 to 800. In Anhwei one tael became Taels 1.3.0 to Taels 1.4.0

Honan, 2,500 to 2,600 per tael.

Kiangsi, 2,582 per tael.

Shantung, 2,400 per tael.

In other provinces 700 or 800 cash above the exchange rate are collected. The Board is of opinion that uniformity cannot be attained. It is necessary for the amount of additional taxes to be settled by the governor in consultation with his circuit superintendents. They must have an eye to the exchange value of silver when deciding. The picul of grain was in 1897 estimated variously at 3,400 to 3,700 cash. During 1898 it was as high as 5,700, but in November, after the harvest, it fell to about 3,600 cash.

CONTRACTING TO LEVY TAXES. *Chung-wai-pao*, DECEMBER 4TH, 1901.

When Kang Yi went to Kiangsu and Canton to increase the revenue in those provinces for the central government he first removed the abuses he found in the land revenue of Kiangsu. He then went to Canton to improve the lekin revenue. He at once changed the contract system by farming for the direct collection by official tax-gatherers. This led easily to perfectly unnecessary waste in salaries given to persons who could be spared and the levy of taxes too often to enter not the public treasury but the pocket of the collector. Many evils sprang into life from the change. The addition to the national revenue was small. The pressure on native merchants was lamentably heavy. To correct the system would have been very difficult. He appealed to men of substance to consult and undertake to farm the taxes. They opened tax offices and paid in a certain amount every quarter to the treasurer. He fixed on Taels 200,000 as the amount for which they became liable. They would thus increase the collection from this source beyond the sum formerly fixed by the Board of Revenue. The special commissioner was proud of his success and the collection of taxes by farmers acquired for the time a high reputation. But after trial it is found that there are hopeless delays in making payment. If the farmer use the money paid him he has it not to give. His quarterly instalment is not punctually credited to the revenue. The consequence is that the viceroy will ask the emperor to allow him to return to the principle of direct taxation, so that by this method the money may be ready at the proper time to forward to the Board.

The contract is not made for a round sum of taxes levied on a large variety of dutiable articles. If $3,000 are collected at one place, the whole province may with difficulty yield $200,000.

Port Dues, or Lo-ti-shui.

The tax office at Shanghai which collects lo-ti-shui on goods is called 貨捐局 hwo-kiuen-chü. There is a staff of 巡丁 siün-ting searchers, who may detain boats on false pretences in order to obtain bribes from the boatmen or the boat firm. A boat may have a registration certificate, 船牌 ch'wen-p'ai, and pay duty after the application for sailing permit. The cargo of say thirty tons of Japanese coal destined for Kia-hing may be shipped under permit and all formalities may be discharged, and yet the tax office police may come and pretend that there is intent to smuggle or to pass the barrier without inspection. This is a case in which the boatman and boat firm may ask the commissioner to help them. See petition, June 30th, 1899.

TEA TAXES IN THE YUEN DYNASTY.

Copper was less used in the Yuen dynasty than before. Paper notes took the place of silver and card board tickets were substituted for copper. In the public accounts of the Yuen dynasty fifty taels of silver were called a ting and represented in paper notes. As government notes represented silver and copper, so certificates represented salt and tea. For example one tea certificate represented ninety catties of tea.

In the year A.D. 1336 the Viceroy of Hukwang and Kiangsi sent a despatch to the Peking government making a proposition for the improved administration of the tea trade. He stated the views of Wan-chia-lü, tea commissioner. The annual revenue from tea collected by him, according to the amount fixed in Peking 歲辦額課, was 289,200 ting, or taels 1,446,000. Beside the amount collected from tea hawkers the number of tea certificates 引 was 1,000,000. These at Taels 12.5.0 each, yield taels 12,500,000, represented by 250,000 money notes.

Tickets represented common kinds of tea 草茶, and were printed annually to the amount of 13,085,289 catties. These were of card board. They answered to 29,080 ting in money notes, that is to say, 1,254,000 taels in that form of currency. The proposition of the tea commissioner was that since there were too many certificates there should be an addition made to the tickets in the proportion of two to ten. Tea remained in official hands unsold at the end of the year. To remedy this inconvenience tickets should be printed to the amount of 2,617,058 catties. The whole amount of tea, by adding this quantity, became 15,702,347 catties.

The money notes when 7,269 ting, seven taels, were added, would become 363,457 taels more than before.

To this proposition the government agreed. The salt and tea commissioner was ordered to issue 100,000 permits 公據 and one million certificates representing 90,000,000 catties and 289,200 ting, or in taels 14,460,000. *Vide* 元史 Yuen-shih, 97, 18.

Five centuries and a half ago the tea trade was carried on by the use of government money notes only. Neither silver nor copper cash were much used in payment. Large certificates issued by government represented tea in large quantities. Small cardboard tickets were used by the common people for buying tea. There were money tickets also which could be exchanged for tea certificates or salt certificates at the official price. Fifty taels of silver were a ting in paper money, and twenty-five ting corresponded to 1,250 taels of silver.

If we assume the population to have amounted to sixty millions, each person would consume one-fourth of a catty of tea in a year. If we assume the population now to be four hundred millions, the tea consumed in China will be one hundred million catties, which is about half the amount of the foreign export.

Dust tea, now used to make brick tea for the trade with Russia, was packed in bamboo cylinders with a special seal. Beside this powdered tea there was also coarse tea, in buying and selling which card tickets, 草茶由占 Ts'ao-ch'a-yu-t'iê, were used. Copper cash went almost out of circulation at that time in such markets as Hankow. The annual amount of catties of tea was 13,085,289 as stated above.

If we compare this amount of tea with the modern export, the increase has been remarkable on account of the growth of foreign trade. For example, in the year 1885 the total export was 212,875,075 catties, which is nearly twenty times as great. Each tea certificate in use six centuries ago represented ninety catties of tea. They were used by traders in commercial centres. The tickets went to small dealers and circulated in the hill districts where the tea shrubs grow. When tea was retailed the tickets took the place of money. They were sold in spring. If too few in number, the people could not buy tea when autumn came. On this account it was found necessary to make two-tenths more of these cardboard tickets. If the number of tea certificates was too great the tea was stored in winter, because it remained unsold. The tea which was represented by these tickets became 2,617,058 catties.

On each catty the duty was in silver taels 0.1.3.8.8.8 On ninety catties represented by one tea certificate (yin) the duty was taels 12.5.0. This was the case when silver was one-tenth the value of gold and 109 times the value of copper.

The government made it obligatory on the commissioner who had charge of the salt and tea collections for the Yangtsz river to issue one million tea certificates and notes to the amount of 289,200 ting or thereabouts. The number of tea tickets represented 13,085,289 catties. Each catty was charged taels 0.1.1.1.1.2. The number of notes representing this tax was in the fifty taels per ting nomenclature, 5,816 ting, seven taels, four mace, one candareen. The issue of certificates was fewer by 23,264 certificates. The oppressive burden on the country people who had to manufacture sufficient tea to correspond to the number of certificates, was thus lessened.

Certificates, money notes, and retail tickets of cardboard were the three factors by which the tea trade and the levy of taxes on tea were then conducted. The system allowed much oppression of the traders and of the farmers who worked on the tea plantations.

Special Contributions.

Recently the government has felt the need of special expenditure.

In 1897 it was proposed in a memorial to the emperor that treasury notes bearing interest at five per cent. should be offered by the Board of Revenue to rich men. They were from patriotic motives and also from the security of the government guarantee largely applied for in all the provinces. The name given to them is 昭信股票 Chao-sin-ku-p'iao. The memorialist who proposed this important measure in the story of Chinese finance was 黃思永 Hwang Sz-yung, a Chwang-yuen doctor of literature, native of Nanking, and now a censor in Peking.

There are other special contributions which have been given to aid the government. The 籌餉 Ch'ou-hsiang was to assist in quelling the Tai-ping rebellion. The 海防 Hai-fang was to provide funds to resist foreign invasion. The 鄭工 Cheng-kung contribution was intended to obtain funds for the restoration of the Yellow River embankment after its giving way. All these are modes of raising funds by free contributions without interest. The Chao-sin-ku-piau contributors receive interest. The other classes of contributors are rewarded by official appointments. The wealth obtained by these appointments far exceeds in amount the interest at five per cent. of the Chao-sin-ku-piao.

Japan Land Tax.

In Japan land tax is three and a half per cent. on the assessed value of the land of a buyer,—*Japan Mail*, April 21st, 1900.

If a buyer A purchases land for 10,000 yen and borrows 8,000 from B to pay for the purchase he may also borrow

10,000 from C. With this sum he builds houses and lets them for 2,000 yen annually. In addition to the land tax he will have to pay income tax on 8,000 as a loan. He also pays income tax on 2,000, the amount of his rents, and C pays income tax on the interest he receives. It would be more equitable for A to pay two-fifths of the land tax and three-fifths of the income tax and A should pay income tax only on the residue of the rents after deducting the interest to C. But this is found to be impracticable.

Land tax is land rent. Land in Japan was made over to occupiers for a payment of three per cent. on the assessed value of the land. This was reduced to two and a half per cent. and afterwards was raised to 3·3 per cent. This tax of three per cent. was, however, twenty-five years ago really not more than one and a half per cent. of the value, and the present tax of 3·3 per cent. is only 1.65 per cent. of the value. In New South Wales a homestead can be obtained for 1·25 per cent. of the assessed value of the land for five years. After five years the tax is 2·5 per cent. till the next reassessment at the end of ten years.

The agricultural land in Japan as now registered has the value of 1,350,000,000 yen. The produce has the value 650,000,000 yen. The assessed value is then only double the gross annual produce or about four times the net produce. The equivalent to this would be in England the letting of land for £1 an acre which was valued for sale at £4 an acre.

In Corea the only tax is a land tax collected everywhere by the city magistrate.

Hu-pao, March 27th, 1899.—A letter from Japan stated that the revenue was very large from land tax in that year and amounted to $189,000,000.

Chinese Local Taxes on Tea.

The *Chung-wai-pao*, May 18th, 1900, says the taxes on tea are as follows:—

Chekiang, Taels 0.6 per picul; Haugchow, Taels 0.1.3.4.

Anhwei, Taels 2.0.8 per 120 catties.

姑塘 Ku-tang, Taels 0.4.0 per picul.

Hupei, Hunan, Taels 1.2.5 per picul; Hupei ramparts, Taels 0.0.4 per box of 40 斤.

Mountain duty, *ad valorem;* forty cash for tea of the value of 1,000 cash.

Kiang-yi, Ning-wu tea, Taels 1.4.0 per picul; Ho-kow, Taels 1.2.5.

Ku-tang, Taels 0.5.0. Tea dust and tea stems, half duty.

Formerly tea was worth Taels 50 to Taels 60 a picul. It is now worth 30 to 40 taels.

Traders cannot compete with Ceylon and India. There ought therefore to be a reduction in these duties.

Memorial of Li Ping-heng on the Opium Tax.

The amount of the tax on opium is mentioned in a memorial of the late Shantung Governor, Li Ping-heng.* In that memorial he gave reasons for opposing the collection of taxes on native opium by the foreign Customs establishment. The proposition of Sir Robert Hart was to levy sixty taels on each picul. The whole amount of native production was stated to be 334,000 piculs and the proposed levy would yield twenty million taels to the government. He argued that with a rise in the price of opium the temptation to plant more land with the poppy would be irresistibly great. The price of grain would rise as the area of cultivation became contracted and distress would prevail among the people. Our dynasty, he said, ought not to encourage the increased cultivation of the poppy.

* Replaced as governor by Chang Ju-mei, 1898.

He then says the whole revenue ought to be from land and grain—thirty-six million taels. This sum also includes some other taxes. Recently, he says, the portion of this amount collected has been only seven-tenths. Eleven million taels is the amount of the deficiency.

He adds that his predecessor, Chang Yau, when governor of Shantung, sent wei-yuens to the poppy-growing districts to collect eight per cent. *ad valorem* on the opium produced. They learned that the price was 200 taels a picul. The collection, was sixteen taels. Adding lekin and the customs collection, when the opium reached any port, the whole was forty-eight taels a picul. He states that in Shantung the amount raised has been Taels 70,000 as a maximum and 40,000, 50,000 or 60,000 in some years. How then could the foreign Customs raise the collection to Taels 600,000 from Shantung? He uses the same argument in reference to Yünnan, 80,000 piculs; Szchwen, 120,000 piculs; Kweichou, 40,000 piculs; Kirin, 6,000 piculs; Kansu, 10,000 piculs. He does not think it will be possible to collect Taels 7,200,000 from Szchwen. At present that province yields Taels 600,000 or 700,000. Nor will it be possible to collect Taels 480,000, Taels 24,000,000, Taels 360,000, in the other provinces mentioned upon their opium yield. They are obliged to obtain help from the Board of Revenue to defray their military expenditure. This, he thinks, proves their inability to pay.

Besides, he adds, the trend of policy during the 250 years of the duration of this dynasty, has been in the direction of diminished taxation. It would be inconsistent with the benevolence of the government to lay so heavy a tax on a large portion of the land. The government ought not to seek for gain or compete with traders. If the government engages in trade the people will cease to trade. The people too must be kept in a loyal and loving frame of mind, because Burmah and Cochin China are in the hands of powerful foes. The Taels 20,000,000 of which Sir Robert Hart speaks as possible to be raised from native opium, certainly cannot be collected.

Increase in Native Opium Revenue.

In the Returns of Trade for Ichang in 1897 the Commissioner says this year shows a gain of thirty per cent. over 1896, but a loss of eleven per cent. as compared with 1895, our most prosperous year. Yünnan opium steadily increases in favour. On the river 12,600 piculs passed Ichang in 1894, 17,000 in 1895, 17,200 in 1896 and 22,000 in 1897. Constant lowering of lekin charges on opium, both river-borne and by overland routes, tends to contract the volume of trade at the Custom House, controlled by the Commissioner. At Wuhu the Commissioner remarks that the tax in native opium is extremely light, while the tax on rice is heavy. He thinks the Anhwei farmers will grow more opium and less rice as the result of this. He suspects that native opium production is purposely encouraged.

The Commissioner at Chinkiang says the import of foreign opium diminishes at that port at a rate of 400 piculs yearly. This is partly because Nanking is supplied largely by native craft from Shanghai, but it is mainly due to the gradual and inevitable displacement of foreign opium by the native drug. The price of the opium of Hsü-chou he states to be 288 taels per picul.

The *Sin-wen-pao*, November 29th, reports that in Canton an official offer was made to capitalists to undertake the collection of prepared opium duties for the province at a fixed rate. The offer has not been accepted. The collection of duty on native opium by the Canton lekin contractor is $160,000 for the province. Whatever capitalist brings $90,000 ready money will receive the contract.

In 1881 Mr. Donald Spence was Consul for Great Britain at Chung-ching. He stated the Szchwen production to be 54,000 piculs. Out of this total 723,000 piculs were sold to neighbouring provinces and 70,000 to eastern China. Of this amount 40,000 piculs paid duty and 30,000 piculs were smuggled. The Yünnan production was at that time 35,000 piculs each year. Kweichou produced 10,000 piculs, Hupei 2,000 piculs. The grand total is 220,000 piculs. Indian opium at that time was imported to the amount of 66,900 piculs. The authority for these statements was not given.

The collection in Chihli on native opium from the ninth month of 1896 to the third month of 1898 amounted to Taels 50,000. Subtracting a part employed in military training the remainder was to be sent to the Shanghai Customs to repay foreign loans.

In the *Shen-pao*, December 28th, 1898, a memorial of Chang Ju-wei, the governor of Shantung, stated that the production of native opium has fallen off this year to the extent of one-fifth compared with what it has been for several years past. The cause of this was unpropitious wind and rain. There is in consequence a serious fall in the revenue. The memorialist has directed the officers in charge (Wei-yuen) in offices and at barriers to be diligent in securing as large a revenue as possible.

Lamp Tax in Shanghai and Shantung.

In Shanghai twelve dollars are paid each year for two opium lamps.

In Shantung the 籌欵局 Ch'ow-kw'an-chu has, says the *Chung-wai-pao* of July 29th, 1901, commenced the levy of a tax on opium smokers' lamps, on wine, on opium shops, and on houses.

Yarn Tax.

The foreign yarn tax is levied at an office at Shī-lin-pu, beyond the French concession at Shanghai. The collection of the yarn tax of two-tenths on the value began December 25th, 1899. Previously the lekin collection had amounted to not more than 40,000. So says the *Chung-wai-pao* of December 24th, 1899. This is insufficient for present needs. The loti tax amounts to 7,000 taels. It is collected at the Wusung-kiang barrier,* twenty li west of Sin-cha Bridge and at Min-hang. Chien Taotai is the chief manager of the Sungkiang and Shanghai taxes and lekin. It is he who has made this new settlement, by which in future two-tenths are to be collected on all yarn, native and foreign.

Shop Tax in Shantung and Ichang.

In Shantung the Chow-kwan-chü collects duties on shop sign boards.

In the *Chung-wai-pao*, August 13th, 1901, a letter from Ichang says the shops in Ichang are resolved to shut their doors. The Taotai and prefect issued a proclamation recently saying that on account of the heavy indemnity to the foreign powers the duty on native opium was taken out of their hands. The revenue is not sufficient. Funds to maintain troops are wanting, and on this account it has become necessary to levy a house tax. When the gentry had read this proclamation they met in conference. They agreed that there is need of a house tax, and united in proposing that each year large shops shall pay 1,000 cash, small shops 200 cash and moderately large shops a sum between these amounts. The Taotai on receiving this proposal sent a wei-yuen from his yamên to say that the

* The lekin offices have a collecting station at Chow-t'a-yê-miau. It is called the 北卡 po-k'a. K'a is a new character of the Ming dynasty, a guard house where soldiers collect taxes. The root is kat, to close. It is another form of 關 kwan, custom house.

proposed amount was too small. He wished each large shop to pay 4,000 cash and the others in proportion. On hearing this the shops decided to close business. Yesterday the city magistrate sent a crier round with a gong ordering the shops to open their doors and transact business as before. He was not obeyed. To-day another proclamation is out urging the commercial class to recommence business. If they think the tax too great this will be considered and a reduction is possible. After this some of the shops were seen taking down their shutters.

House Tax in Canton.

Chung-wai-pao, October 17th, 1901.—The house tax has been very successfully collected by Li Sien-chow, an expectant city magistrate. He first visited the leading gentry of his district to obtain their assistance. He then divided the land, where his collection was to be made, into ten districts. He appointed a man of good repute and sufficient means to find shop security. In making inquiries into amounts of rent he directed him to commission the local constable and the wei-yuen in office in that locality to inquire the amount of rent at each house. The constable collected the tax and delivered it to the tax office. In ten days the collection was completed.

Shen-pau, December 17th, 1901.—The viceroy fixed the first day for collecting house tax for September 13th. The first month's collection amounted to Taels 781.9.6. The next month it reached Taels 4,002.2.7. The high officers are much pleased.

Deed Tax.

The tax on deeds is an old impost, the revenue from which had been neglected through the difficulty of collection. The proprietors of houses and lands evade the payment, and the deeds are often lost through war and consequent migration.

In 1899 a large amount of additional revenue was collected in Kiangsu by Kang Chung-t'ang when sent to that province. This was done by instituting an inquiry into the number of deeds of purchase in that province on which the tax had not been paid. In the *Shen-pao*, February 9th, 1900, it is stated that at Woo-chang orders had been given that holders of deeds should all present them that it might be known if the tax had been paid. The uneasiness was great. A memorial was presented in Peking recommending that this mode of proceeding should be stopped. Also the Viceroy Chang was unwilling to see the people's sentiments roughly overridden. He ordered the treasurer to consult with the Defence Board (Shan-how-tsung-chü) and give with them a united order to officers under their jurisdiction to cease from the collection of this tax.

But the people are legally liable to pay this tax. The principle at present adopted is to collect the deed tax now due but not to enforce payment for past years, when from various causes the collection was neglected.

The deed tax was originally imposed to obtain Taels 300,000 additional revenue. Kang Chung-t'ang in 1897 in a despatch to the Soochow prefect, stated that the grain tribute should be cleared of abuses and land deeds should pay a tax. In the three districts—Chang, Yuen, and Woo—those who have land according to the entry by the grain tribute Shoo-pans in their account books are named and the amount of their land may be roughly known. In levying a deed tax the government officers and gentry should consult together and fix the value of the land. This should be done on the principle that one mow is valued at five dollars. In this way it will be found that the landed proprietors of the three Soochow districts possess 2,000,000 mow and that the tax should be three candareens each mow. Each mow will yield Taels 0.1.5 and two million mow will yield Taels 300,000. If this system be extended to all the cities of the province a large increase to the revenue will be secured. *Sin-wen-pao*, July, 1899.

Barrier Charges Near Shanghai.

Two boats laden with foreign oil leave Shanghai with four duty paid certificates, Tsz-k'ou-tan 子口單. They obtain a certificate in return on their being inspected at Sin-cha bridge. There they pay a Soochow Creek barrier duty of twenty cash a box. It was 4,800 cash in all for 240 boxes or about five and a half dollars. On reaching Nanzing there was a charge of 5,000 cash lo-ti-shui, and fifty boxes of oil were retained by the collector. The remaining 190 boxes went on to Shwang-lin, forty were addressed to Shwang-lin, forty to Ling-hu and 100 to Hu-chou. All goods from Shanghai on passing the frontier of Chekiang are stamped and released. At Shwang-lin $3 were paid and fifty boxes landed. The rest were detained on a charge of smuggling.

The selling price of a box is $1.5.0 to $0.9.5 at Shanghai.

Sungkiang Prefecture Land Tax.

In the reign of Tung Chi a reduction of three-tenths was made in the land tax. This was to be perpetual. It is mentioned by Tseng Kwo-ts'inen in his preface to the supplement, published when he was viceroy of Kiangnan, of the Sung-kiang-fu-chi. This book was prepared by Po Jun, the Manchu prefect of Sungkiang, during his leisure after the expulsion of the Tai-pings from Kiangsu. It was published in A.D. 1884. The perpetual reduction of land tax was granted because the people of the prefecture had suffered so severely during the Tai-ping occupation.

Soochow Grain Tax.

The *Sin-wen-pao* of September 6th, 1899, says that the amount of grain tax fixed by Kang Chung-tang was in 1893 to be 141,400 piculs for the Ch'ang-chow and Chau-wen districts. Six-tenths of this were paid. When petitioned by landowners the treasurer refused to lessen the amount legally due. Some paid nine-tenths, others eight, seven, or six-tenths. The city magistrate gave the required amount in figures to the head Shoo-pan.

Kiangsu Taxes on Grain.

In the year 1897, June 2nd, appeared a proclamation from the Soochow provincial treasurer to regulate the summer and autumn grain taxes. Two thousand cash for every tael were to include all charges. Silver is still required by law, but silver is estimated according to the rate for this year of 2,000 cash, including expenses. Next year there will be another inquiry into the market rate of silver, and the fixed amount of 2,000 cash will either be confirmed or modified. accordingly.* By this proclamation the people know the amount of extras which are required from them beyond the legal tax. At present (December ,1897) the tael is 1,170. Beyond this the tax payer is charged 830 or about 70 per cent. to cover all charges.

Hu-pao, July 31st, 1897, Shanghai.—White and coarse rice, 10,464 piculs. The people really pay silver and copper cash. Thirty-two years ago (1865) it was decreed that six-tenths of the grain tax should go to Peking in kind and four-tenths in silver. Times have changed, and the whole should now be paid in silver. Such is the opinion of the people themselves as expressed in newspapers.

---

* These extra charges are for provincial as well as for Hupu expenditure. The Hupu pecuniary needs have to be met in addition to the local expenses. When about twelve years ago the governor of Shantung, Chang Yao, received one million taels for Yellow River expenditure, a large reduction was made. Of this Chang Yao complained in a letter to a vice-president, who showed it to the emperor. The emperor punished Chang Yao and the Hupu officers. The amount appropriated by the Revenue Board officers on this occasion was ten thousand taels. This is not considered a crime. They must live; but they must not take too much.

Tax on Brokers.

The number of certificated brokers who pay brokers' tax in Wu-hien in Soochow was in A.D. 1735 fixed at 833. In the Chang-chow district the number was 551. In Yuen-ho the number was 902. In the fourth year of Tau Kwang, when a new topography was published, the brokers of Wu-hien were 1,043 and the tax yielded Taels 328.5.0. In addition to this the waste tax rated at one-twentieth to the tael, yielded Taels 16,4,2·5 In the reign of Tau Kwang, 1824, the Chang-chow tax-paying brokers increased to 600. Those of the Yuen-ho department rose from 902 to 912.

There was a remarkable increase in the business of the brokers in Wu-hien. Consequently the number of brokers paying taxes amounted to 1,043 in place of 830 in the year 1735. Business increased during ninety years so as to occasion this addition to the activity of the manufactures of Soochow. It probably was connected with the two British embassies—that of 1793 and 1816.

The weavers live chiefly in the north-east quarter of the city of Soochow. The goods they manufacture are sold for them by the brokers. They must have had more to do through the new demand occasioned by British trade after the two embassies conducted by Lord Macartney and Lord Amherst.

Soochow Taxation.

The tax offices in Soochow include the 機 捐 局, the loom tax office, and six gates tax office 六 門 捐 局. Every loom pays to the first of these offices 1,000 cash a year. There is also the 牙 釐 局 Ya-li-chü. There are many thousand weavers in the city. The exaction at the octroi office is much complained of. On paying a tax a permit to export the goods is given. *Chung-wai-pao*, November 28th, 1901. One main reason why a less amount of silk piece goods do not add to the revenue of the Soochow and Shanghai customs is the oppressive nature of the local taxation. Recently four boxes of silk piece goods destined for Corea had reported for duty at the customs. The six-gate octroi wei-yuen was angry, and ordered a paper to be pasted on the door of the reporting firm forbidding them to do business. The foreign officer was preparing to arrest the wei-yuen and institute legal proceedings, when the owner of the goods procured his release by paying duty at both places. On this account the wei-yuen who collects the local tax is more eager than before to detain goods and hinder the prosperity of the foreign Customs.

The Ya-li-chü is the office for collecting the lekin tax paid by the certificated brokers who sell goods for their constituents and charge brokerage.

SOOCHOW LAND TAX.

1736	Wu-hien, Taels	328.5.0.	Extra Hao-sien, Taels	16.4.2.5
	Chang-chow „	194	„	9.7
	Yuen-ho „	275	„	13.7.5
	Kwun-shun „	103	„	5.1.5
	Sui-yang „	50.7	„	2.5.3.5
	Ch'ang-shu „	87.9	„	4.3.9.5
	Chao-wen „	91.2	„	6.5.6
	Wu-kiang „	135.4	„	6.7.5
	Chên-tsê „	119.8.2.5	„	5.9.9.1
	Total Taels	1,385.0.2.5	Total Taels	71.2.5.6

This was before the loss of Suchow to the Tai-pings. In 1863 on the recovery of Suchow the best land was rated at 200 taels. Second class, Taels 150; third class, Taels 100; inferior, Taels 50. The tax was (1) Taels 2.1.0, (2) Taels 1.5.7.5, (3) Taels 1.0.5, (4) Taels 0.5.2.5. But the land changed owners without announcing the new proprietor's name, and it followed that there was no regularity in the collection. What was received was forwarded.

In 1871 to 1874 the collection was as under:—

1872	Wu-hien,	Taels 90.	Extra, Taels 4.5
1871	Chang-chow	45	2.2.5
1872	Yuen-ho	65	3.2.5

At Kwan-shan there was no collection after the recovery of the city.

1871	Sin-yang	5	0.2.5
1873	Chang-shu	30	1.5.0
1874	Chao-wen	35	1.7.5
1874	Wu-kiang	50	2.5.0
1874	Chen-tsê	30	1.5.0

Vide Su-chow-fu-chih, Ch. 17. See Kang Chung-t'ang's financial plans.

THE CHANGES EFFECTED BY KANG-YI.

In the *Sin-wen-pao*, July 18th, 1899, it was stated that the special commissioner Kang, while at Nanking, sent a despatch to Soochow directing the governor to appoint an officer to establish a board for collecting the grain revenue and the still uncollected tax on land deeds. The collectors have visited every homestead to obtain the grain tax. The gentry have consulted on the land deed duty. On each mow should be collected a deed tax amounting to one mace five candareens. There are about two million mow. This will yield Taels 300,000 for the three districts of Soochow. This is not a new tax. It is an old tax not collected. By extending this collection to all prefectures and districts a very large addition will be made to the revenue.

Thus, 2,000,000 × 15 = 30,000,000, *i.e.*, Taels 300,000, known as 清賦. This is the proposition. On account of Kang Yi's visit it became law.

The *Shen-pao* of July 29th, 1899, says that Kang Chung-t'ang has arranged that the house tax at Soochow shall be one month's rent in a year. Of this sum the landlord receives rent for eleven and a half months. The tenant pays rent for twelve and a half months.

Also house deeds are taxed three candareens on every tael of the purchase money. If the deed duty is not paid the property will be confiscated. In the *Shen-pao* of September 7th, 1899, there was a proclamation from the treasurer (Nie) and the lekin chief manager Chu, stating what are the new taxes appointed by Kang Chang-t'ang. House or land deed granted, 240 cash. On September 5th, 1899, at Sung-kiang the collection was made. Six months' limit was allowed. All who did not bring their deeds for payment within that time would be punished. The tax is then three candereens for every tael of the value. Sixty cash are received as three candareens. The surplus tax, han-fei, is not required. One thousand cash are received for eight mace. One dollar is seven mace. The tax on a dollar is two candareens and four-tenths. The city magistrate appoints Shu-pans to receive these taxes at his office on days appointed.

On October 11th the *Chung-wai-pao* says that when the deed of sale is for 1,000 taels or more the Shu-pan in charge at the prefecture claims $10 or more. The owner has the right of appealing to the district magistrate to correct any overcharge.

Ch'ang-shu Rice Tax.

This tax was first imposed in 1891 when money was needed for the Yellow River repairs, then called for by the bursting of the river bank. In January, 1901, the whole amount of the collection continued during ten years was 83,000 or 84,000 strings of cash. In 1897, in consequence of a petition from one of the literati named Lu, 30,000 strings were spent on rebuilding the pagoda. Afterwards another of the literati named Sun asked that an endowment might be set apart for the college named 常昭學堂 Ch'ang-chau-hio-t'ang. Subsequently Lu asked the city magistrate to continue the rice tax, because 20,000 strings more were needed for the pagoda. When this was reported to the governor he wrote his decision. "The matter must be inquired into." He directed the treasurer to send a wei-yuen to confer with the parties concerned. When the report is received the governor will decide on the course the law must take. He fears that the two literati—Lu and Sun—are both guilty of enriching themselves from public money.

Rice Tax in Kiangsu.

When Kwei Chiün, now viceroy of Szchwen, was governor of Kiangsu he asked for a removal of the rice tax as a relief to traders. At present the lekin receipts at Soochow and Shanghai are insufficient. The quota due for the foreign indemnity cannot be paid. Governor Lu and Viceroy Liu have asked to have the rice tax again imposed. It was accordingly to be collected from November 1st. The Ya-li-chü office has asked for a postponement. It will therefore be collected from November 13th onward. *Chung-wai-pao*, November 14th, 1899. The lekin on rice at 150 catties is Taels 0.1.4. This was the rate at Wuhu and Chinkiang during the Japanese war.

Tax on Native Opium in Szchwen.

The *Chung-wai-pao* of June 21st, 1899, says Pa-hien in Szchwen produces opium in large quantities at Lao-ch'ang. The wei-yuen in charge wished to establish a branch office at Ma-kia-tien to collect the tax. The residents are not pleased. They have petitioned the superintendent not to allow this.

The *Chung-wai-pao* of July 29th, 1901, says the superintendent has commenced the collection of a tax on lamps used by opium smokers.

Camphor Monopoly in Formosa.—Messrs. Samuel Samuel & Co. have taken over 700,000 catties of camphor from the government and are beginning to export it. Any officially recognized securities it was agreed would suffice. *Japan Mail*, April 21st, 1900.

Tax on Native Opium in Canton.

Shen-pau, December 27th, 1901.—The journal 世說編 of the *An-ya-shu-chü* states that the tax on native opium will now amount to Taels 23.6.6 a picul. A label affixed will free it from further taxation. This sum includes three-tenths of the value now added to provide funds to pay the share of the indemnity now charged to Canton province. Several years ago the tax was Taels 11.5.0. It was afterwards raised to Taels 14.0.0. In 1899 it was raised to Taels 18.2.0.

Shop Tax in Foochow.

A wei-yuen visits the shop to ascertain from the books the amount of rent. The annual tax is charged on the monthly rent. The landlord is not charged. A proclamation states the obligation to pay the tax. A book is prepared in which the entries are made in tabular form. Recently many persons have sought to evade the tax, and have reported the rent to be below the true amount, or they are absent and the books are not presented for reference. The penalty for offences is fixed. The case is judged by the city magistrate or by the wei-yuen at his Kung Kwan. When a fine is charged the tenant still pays rent to the landlord.

Foochow Taxes on Pawn Shops, Cash Shops, Oil Shops, etc.

The expense of the volunteer corps is met by the tax on pawn-brokers, on cash shops and with the help of the heads of the colleges from the dealers in oil, $8,000 a year ; paper, $5,000 a year; and timber, $5,000 a year. This money supports twelve volunteer officers, whose pay is not yet fixed, and 3,000 volunteers who have all of them great physical strength, so that they can lift stones weighing 320 catties, and using both hands, pass them over both thighs. If they cannot do this, they cannot enter the corps.

HANKOW HOUSE TAX.

The house duty is now (July 5th, 1899, *Universal Gazette,*) by the house tax wei-yuen under the order of the customs' Taotai. The habit of the tax office underlings has been to keep house deeds in concealment. This abuse the wei-yuen is to set right.

SHOP TAX IN HANKOW.

The shop and house tax imposed in the spring of 1898 amounts to one-tenth of the rental. Half is paid by the landlord and half by the tenant. In 1896 viceroy Chang imposed this tax in Hankow temporarily. Thirty or forty years ago under Hsien Feng and T'ung Chih a similar tax was levied in Peking, in Kiang-su, and in Canton. The landlord receives in rent less by one-twentieth. The tenant pays one-twentieth when called on by the wei-yuen. The wei-yuen looks to his superior for his own salary, and it is deducted from the amount collected. This house tax was proposed for adoption by the Board of Revenue. The collection began May 20th, 1898.

This tax and that on opium had to be abandoned; they gave occasion to rioting in more than one city in Chekiang. On finding this to be the case, the collection of these taxes was brought to an end by the authorities.

TIMBER YARD TAX IN SHANGHAI.

The Taotai has directed that the tax on timber yards shall be $2 a month for each frontage compartment. Other shops pay forty cash on every thousand cash of the rent, which is one twenty-fifth part. *Sin-wen-pao*, November 13th, 1898. This is an extension of the system now current on the foreign concession in Shanghai. Timber occupies a large amount of space. Foreign taxation is in this instance adopted by the Chinese on the river side south of the foreign concession.

Tax on Distilleries in Chihli.

In Chihli there is an annual levy of Taels 32 on all distilleries. The *Shen-pao* mentioned on May 6th, 1899, that the Board of Revenue requested the Emperor to enact an extra import of ten taels on distilleries. This was approved.

The superintendent of the Hatamen customs in Peking (*Shen-pao*, December 17th, 1901) has posted up a proclamation threatening smugglers of spirits with severe penalties. The price of spirits has risen in consequence. Some of the twenty firms dealing in spirits had shut their shops through their being undersold by smuggling firms. They have now resumed business.

Shantung Taxation.

Shen-pao, August 22nd, 1901.—T'sing-chow and Ts'i-chow letter. The governor has instituted a new system of taxation. For a tael of land tax he requires 4,800 king-tsien=2,400 cash. This will yield Taels 500,000; wine, Taels 100,000; salt, native opium and coal, Taels 300,000. Opium lamps at twenty cash a day each, in Tsinan and neighbourhood, 300,000 cash a month. The governor is also considering the question of a shop and house tax.

Shen-pao, September 12th, 1901.—Prepared opium tax in Foochow. The prepared opium tax has in Foochow hitherto been contracted for by natives. They paid Taels 44,000 to the viceroy; they now withdraw, and an Italian has offered Taels 64,000 for the right to collect this tax. To this the viceroy has agreed.

Wine Tax in Chekiang.

The *Chung-wai-pao*, June 21st, 1899, says at Ningpo the wine tax ought to be paid at the same time with the land tax. Last year the wine makers refused to pay, so that the wine tax office could not forward the required amount to the provincial treasurer. This was the reason he gave for requesting the magistrate to issue proclamations requiring prompt payment of the tax.

Chung-wai-pao, July 29th, 1901.—In Shantung the 籌款局 *Ch'ou-kwan-chü*, newly established tax office, is collecting a wine shop tax.

Taxes in Shansi.

The amount of the taxes in this province may be estimated approximately by the statistics given in the *Shen-pao* of October 24th, 1898. The poppy is cultivated chiefly in Tai-yuen, Yü-tsz, Kian-ch'eng, Wen-shui, Tai-chow, and Kwei-hwa. Land tax on poppy fields in these departments is Taels 109,400; lekin, Taels 96,000; drug tax levied on travellers, Taels 57,700. Taels 263,100. The villages of Tai-yuen are 176 in number, and the poppy is grown over 4,535 mow or 756 acres; the villages of Yü-tsz are 150, and the number of mow is 3,013; the villages of Kiao-chow are 145, and the number of mow is 3,571; the villages of Wen-shui are 175, and the land occupied is 4,302 mow; the villages of Tai-chow are 194, and the land occupied is 5,096 mow; at Kwei-hwa in Mongolia the villages are 161 in number, and the land occupied is 4,885 mow. The total number of acres is 4,232, and the land tax on the poppy grounds is twenty-three taels or $3 an acre.

An-hwei Taxes.

Out of the proceeds of these taxes Taels 200,000, together with lekin, Taels 50,000. Wuhu native customs, Taels 40,000; Feng-yang native customs, Taels 30,000. Total, Taels 320,000, are applied to aid the Peking army expenditure and the imperial household expenditure.

Wuhu Rice Export Duty.

In 1899 the export of rice, November 14th to December 12th, amounted to piculs 246,670; the duty was Taels 4,300.

Amoy Customs Collection.

In the *Hu-pao*, October 31st, 1898, there is given the following information regarding the Amoy native customs collection. Rich men undertook the collection according to the system hitherto pursued. It amounted to about 20,000 taels. Half of this was placed to public account, half was retained by the collectors. The wei-yuen, Ch'en Shu-hiün, who inspects weights at Amoy, saw this to be the case, and thought the public revenue might be increased by the introduction of a new system. Last month he went to Foochow, saw the Tartar General Tseng, who at that city has charge of the customs and stated the bare facts. The general approved his statement and sent two wei-yuens—Chen Shu-hiün and Huang Tsu-an—to Amoy to dismiss the collectors and to collect the duties themselves. From the 26th, of last month, September 11th, the whole of the customs' duties are to be applied to increase the revenue. Each day they now receive from Taels 150 to 200; this will amount in a year to 60,000 or 70,000 taels.

The amount in the Red Book is Taels 73,549. The Red Book numbers are the same every year, and they were probably the same last century as now. Private printing firms pay a sum for information furnished them by the servants of the government. With this information they compile a new Red Book every quarter. The Hupu statement of the native customs' collection for the province of Fukien is Taels 193,408 for the year 1893. The collection at the foreign customs was Taels 2,846,485 in the same year. This included Formosa, now ceded to Japan.

TOTAL TAXATION IN MOUKDEN PROVINCE.

On June 17th, 1899, the *Chung-wai-pao* stated that the lekin office at Moukden collected in 1898 Taels 179,240. Opium and wine, Taels 10,540; salt, Taels 302,640 (4th and 8th months); salt, Taels 15,132 (2nd and 4th months). School expenses tax began to be collected in the 11th month and finished in the 12th month, Taels 9,960. These are the whole of the taxes in this province for the 24th year of Kwangsü. Total, Taels 517,512. In the memorial of Sü Tung in the *Shen-pao*, August 5th, 1899, he says if crafty subordinates demand too much when tax gathering, they should be accused and punished.

EXEMPTION FROM DUTIES IN THE CHINESE CUSTOMS.

The *Peking Gazette*, May 1st, 1902, says King Sing Manchu general at Foochow, reports the times are hard. The indemnity presses heavily. It is necessary to repress smuggling by correcting the abuses of the customs. The Foochow customs in 1883 received an order from the Tsung-li yamên that artillery stores from abroad and articles for official use are to be exempt from duty. Acting on this rule all articles, whether foreign or native, needed by official persons or for use in the various official boards, were accompanied by an exemption certificate when examined by the customs. In this action no hesitation was felt. This system naturally led to much smuggling, because other goods were surreptitiously sheltered under the official certificates of exemption. Such covert smuggling went on for a long time unnoticed. The order of the Tsung-li Yamên at that time only referred to foreign munitions of war and foreign imports. It did not refer to native goods having a place in the tariff of the Board of Revenue. There was great reason to correct this abuse. How could I be slow in taking action at such a time as this when money is so much needed?

Beside this there is the exemption which prevails in the Foochow arsenal. This is different, but it also should no longer be allowed. The needs of the present time do not warrant this indulgence. The new treaty contains the rule that goods are to pay duty to the amount of an effective five per cent. on the value, and all imported goods which hitherto have been exempted, are liable to this charge. The Emperor refers this memorial to the Board of Revenue for its consideration.

REVENUE FROM SALT.

The Salt Administration of China.

Now and then, in the Chinese laws, passages occur of kindness to the poor. Old men of fifty-nine years and more are allowed to carry salt from the salt-pans and sell it for a living. Children under sixteen years of age are allowed the same privilege. All persons belonging to these classes as well as aged women and maimed persons may carry on their backs a load of not more than ten catties of salt to sell for their livelihood. They must not make use of a boat. The burden must be carried on their backs by themselves. But in contrast with this philanthropy are many very severe enactments. Whoever sells salt clandestinely, whatever the quantity, is liable to be exiled for three years and receive a hundred blows, also losing the salt, which is confiscated. If a woman sell unlicensed salt her husband will be punished in her place, whether he knew it or not, if he were in the same house with her. In the absence of her husband, if she had with her a son of more than fifteen years he will be punished in her stead. In every other case the woman bears the penalty. Whoever assists the seller of unlicensed salt, by receiving it on deposit or pointing out the way by which the smuggler can effect his purpose, will be exiled for two and a-half years with eighty blows. To buy unlicensed salt is a crime to be punished by one hundred blows and three years' banishment. Such is the law; but in fact it does not appear to be carried out. At Shanghai the salt bought and sold ought to be the Chêkiang salt, which is produced in abundance to the south and, by law, is the only salt saleable there. If the salt of Northern Kiangsu should be sold here the punishment is one hundred blows and confiscation of the salt. Perpetual exile to some place distant three thousand *li* is the punishment if the quantity of salt be more than three thousand catties.

These severe rules cannot be carried out, and salt is smuggled to an enormous extent. It is said that very little licensed salt is sold in Shanghai. The salt laws procure a million taels to the central government and maintain a very large staff of officials at the expense of the general population. The price is nearly that of rice. This high price is caused by the large amount of fresh water carried into the sea by the Yang-tze-kiang and formerly by the Yellow River. It was only in the Sung dynasty that the Yellow River coming down from Chihli poured a vast volume of fresh water into the sea at the mouth of the Huai River, thus raising the price of salt. At present rice costs about twenty-eight cash a catty, if we take 890 cash as the exchange for a dollar and regard the price of 160 catties as $5. But $6 are often asked, and then the value of a catty of rice is thirty-three cash. In that case salt is just as dear to buy as rice. This anomaly happens in a country very thickly populated, where rice, wheat, and cotton are the chief products of the soil. The poor all around suffer by this high price of salt; it is one of the elements which increases the dearness of living, and it falls heavily on the poor. In Fukien, Mr. Jamieson tells us in his account of Chinese Revenue and Expenditure, salt costs to produce it from one to two cash a catty. By a favourable system of administration, salt ought to be made cheap for the people's use. But is this possible where the ocean is fresh for many miles as at Shanghai? The water all along the Kiangsu coast is freshened by the Yang-tze-kiang water. Formerly it was freshened by the Yellow River water also. It was in the year A.D. 1144 that the Yellow River floods first came down from the north to join the Yang-tze-kiang in freshening the sea. Before that year, from the beginning of Chinese history, the Yellow River had always found its way to the Gulf of Pechili. During six centuries and a-half vast volumes of fresh water came to increase the flow of the Huai River, till nearly half-a-century ago the Yellow River returned to the north and was again as of old emptied into the Gulf of Pechili.

This then is the historical origin of the Huai Salt Administration. The province of Kiangsu was always populous, and when sea salt ceased to be abundant the people found a substitute in salt deposits of older times. When the Yellow River, a little before A.D. 1200, changed its course, it was at Chi-ning in Shantung province that it took for its channel what afterwards became the Grand Canal. This channel was scoured out by the Yellow River when its mighty stream took a southern course from Shantung towards Kiangsu. As a natural result of this event the Liang Huai salt system was originated. In the year A.D. 1462 another great event took place. The Chinese records tell us that in that year the Yellow River left the north at a point fifty miles west of Kai-fêng-fu, in Honan. The new river divided into two branches at Kai-fêng and each passed its course by a separate channel till they united again at Tsing-kiang-pu and proceeded together along the old channel of the Huai to the ocean. The northern branch passed by Hsü-chou, where opium is now produced in large quantity. The southern branch passed by Fêng-yang, where it was fed on the south-west by the hills of An-hui. It was the former of these two branches proceeding by Hsü-chou that became the Yellow River for four hundred years. This time was long enough to prevent any sufficient supply of salt from the Kiangsu sea coast. These conditions are unique. There is in no part of the world a second instance of a river of first-class magnitude undergoing so great a change in its course. Raphael Pumpelly thought the change was due to subterranean oscillation on a grand scale. If there was no oscillation why should the river move to the south and then go back to the north? Richthoven describes silting as leading inevitably to great changes. Flowing through a country where the soil called *loess* is easily washed away, every river channel rises with comparative rapidity. A sudden flood causes an overflow and a change of direction. In this way this excellent geologist, if appealed to, would explain changes of course when rivers go through a country where the soil is light with vertical cleavage of subaerial formation. We may adopt this explanation, for a freshet has enormous hydraulic power and can force a way through strong embankments. It was under these peculiar conditions that the salt system of the Huai-pei and Huai-nan Administrations became inevitable, if Kiangsu was to continue to be a salt-producing country.

When a salt ocean disappears it leaves salt lakes behind, of necessity, because salt does not evaporate. Such was the origin of the Great Salt Lake of the Mormons. "It has been shown," states Professor Whitney, "that this lake hasdiminished greatly in size. Water marks have been discovered two hundred feet above the present surface of the lake." He holds the doctrine of extensive desiccation to account for the small dimensions of salt lakes. It is the remains of such a salt lake that may prove to be the best explanation of that portion of the Kiangsu salt which is collected from wells of great depth to the north of the city of Hwai-an-fu.

Officers Charged with Salt Administration.

The administration of salt is directed by the salt commissioner 鹽運使 Yen Yün-shï, of whom there are in all five vacancies to be filled when the holders of these posts die, resign or are dismissed.

The Chang-lu-yen-yün-shï administers the salt of Chihli. The others are those of Shantung, of the two Hwai, of Chekiang, and of Canton.

Among the other salt administrators are the deputy salt manager or 盐運同. There are three officers bearing this title. Next there are three officers named Yen-ti-chü 盐提舉. There is one officer named Yen-yün-fu 盐運副. Five officers bear the title Yen-yün-p'au 盐運判. Six officers have the name Yen-king-li 盐經歷. Six have the title Yen-ku-ta-shï 盐庫大使. Thirteen are styled P'i-yen-ta-shï 批驗大使. A hundred and fifteen officers have the title Yen-k'o-ta-shï 盐課大使. Three officers are styled Yen-chï-shï 盐知事.

Thus there are 160 officers engaged in managing the salt revenue under the direction of the viceroys and governors mentioned below.

The Board of Revenue receives the salt revenue at certain fixed dates from the treasurer of each province.

Among the eight viceroys there are six who control this branch of the revenue, viz., Chihli, Szchwen, Liang-kiang, Min-che, and Liang-kwang. There are two viceroys who do not manage the salt revenue, viz., Liang-hu and Shan-kan. In this case salt is conveyed from neighbouring provinces sufficient for the consumption of the population of their provinces. Shansi lake salt supplies Shensi and Mongolia supplies Kansu.

The Shantung governor manages the salt of his province. So doos tho Chckiang governor.

The 鹽公堂 public salt office is established for the sale of official rice. At Shanghai it is outside the great east gate.

First Mention of Salt.

Salt baskets 鹽筴 were in use to limit the quantity of salt in the time of Kwan Tsï, B. C. 600. In the work 晏子春秋, a Han dynasty book the salt baskets 㡿 on the sea shore were kept by Chi-wang. This is the first mention of salt farmers.

The price of salt is mentioned in A. D 1033. A hundred catties cost 2,000 cash. At Hwai-nan in Kiangsu it would be possible to obtain 30,000,000 strings of cash for the revenue by selling to the people 15,000,000 piculs of salt. The people on both sides of the Kiang could possess white salt.

Historical Extracts.

Ku Yen-wu mentions that in his time the salt revenue was 6,000,000 strings of cash. This was 250 years ago. He adds that in history the amount recorded was 400,000 strings of cash. It had risen from 400,000 taels to six million taels. He also remarks that it is well to levy a duty on salt at the place of production. Then it ceases to be contraband and the circulation of all salt becomes legitimate.

The poet Tu Fu twelve centuries ago said the hemp of Szchwen has from ancient times been exchanged with the salt of the Wu country. Another extract from Tu Fu is 風烟渺吳蜀, 舟楫通鹽麻. The winds and clouds separate widely the Wu kingdom from Szchwen or dim the distance between them, but the swift ship exchanges the salt of the one for the hemp of the other, 蜀麻久不來吳鹽擁荆門. When the hemp of Szchwen for a long time is not brought to market the salt of the Wu country is stored up at King-men. It should be noted that King-men is on the Western frontier of Hupei province. Ku Yen-wu remarks that the salt administration must have been different at that time. At present it is illegal to sell Kiang-su salt in Szchuen. The salt wells of Szchwen would be unknown in the Tang dynasty. Probably they were discovered in the early Sung.

The Salt Certificate of 200 Catties.

In Shansi it was arranged in the year A. D. 1370 that a merchant should bring one picul of rice to the Ta-t'ung granary and one picul three-tenths to the Tai-yuen granary. He would obtain a salt certificate for 200 catties. When this was sold he would give up the certificate to the official superintendent. He would be saved the cost of conveyance from Tai-yuen to Ta-t'ung and must therefore pay a larger tribute at the nearer city. We learn that the cost of conveyance for a picul over 620 *li* was in A. D. 1370 three-tenths of a picul of grain. Ta-t'ung is 720 *li* from Peking and 620 *li* from Tai-yuen. Forty-four pounds weight of any grain would be compensation for a muleteer and mule carrying grain for 600 *li*. That is to say, five hundred years ago twenty-two pounds of grain would pay for conveyance over 100 English miles. The extra tax was levied when the city was near the salt lake. This was called the 中鹽之法, "Salt tax equalization system." The governor 行省 of Shansi recommended this arrangement in the case of the grain Taotai of Ta-t'ung (大同糧儲) who superintended the conveyance of Lu-t'ai salt into Shansi. The city of Ta-t'ung is as far from the Tientsin salt depôt as it is from the salt lake of Shansi.

In Honan at present the salt of five producing centres meets. They are: Hwai-pei, Hwai-nan, Shantung, Tientsin, and Shansi.

The Name of Salt Certificate Explained.

A salt certificate is called Yin 引, because the merchant who receives it in return for its value in the form of silver, acquires a certificate which authorises him to obtain information as to where he may sell his salt in the provinces mentioned on the certificate. Yin means chen, true.

Price of Certificates.

Chang-lu salt	...	...	... Taels	0.5.1	for each certificate.
Shantung "	...	...	... "	0.2.4	"
Honan "	...	...	... "	0.4.1	"

Liang-hwai salt	Taels	1.1.7	for each certificate.
Liang-che "	"	0.3.9	"
Liang-kwang "	"	1.3.3	"
Fukien "	"	2.8.3	"
Szchwen land conveyance certificates	"	0.2.7	"
" river " "	"	3.4.5	"

These prices are taken from the Hu-pu-tsê-li.

QUANTITIES OF SALT REPRESENTED BY CERTIFICATES.

Chang-lu	300 catties.
Shantung	225 "
Shansi	240 "
Liang-hwai	364 "
Liang-che	335 to 400 catties.

The yin contains 400 catties in the three prefectures—Tai-chow, Wen-chow, Chu-chow—and a part of Kiu-hwa. It also contains 400 catties in the Sung-kiang and Soochow prefectures. It contains 335 catties in the remaining prefectures of Chekiang and Kiangsu.

In the seventeenth century each yin weighed 200 catties. About 1730 the weight was made 344 catties. It was from time to time increased. In 1830 it was made 400 catties. Thus seven yin of the old weight became six yin of the new weight nearly.

Hunan and Hupei had a population of 50,000,000 as reported to the Board of Revenue. Each person uses daily three mace of salt. At this rate each yin will suffice for the consumption of sixty persons for a year.

The Szchwen salt is sold in bags of 135 catties weight The Lu-an-fu salt coming from the salt lake and amounting to 120 yin is known by the name 名 ming.

The Chang-lu salt at Tientsin was valued in 1827 at sixteen cash a catty; one tael of silver was exchanged at that time for 1,300 copper cash.

Salt Tax in the Eighteenth Century.

In the year 1723 an imperial edict ordered that when the salt censor in conjunction with the viceroy and governor cannot agree as to the price of the salt bag they should apply to the Board of Revenue to settle this point and fix a uniform rate. On this the Hu-kuang viceroy wrote stating that thirty years before the selling price was one mace or 100 cash, and this was fixed by the viceroy. The Board raised objections. The salt farmers said the price varies with the season. They could not afford to sell at the rate proposed, because expenses have increased during thirty years. The Imperial factory requires money. The river repairs and purchase of copper for the mints create a demand for money. The amount required has increased by several thousands of taels. The viceroy says that the Hu-kuang salt farmers' receipts amount to Taels 150,000. By making the retail price less by six-tenths of a candareen a contribution can be levied of 150,000 taels. They will not suffer loss. The result was that when the retail price was announced certain small traders bought up the salt and stored it to sell at a higher price when the market allowed. To prevent this in future the viceroy advises the adoption of the rule that salt be sold at the current market price.

Soon after this the same censor states in a memorial the case of the Liang-huai salt farmers. When the south wind blows in the summer, junks cannot ascend the river with salt to supply Kiangsi and Hu-kuang. Speculators buy several tens of thousands of salt certificates beforehand in order to keep up the supply of salt in these provinces. The cause of difficulties felt by farmers was the diminution of the retail price by the Hu-kuang viceroy. In these circumstances the censor asks if the farmers may borrow public money to enable them to carry on salt farming without loss. If they were allowed to receive a loan from the salt commissioner, they would repay it in ten years with interest. The Emperor refuses this request. "It involves your successors in the salt censorate. You should exert yourself in harmony with the viceroy to give salt to the people at a low rate, and at the same time you should not be too severe on the salt farmer." The system pursued on the river and in Chekiang as well as at Lu-t'ai, in Chihli province, was in each case to be on the same footing.

On the 37th page, chapter 13th, it is stated that for the prefectures of Kia-hing, Hang-chow, Shao-hing and Sung-kiang the customs' expenses were made a charge on the salt farmers. This charge amounted annually in A. D. 1726 to Taels 400,000. After deducting this sum the amount which went to the treasury was Taels 258,690. The system of farming allowed the farmer to reimburse himself by various charges made by him on retail dealers and in other ways known by the term *Lou-kuei*, extortionate exactions.

In the Tung-hwa-lu, A. D. 1736, Chapter I, p. 52, it is said that salt in Chekiang was by edict for each certificate increased fifty catties, so that the amount of salt represented by one certificate would be 335 catties, including the weight of the bags and ropes. This refers to the three prefectures—Hang-chow, Kia-hing, and Shao-hing. At the same time in the Sung-kiang prefecture, in which Shanghai is situated, the weight of salt represented by one certificate was 400 catties The tax and extra charges made up Taels 54,000, as the contribution under the head salt tax from this prefecture. The number of certificates (yin) was 90,000.

Commutation of Salt Tax into the Land and Personal Service Tax.

In A. D. 1736 each person in Formosa would pay, previous to the edict of that year, Taels 0.4.7 in a year and with expenses Taels 0.5.0. On the mainland the tax was Taels 0.1.0 or Taels 0.2.0 or Taels 0.3.0 The Emperor reduced the charge in Formosa to Taels 0.2.0. This was the new form then given to the personal service tax.

In A. D. 1746 (Tung-hua 7, 23) the Emperor ordered that women should not in future be separately counted as liable to pay the salt tax. The salt tax was ordered to be included in the land tax and grain tax. From the statements given the commutation edict must have been before the year 1736. In earlier times when women were counted in the number of those on whom the salt tax was levied, it was necessary to inquire if they were living or dead and to learn what additions or subtractions should be made in the tax registers in the names of men and women liable to the tax. The subject is again referred to because the Kiangsi tax gatherers went by the old rule and collected a salt tax separately. The emperor ordered Kiangsi for uniformity to follow other provinces in adding the salt tax to the grain tax.

In the year 1806 the salt tax was changed to a land and personal service tax. Tung-hwa-lu, ch. 7, p. 30. The Alashan salt in Mongolia could no longer be dug out and conveyed to a distance. The governor of Shansi requested the Emperor to allow the salt of the Ho-tung superintendency in Shansi to be used, and the salt farmers to collect it. Formerly on account of local disturbances the salt tax was commu ed to become part of the land and personal service tax. Lake salt yields very small profits, and traders do not very readily offer to farm it. The Mongols, through natural indolence, neglected to collect salt in their neighbourhood. He therefore urged the inauguration of a new system uniform for Kansu, Shensi, and Shansi. The governors and other high officers were ordered to consult. After doing so they replied, recommending the system of 1746. Let the traders themselves fix a low price for salt. Returns should be sent in to the Revenue Board, stating the prices of salt for each month, so that the Board may have data from which to fix the price.

In chapter 7, page 36, it is stated that difficulty arose in Shansi from the fixed amount of the Board having been based on too low a retail price for salt. When the salt revenues are contracted for it is better for the shipping merchant to buy timber and build his own boats for conveying the salt. He also provides rice and other provisions. There is simply an official inspection of these. The Shansi salt is managed by the Ho-tung Taotai under the control of the governor. The Kansu salt is managed by the Ning-hia Taotai. The Shensi salt is under the management of the Feng Pin superintendent.

Salt Lake Administration.

In the year 1846 Tao Kuang, 26th year, Tung-hua-sü-lu, ch. 12, page 16, the Emperor in an edict says that a censor has recommended a change in the salt system in Shansi. It has been found distinctly beneficial for the salt administration to levy duties and leave the collection of salt and its distribution in the hands of merchants. Prices, however, need revision by authority from time to time. The Shansi salt farmers are in difficulties.

He recommends the Emperor to adopt the system of last century in the Ch'ien Lung period, when the Honan salt tax was commuted and became a part of the land tax and personal service tax of Honan, Shensi, and Shansi.

The Emperor ordered the governor, Wai Chi-chiün, to give his opinion on the censor's recommendation. In the governor's reply it is stated that from the Tang dynasty for a thousand years there has been a wall round the Shansi salt lake to keep out smugglers who would carry away the salt for their own profit. There have also been banks to prevent fresh water streams flowing down surrounding heights from entering the lake. The salt farmers contribute funds to keep the wall and banks in repair. If the monopoly were abrogated and the manufacture thrown open to the public no one would make these repairs. The production of salt would be ruined because the artisans engaged in the manufaoture would have no money to carry through the repairs. Natron and saltpetre would enter from the tributary streams which would flow into the lake, a danger from which the lake ought to be carefully protected. The salt would not be suitable for public use. The gift of heaven would be lost to the people and a source of the salt revenue cut off. The salt trade should not be left to the people to manage entirely themselves.

Further, the proposal to commute the salt tax by including it in the land and personal service tax and to make this change in three provinces and not elsewhere emanates only from one province. No consultation on the propriety of this measure has yet been held with Honan and Shensi. The Huai and Tientsin salt administration might become seriously affected it this change in regard to the Shansi lake salt were made abruptly and the avenues of distribution closed to salt from the ocean salt lake administration.

In 1807 the administration of the salt lake was, after many years' trial of a new system, again farmed out to capitalists as it had been originally. It was a measure not well considered at the time. Looking at the present aspect of the Shansi salt question and the revenue of Taels 280,000 which it yields annually and which is much too large a sum to be paid by a number of poor persons, the proposed change in system cannot be recommended.

The size of the lake is given as fifty-one *li* in length and seven *li* in breadth. Circumference 116 *li*. The salt of this lake was used in high antiquity, for it is mentioned in the Chou-li that there was an officer appointed to superintend the provision of salt. Salt is required for use at sacrifices, and this circumstance led to its early mention.

Moral Aspect of Salt Tax.

The moral aspect of the salt tax is important. The high price of salt leads to smuggling. The smugglers are desperate characters who risk all for a little gain. Near Shanghai, where smuggled salt is used almost exclusively, there are stores of it collected by bands of dangerous smugglers. In the *Hu-pao*, December 10th, 1898, it is said that at San-ling-dong and Po-ts'a salt smugglers lately resolved to take out the eyes of a confederate who informed against them.

Fukien Salt Tax at One View.

According to the old system the taxes were as under:—

Western district, yin of 675 catties	Taels	2.8.3.3.3.3.6
South Eastern, yin of 100 catties...		0.1.5
Eastern, yin of 100 catties ...		0.0.7.5
Southern, yin of 100 catties ...		0.2 3.2

New System with Duty-paid Certificate (P'iau).

West district, 675 catties... ...	Taels	2.8.4	30 yin.
Waste tax		0.2.8.4	
Lekin		1.4.2	
	Taels	4.5.4.4	
South East, 100	Taels	0.2.8	100 yin.
Waste tax		0.0.2.8	
Lekin		0.1.4	
	Taels	0 4 4.8	

Half the tax is to be paid when the certificates are purchased. The remaining half is to be paid when the salt has been sold.

The viceroy of Fukien reports annually the amount remaining at the end of each year in the salt tax treasury.

Hu-pao, May 27th, 1902. In an edict it is said that the Fukien salt tax Taotai had stated that it is the rule to examine the salt tax treasury at the end of each year and to report the amount found there. Accordingly at the end of the 27th year of Kwang Sü he found that from December 29th, 1901, to March 1st, when the Yamên commenced business after the new year holidays the amount of silver paid into the treasury was Taels 304,541.3.0. This was independent of the sums forwarded.

Salt made at Sixteen Points on the Fukien Coast.

In Fukien there are sixteen salt manufacturing centres. The earthenware moulds there in use are called 漏 leu, funnel. Of these there are 1,361. Other moulds in use are called 埕 ch'eng. Of these there are 241,109. The mould is a pear-shaped earthen jar. There are other shapes called 坵 k'iu, "mound." Of these there are 38,491. The amount payable each year to the treasurer of the province for the funnel salt is Taels 133.1.9.3. The kiu or "mound" salt pays annually to the salt Taotai Taels 4,136.6.6.1.

History of the Fukien Salt Tax.

In the 17th century the salt tax in the province of Fukien was Taels 85,000 in amount. In 1723 the salt collection was made by special officers, and in 1742 amounted to Taels 141,000. The magistrate placed barriers on the roads and the special officers collected duties at the barriers. Duty paid tickets were given (單 tan) to tax payers, and with these they could sell their goods wherever they pleased.* According to the old system in the time of Kang Hi a 引 yin certificate covered 400 catties. This system fell into disuse. The duty paid *tan* took its place. Sometimes contractors undertook the collection. At other times the officials were themselves the collectors The contractors might lose money by gifts to the importunate, by putting out public money to interest, as well as by losses through storms and other causes. When private persons declined to farm the tax collection it fell back on the officials. Things moved smoothly at first, but soon there would be those who appropriated every surplus sum as falling to them or caused disorder by borrowing and lending the funds of this station to be met by the expected receipts of that station.

It was not always with success that private persons undertook to farm the collection. When they found themselves in difficulty, the salt boat business was offered to new collectors. Failing these it went back to the officials to manage it. In their case corruption took many forms. The charge for expenditure varied from one station to another and unreal statements were made; the fact being that the manager was taking advantage of his position to fill his own pocket. This is what is said by Tso Tsung-tang, from whom this memorial emanated in 1865. The private appropriation was called reduction for expenses, 扣費 k'ou-fei. The manager, it is added, also sold contraband salt, on which duty had not been paid, so as to obtain for his own profit the difference between the prices of contraband and official salt. This difference is called 盈 ying 餘 yü When the Hupu rule leaves it open for the manager to do so he wrongly reports loss by water or by robbery and waste. Then the salt officers of upper and lower rank divide between them any large surplus that may remain

* The barrier 卡, in mandarin chia, is in Kang Hi's Dictionary pronounced dzap. mixed. A bridge across a river with draw bridge boards between the piers is called 閘 cha or dzap. The real etymology is in the root *dab*, to pass.

when the Peking contingent has been sent away. The salt under their care, viewed as capital, gradually disappears altogether. Such are the characteristics of official corruption in the salt administration.

The salt administration meets with difficulty from the production of salt being distributed over so many points. Contraband salt finds its way everywhere, and the conveyance being very profitable the practice of smuggling is boldly conducted by armed bands, who take advantage of every instance of laxity in the preventive service. There is universal competition between those who sell smuggled and official salt, and the smugglers are the declared enemies of officials and of trading salt contractors. The salt collection in south Fukien, in the prefectures of the coast, Foochow, Hsing-hwa, Changchow, and Chiuen-chen, is distributed among twenty-one districts. The magistrates are the collectors. The money has to be paid by a certain day. The magistrates are indolent. They entrust the collection to persons known as Po-hu. The people are unruly. The money is not paid, and there is a deficit, or there is a surplus, because this year's collection is to be forwarded, it may be, next year. The collector forwards two-tenths or three-tenths to the treasurer, who enters it in the military expenditure book and does not represent him as behind in his accounts. The remainder he keeps for himself. Orders come to him to pay the salt gabelle. He pays no attention. The local payment is not made. This is an example of the faults in the administration of salt revenue in the hands of officials.

Another difficulty is in the want of offices. The officer cannot live at the salt pans if there is no house there. He lives in the provincial capital in hired lodgings. Salt smugglers come in boats. Traders take salt from them and distribute it for sale. The official salt officers are anxious to enrich themselves. They point to smuggled salt and assert that it is official salt taken from the salt pans in their charge. Their own salt pans are neglected, and through the country there is in circulation in many instances smuggled salt only. If the salt pans are managed by the officials this is the result too often, because they take bribes from the sellers of smuggled salt.

Salt furnishes one-fourth of the revenue of Fukien province. When there was war during more than ten years Fukien suffered little comparatively. The salt gabelle of Fukien is less than in other provinces. Yet it disappears and cannot be paid when due. The Emperor was petitioned by the Board of Revenue to allow a change to be made. It was recommended in 1851 that there should be a duty levied on each bale of salt where it is manufactured.

Salt Tax of Hwai-pei.

In 1861 it was decided by edict in response to a memorial that the kang* salt of Hwai-pei should be, as is the case in Shantung and Chekiang, placed in the hands of substantial traders acting under official control, and the salt of Hwai-pei with the p'iao certificate (票), could be distributed along with the salt of Hwai-nan with the old yin certificate. The Hwai-pei and Hwai-nan salt could in fact be sold in the same places. At the three salt manufactories of Hai-chow on the north of the Hwai river salt shops were established. The people were permitted to buy and to sell as they pleased. Also a custom house was opened and certificates called 照 票 chau-p'iau were there given when duty was paid. This duty-paid salt is known as p'iao-yen. In the year 1865 Tseng Kwo-fan, at that time Nanking viceroy, arranged the regulations of the Hwai salt, and they were approved by the Emperor. These regulations included those which concern the certificated salt of Hwai-pei 淮北票鹽.

* 綱 kang, head, chief. The head of the salt department in any city is called the kang-tung, or chief of the salt administration in that locality.

Previous to the action taken by Tseng Kwo-fan, a censor, Tsai Cheng-fan, had in 1853 recommended the adoption of a duty at the locality of production, the amount to be calculated so as to be in proportion to the sum hitherto payable by the salt farmers. It was in fact a salt pan duty, 塲稅. The edict however, merely directed a new consultation to be held and a careful memorial to be presented. Soon after the viceroy and governor of Fukien requested that trial should be made and traders invited to convey the salt in about 750 junks as an experiment. Whether the plan was successful or not we do not know. The change to the levy of duty at the salt pans, made in Kiangsu, occurred at a time of peace. Sales of salt became very abundant. Lately Anhwei and Chekiang have been wasted by civil war. The traders became scattered and the people poor. The Piau-yen certificates were used and lekin collected at the same time. The system was quite effectual, so far that the army was supported.

Gradual Increase in the Salt Tax.

Salt in Great Britain costs a farthing a pound. In China it costs in some places thirty-three cash a catty. In England salt costs a tael of silver a picul. In China salt costs two taels, seven mace a picul. The dearness of salt is caused by the collection of a revenue of Taels 7,679,820 on this commodity. This amount is given in the published accounts of the Board of Revenue for 1893. In 1899 it was Taels 11,547,200. This includes additional taxes, and is nearer to the present collection than that of 1893, which in fact gives the salt tax proper without the additional imposts.

The salt administration is specially open to corrupt practices in any country where the population is always rising. In the sixty years of the reign of Kang Hi, 1662 to 1742, the salt collection in Fukien rose from Taels 85,000 to Taels 141,000.

In that year the amount fixed by edict was raised to this latter sum. The cause could only be in the increase of population during about seventy years. The salt collection was nearly doubled because the population had nearly doubled. This would be the reason that the Board of Revenue in 1742 found that the salt revenue sent from Fukien admitted of the amount to be paid by farmers of the salt tax being so greatly increased.

In the year 1893 the salt revenue of Fukien was Taels 108,654 as stated in the Board of Revenue registers. After 151 years the quantity of salt consumed in Fukien should have been much greater each year with the increase of population, yet the revenue has not increased.

Two cash a catty were added to the price of salt by the Hu-pu three times in Chihli and Honan during the last fifty years. On this account on May 9th, 1899, in the *Shen-pao*, it is stated in a memorial by viceroy Yü Lu that it will not be advisable to add to the price now by an additional impost. If this were done, the price of official salt being very high, there would be an increase in the amount of contraband salt. In 1859 two cash were added in both the provinces mentioned. In 1867 two more cash were added in Honan. In 1874 a like addition was made in Chihli. In 1895 two more cash were added in both provinces. Salt was rendered six cash dearer in all throughout these two large provinces, both using Tientsin salt. By levying a new tax the government would sell a less quantity, because they would be undersold by dealers in the contraband article. In 1895 it was arranged that the salt merchants should pay every year, during five years, an additional sum of Taels 20,000 under the heading Chihli famine relief. The five years soon passed away and the exemption was continued.

The addition of two cash on Chihli in 1874 was on account of the high price of silver. Revenue is paid in silver and the salt merchants were losing on a large scale. Viceroy Li Hung-chang arranged that they might sell salt at two cash more a catty to reimburse themselves. In the year 1879 the addition of two cash was continued for another five years, and the merchants would, on account of this addition, pay annually 20,000 taels. In 1884 the amount paid was short of the required sum. Again on account of the succession of bad harvests in Chihli the favour of the two extra cash was continued. But silver fell in value and the salt merchants could more easily make up the amount required. Meantime the twenty years of payment had accustomed the people to the increased price of salt. It was farther arranged that out of the receipts on salt seven-tenths should go to the revenue and three-tenths be retained by the merchants to lighten their burden. On every ordinary certificate six mace were paid to public account. On the Peking certificate two mace were paid.

The salt certificates issued by the treasury are in some years more numerous than usual. The amount received will in that case be more than Taels 20,000. The amount, Taels 20,000, intended to repay the Chihli famine expenditure will, as before, require to be paid each year.

Latest Additions to Salt Tax.

The *Chung-wai-pao* of May 3rd, 1899, published the proclamation of Viceroy Liu and the Hunan Governor Yü, stating that orders had been received from the Cabinet to raise a new force at Nanking of 2,000 men. They were directed to investigate in what way the necessary expenditure could be best provided. In Hunan a fund existed to purchase rifles and cartridges, and two cash a catty had been levied on salt to meet the expenditure. Out of this additional amount of revenue it is proposed to transfer to Nanking a sum to meet the new expenditure for troops, and an edict commanding this to be done, will be asked for accordingly. By this arrangement no fresh burden is borne by the trader. The expense to the consumer is increased by a very small amount. It is indispensable to put down smuggling. The sale of Hwei salt certificates not only benefits the Hunan army funds, increased as it is by the new tax, but the Kiangnan expenditure is also assisted to no small extent. This addition to the salt tax is temporary only. It is required for training troops. When army funds are sufficient the Emperor will be asked to terminate the levy of this additional salt tax. Two cash on the selling price of each catty of salt will be required from April 1st, 1901, onward. This is independent of previous additions to the salt tax not yet abrogated. Since the number of certificates is 600 for Hunan, the contract price, in all 721,000 cash, will need to be paid in instalments to provide for fresh military expenditure at Nanking.

This certification is issued to the Hwai-an contracting salt merchants in order that they may pay duly the regulation amounts to the salt department.

The *Sin-wen-pao* of July 19th, 1901, says: Information has been received that an addition to the price of salt is permitted. The deputy inspector 巡檢 Lu has presented an elaborate argument for diminishing the price of salt. The method proposed by him will be successful in reducing the amount of smuggled salt. It will also be useful in opposing the introduction of foreign salt. Quite recently the salt commissioner at Yangchow has posted a proclamation acceding to the petition of the traders. The price of Hwai-an salt at ports on the Yangtse will be one tael one mace more for each certificate. The manufacturing merchants, 塲商 Ch'ang-shang, may add one mace and five candareens to each certificate; the effect will be to raise the price of salt to the buyer five cash a catty. The buyer of the 內 Nui-ho 河 salt (that of Shansi) will pay two cash more for each catty. Thus two million taels will be added to the revenue. This addition to the salt duty is announced at Yangchow in a proclamation by the salt commissioner, above mentioned.

How the Salt Tax is Applied.

The following instances show in what way the proceeds of the salt tax have been usefully applied :—

In the year 1806, in the historical work Tung-hua-sü-lu, ch. 7, p. 22, it is stated that for the Yellow River repairs 400,000 taels were needed. The Chihli viceroy asked that the Lu-t'ai salt farmers may be permitted this year to add one cash per catty to the retail price of salt. This the Emperor refused to allow. Formerly for a brief period when cash were low in price and the salt farmers were not able to bear the burden of the required contribution, it was allowed. This exceptional instance ought not to be regarded as a precedent.

In 1826 a contribution of Taels 2,000,000 was levied on the Huai-an salt farmers. The special object was the suppression of a Mahommedan rising in the West.—Tung-hua-sü-lu, chap. 4, p. 25.

The Chang-lu Salt Department.

This is the name of the Tientsin salt department. There are 40,000 certificates allowed. The Viceroy of Chihli, in a memorial published in the *Shen-pao*, April 20th, 1898, mentions that the Board of Revenue had petitioned the Emperor to direct the viceroys and governors of the provinces to inquire whether it would be possible to add to the salt gabelle in their jurisdiction, Wan-pei. The salt commissioner of the Chang-lu department reports that about A.D. 1850 two cash a catty were added to the price of salt.

Sin-wen-pao, July 9th, 1901.—A Peking letter says Li Chung-tang has given orders that when there is no permit to convey salt it must be detained. Li Chung-tang has arranged with the foreign plenipotentiaries that sea coast salt shall not be conveyed by Chinese traders to any point to sell for their own profit. The Lu-t'ai salt stored in heaps on the east of the Peiho at Tientsin and taken by Russia was the property of the Lu-t'ai merchants. Russia and Italy had to be consulted. The Russians wished the place of storage to be changed. Italy thought this salt was lawful spoil taken in war. Viceroy Li replied in gentle terms saying the salt was private property, and it did not concern the government.

The salt stored in heaps at Tientsin, which had been taken possession of in 1900 by Russian troops, remained with them till in the spring of 1901 they invited traders to buy it; the traders offered Taels 300,000. This was accepted, and the salt was sent away and sold under the protection of foreign flags. Some of it was bought in Peking, and there was an Italian proclamation of a protective character posted at the door of the salt guild merchants in the street Teng-shï-k'ow.

Salt at Tientsin.

Chung-wai-pao, December 21st, 1900.—The British had possession of the salt heaps at first, but they neglected the opportunity. Afterwards the Russians and French took them over and erected their flags upon them. The foreign governors of Tientsin, at that time bearing the title of Tu-t'ung, asked for the salt from them, but in vain. At last they agreed to divide. The white salt, one million bags, fell to the two foreign nations. They consented to pay likin upon it. Each bag is worth three taels. Half of this is the likin tax. The Chinese obtain Taels 1,500,000 as likin payment, beside receiving also the dark unpurified salt.

After the Boxer insurrection the conveyance of salt in the neighbourhood of Tientsin was checked for some months. But (*Chung-wai-pao*, December 20th, 1900) it was stated that traders in Peking persuaded the English authorities to give them protection in their undertaking to re-commence the conveyance of salt. By this arrangement the population of Peking were freed from the inconvenience of taking food without salt. The price was till lately 240 cash a catty, ten cash piece currency, and has risen to 500 recently. The doubling of the price forced the traders to take action.

Smuggling Salt in Peking.

Sin-wen-pao, October 12th, 1901.—Lately sellers of smuggled salt have been arrested. They said that Japanese traders induced them to sell it. The local magistrate informed the Japanese officer at the Japanese Legation. Viceroy Li has consulted with the Japanese Minister and has directed the local magistrate to make a public announcement, stating that if Japanese deal in smuggled salt and Chinese sell the article coutrary to law, they will alike be arrested and brought to trial.

Salt Smugglers near Soochow.

Soochow salt smugglers are bold and violent. They open gambling houses in all the adjoining towns. Two days ago, says the *Chung-wai-pao*, June 22nd, 1899, about ten or twenty soldiers went to ask them for money. The smugglers refused to give it them. The soldiers attacked them with their weapons and tried to apprehend them. In the fight which ensued seven soldiers were wounded. Their captain was afraid to report the incident, lest the high officials should blame him.

Hunan Salt.

Chung-wai-pao, August 31st, 1902.—A memorial from the governor of Hunan states that to pay the new indemnity the share allotted to Hunan is Taels 700,000. He can make up Taels 400,000 in the following manner: Three-tenths of the tax on native opium, some additions to the house and land tax to be made by careful revision of the registers, four more cash on each catty of the Hwai-an salt which is sold in seven of the ten prefectures of the province. To this is added four cash more on each catty of salt as a gift from the people and gentry. As to the remaining Taels 300,000 the governor proposes to establish in the three prefectures where Canton salt is used a sufficient number of salt tax offices to bar out contraband salt and secure as far as possible the exclusive use by the people of official salt. His difficulty is felt to be the unpopularity of tax collection. Over a hundred thousand soldiers have been lately disbanded by edict. They join the worthless characters and members of forbidden sects in each locality. If they hear any person complain of increased taxation they suggest rebellion. The governor therefore is reluctant to require the tax collectors to investigate strictly into deficiencies in the registration of houses and land with a view to add to the taxes. Nor can he venture to add to the number of collectors, because each one will make it his aim to appropriate what he can for himself. Each man consumes three mace of salt in a day. He will require in a month nine taels. He need only pay five cash a month as an addition to the salt tax, and this small sum he will not feel to be a grievance.

HUNAN SALES OF SALT.

In the *Chung-wai-pao* of September 30th, 1899, Viceroy Lin, Governor-General of Kiangnan and Kiangsi, asks the Empress Dowager and Emperor to add sixteen certificates for selling salt at Liu-yang in Hunan. Each certificate covers 500 yin 引. For each certificate Taels 10,000 of silver should be paid for expenses. One-half would be taken by the old merchants and the other half by the new. The salt commissioner, in conjunction with the manager of the Hunan Tu-siao-chü 督銷局 in

Chang-sha, have negotiated with traders, and they report that the number of subscribers is complete. The viceroy adds, it will be well for the Tu-siao-chü to establish branch depôts to sell the salt. Before this there were twenty-seven or twenty-eight certificates. The addition of Taels 160,000 will allow of expenditure on the preventive service in the province of Kiang-su at Kung-yü, in the northern part of the province, and at Hai-chou. Here three or four new regiments are required, and can be maintained out of the new fund. The Board has been ordered to carry out the viceroy's proposal.

Taxes Paid in Salt Wedges.

Salt tablets or wedges are allowed to be paid as taxes in Chekiang on the sea coast. These wedges are of different sizes, and are weighed by the tax gatherer. When rice falls in price, as it did in October, 1899, the people sent a deputation from Chusan to the superintendent to request his permission to pay in grain. The superintendent ordered the Chusan magistrate to inquire into the matter and report.—*Chung-wai-pao,* October 2nd, 1899.

The Salt of Hwai-pei and Hwai-nan.

Hu-pao, August 25th, 1902.—The Hwai-nan salt is inferior. The best salt is that of Hwai-pei. During the last three years the Hwai-pei salt administration has been imitating the mode of procedure of the Hwai-nan administration. During the spring of this year business was active and a new head depôt was established for Hwai-pei salt. The procedure of the Hwai-nan depôt was reproduced. From this time traders ceased to combine their business in union. The two systems have become more separate. The head office over both the Hwai-pei and Hwai-nan salt is seriously inconvenienced. Trade is checked. The salt is stored and is not conveyed away. The price asked is high. Buyers calculate and hesitate to conclude negotiations. Salt boats leave rarely for Si-pa, Pan-p'u, Wang-pai-tu, and Cheng-yang-kwan. Generally trade experiences a chilling influence. People complain that they cannot get a living by the salt trade. It is, they think, not a favorable time to add to the price of salt.

Hwai-nan and Hwai-pei Salt Administration.

The salt commissioner stationed at Yang-chow, 運 司 Yün-sï, has a salary of 4,000 taels. He has under him the Hwai-pei and Hwai-nan departments and controls the work of three deputy commissioners, who are stationed one at Si-pa, a large market town, two miles north of Hwai-an-fu, another at Tai-chow, and a third at Tung-chow. The country producing salt on the south of the city of Hwai-an-fu is the Hwai-nan department. It includes that city with Ju-ning and Yen-cheng on the southeast of it.

The Salt Wells of Hwai-pei.

The department of Hwai-pei includes part of Sü-chow-fu and that portion of the prefecture of Hwai-an which lies on the north of that city. Only a small part of this region produces salt. It is that which belongs to Hai-chow and specially the land near Pan-p'u 板 浦, about sixty *li* in length.

The Hwai-an salt is called small salt and that of Hwai-pei is found in wells and is obtained by evaporation in the sun. The Hwai-nan salt is obtained by boiling salt water in kettles. The salt wells are 100 feet or more in depth, but some are less. The salt found in them is in large crystals. The brine is dipped out and poured into vats or pools. After some time the brine is passed into the next pool and from that to the next and so on to the last pool. The water is evaporated by the sun and leaves the salt in the form of a thick crust in the pools. The salt production is most plentiful in the spring and summer of each year.

The salt wells belong to the people of the region who own the land. They pay a fixed tax to the commissioner for the monopoly, and it is they who do the work of producing the salt. The vats or pools are in the charge of the salt merchants, who buy the salt and store it in houses close by. From Pan-p'u the salt is sent down to Si-pa, where the deputy commissioner resides. Here the salt passes into the hands of another class of salt merchants who possess large yards and storehouses and pay a tax for each hundred piculs. From Si-pa the salt is shipped by two routes, under strict inspection of the government salt officers. There is the Hu-yün and the Kiang-yün, or lake and river conveyance. The Hu-yün 湖運 takes the salt across the Hung-tsê-hu 鴻澤 into the Anhwei province as far as Chen-yang-kwan on the Hwai, where the official supervision ceases. The conveyance of salt by river conducts it to Shï-er-wei 十二衙, a large salt depôt between Chenkiang and Nanking. From this point the salt is sent up the river to Anhwei, Kiangsi, Hupei, Hunan, and Kwei-chow. Hundreds of large junks anchoring at Ts'ing-kiang-pu near Hwai-an-fu are used in carrying salt to Shï-er-wei. It is brought down on wheel-barrows from Si-pa to Ts'ing-kiang p'u. From Pan-p'u the salt taken from wells is conveyed by boat to Li-pa.

The whole production of salt and the trade in it are a monopoly carefully superintended by the government, which derives from it a large revenue. The laws against smuggling salt are very severe. A boat caught smuggling is sawed in two, the salt is confiscated and the boatman punished.

In 1898 the crops failed in that part of Kiangsu where the salt is produced. Famine refugees were allowed to buy salt at Pan-p'u and go through the country hawking it on their own account. This injured the trade of the salt merchants, who were, however, obliged to pay their dues to the government as in prosperous years.

The average output of salt at Pan-p'u is 1,280,000 bags of salt, weighing from 100 to 130 catties each; but in 1898 the amount was only 800,000 bags. For this statistical account of the Hwai-nan and Hwai-pei salt trade I am indebted to the kindness of Dr. Henry M. Woods, of Tsing-kiang-p'u.

Salt occurs as brine. What is called *lu* is a thick mixture, half liquid and half solid. It needs boiling, and this is done in iron pans or in bamboo baskets. The apertures in the baskets are large, and allow water to pass easily. Both methods are in use in Chekiang. The salt boiled in baskets is whiter than that boiled in iron pans.

The method of boiling sea water to obtain salt began in the Han dynasty. This made a substantial increase to the revenue from salt.

A letter to the *Shen-pao*, January 17th, 1899, from Yang-chow, says the Hwai-pei and Hwai-nan salt managers have recently gone to the salt manufacture depôts to receive their consignments. On account of delay in selling, through slowness in demand, their capital was deficient. For this reason they have borrowed money from the merchants who undertake the conveyance of salt. This they will return by instalments when payments for sales amount to a sufficient sum to enable them to do so. The time has come for the sixth payment of 40,000 taels. But the Hwai-nan head office receives money in successive payments, and the salt managers can at present only pay one-half of the amount due. The head salt office has petitioned the salt commissioner Chiang Yung-fang to allow the deficiency to be met by an advance from the salt conveyance treasury.

In the petition it is said that when the Hu-pei salt conveyance merchants lent a large sum to the Hwai-nan salt managers, it was stipulated that it should be paid back by instalments at six different times. The last time was the fifth, when Taels 120,000 were due. This was paid. In 1898, for the sixth payment, the amount due is Taels 40,000. Of this sum the managers have paid only Taels 20,130. The amount deficient is Taels 19,860. What we request is that the salt commissioner will allow Taels 20,000 to be entrusted to us, so that we may be able to complete the required Taels 40,000. We also ask that the remainder due from this office, viz., Taels 1,300,000, may remain unpaid. We shall be in receipt of all the amounts due and can make further payments.

HUPEI SALT WELLS.

In Hupei, a few miles to the north of Yo-chow, salt is produced, and an officer is appointed to take charge. The place is under the King-chow prefect, and is called Fen-yen-sï. In Hupei, at Wu-sin, about four hundred *li* from Hankow, salt wells are found. They are also found at Ying-ch'eng 應城, seventy or eighty miles north-west of Hankow. From the wells the brine is pumped by the ordinary Chinese method and then evaporated over furnaces. The salt as sold in Hankow is of a fairly good colour and quality. Lately a special officer has been appointed to control the likin on salt at Ying-ch'eng, where salt wells are numerous.

In connection with these salt wells are mines, from which gypsum is extracted. The Chinese say gypsum and salt are always found in proximity. The shafts are from sixty to a hundred or two hundred feet deep. The miners descend in a basket fastened to a long bamboo cable, which is worked at the mouth of the mine by a huge windlass turned by men. Accidents often occur. The gypsum is sold for use in moderate sized blocks.

Ying-ch'eng belongs to the prefecture of Tê-an-fu. The Rev. Arthur Bonsey gave me the items of information on the salt wells of Hu-pei here given.

Sz-chwen Salt Wells.

The salt wells of Szchwen are at Kien-wei-hien, in Kia-ting-fu, at Shun-king-fu and Kung-chow. They vary in depth from 500 to 2,000 feet, and are only a few inches in diameter. The brine is brought up in a bamboo tube, which is alternately raised and lowered; the contents being retained by a strap at the lower end till the tube reaches the top, when the strap is removed and the brine discharged into cisterns. The brine was formerly boiled in large tubs, but iron boilers are now used. See P. Smith's Chinese Materia Medica, p. 190.

On the sea coast of Chekiang large fields from 300 to 500 yards square are levelled and surrounded with low earthen walls. Sea water is pumped into the fields at high water and left to the action of the sun. This operation is repeated and the salt is scraped off and purified by solution, filtration, and evaporation.

Szchwen salt is sold at Sha-shï, in Hu-pei. *Sin-wen-pao*, July 26th, 1902.—The viceroy of Hupei and Hunan is anxious to obtain an additional sum from the Szchwen salt on sale in Hupei, in part for the foreign indemnity and in part to pay his troops. He has therefore sent Sun Taotai, the manager of the 督銷保商局 at Sha-shï. He is to consult the traders to learn if a few cash can be added to the price per catty of Sz-chwen salt. To aid him the viceroy has also sent Shï Taotai, a native of Sz-chwen. He is acquainted with the salt contractors, and they will listen to his advice.

Shantung Salt.

In the *Sin-wen-pao* of February 15th, 1899, it is stated that Taels 5,000, the amount of the Shantung salt tax had, by order of the Board of Revenue, been sent to Peking. The expense of conveyance was Taels 165. It was ordered to be credited to the Imperial Household account.

USE OF SALT TAX IN QUELLING REBELLIONS.

In the year 1876 the viceroy of the Liang-kiang, Shen Pao-cheng, in a memorial regarding salt, mentioned that on such occasions as the subjugation of Ili and the war against the insurgent Lolos, in Szchwen during last century, the money supplied to the government from the salt of Kiangsu amounted on one occasion to a million taels and on other occasions to three or four million taels. When the Tai-ping rebellion prevented Kiangsu salt from ascending the river to Hupei the Viceroy Chang Ki-liang obtained the Emperor's consent (Sü-pien, 44, 16) to allow Szchwen salt to be brought to Hupei. The consequence was that after the recovery of An-ching by Tseng Kwo-fan some years elapsed before the sales of Hwai-nan salt reached their former amount. There was a diminished demand from Hupei. The demand was only half that which was recognized in the Board of Revenue regulations. At Tung-chow and Tai-chow the Hwai-nan salt was stored in large quantities waiting for a buyer. At this juncture, when the twenty manufacturing stations were waiting in vain for purchasers, the new viceroy in 1875 was beset with petitions from the salt merchants asking him to restore to them the right of sale in Hunan and Hupei. This had been yielded to Szchwen at a time when the right of sale in Yun-nan and Kwei-chow was lost by the Mohammedan rebellion. That rebellion was at an end and the Szchwen salt merchants might resign the right of sale in Hunan and Hupei to the salt manufacturers of Hwai-nan who possessed it formerly.

SALT IN ANHWEI.

In *Sin-wen-pao*, December 16th, 1900, it is stated that the pay office at Ta-t'ung 大通督銷局, after it had been arranged that salt and likin funds should be devoted to paying the foreign debt, estimated the price of salt certificates at 480 taels. Paying the foreign debtor for more than 600 certificates each year the amount expended was at least 250,000 taels. Mr. Wolf, commissioner at Wuhu, received this amount monthly and sent it to Shanghai. By the usual mode of transmission each month money is forwarded before the 15th. Mr. Wolf has, in a despatch to the viceroy, charged the manager of the Ta-t'ung office with improper administration of the funds. For October and November the money, amounting to taels 50,000, has not been forwarded. He urges that another manager ought to be appointed. The viceroy has, in a special despatch, urged the manager to promptitude.

Salt in Chekiang.

In Chekiang the salt duty, 鹾 dzop,* has always amounted to a large sum. Thirty years have passed since Tso Tsung-t'ang obtained the Emperor's permission to change the system, and arranged that there should be official control over the merchant farmers of salt. Beside the chief salt manager there is a salt administration office 鹽政督銷局. The merchants are termed Kia-shang 甲, King-shang 經 and 引 Yin-shang. The salt under their management is boiled or evaporated by the sun's heat. The salt is excellent in flavour. Recently the Japanese Consul at Hangchow, with his interpreter, visited the salt pans at Yü-hang and Sin-ch'ang, with some other places where salt is boiled, to become acquainted with the process in each locality. The salt of Japan, though very white, has not so good a flavour as that of Chekiang. The Consul intends to engage some expert salt boilers to go to Japan and teach the art.

---

* The Mongol word is daboso. Hence tso means salt, and salt duty is a derivative sense. The modern Chinese pronunciation yen is evolved from dem, which is ultimately identical with the Mongol word.

Silver Treasury at Yangchow.

This treasury is under the care of the Yangchow salt commissioner. It is the conveyance treasury of the Kiangsu salt gabelle and is situated at Yangchow. In the *Sin-wen-pao* of May 30th, 1898, it is stated that the time has arrived for the fourth consignment of silver for Peking military pay to be forwarded. The salt board at Yangchow 督鹽院 has directed Tsiang Chi-i, the sub-commissioner 分司, to take charge of the silver. Accordingly he saw it clamped in wood, and commenced his journey to Peking.

Salt in Sung-kiang Prefecture.

The water of the sea is fresh from Woosung to Kintoan Beacon there. There, at the seventh twan or village, or preventive station, the production of salt commences. The salt, boiled, begins to be most abundant in the fourth twan or division. There are nine divisions in all. The salt pans are in great activity at Nan-hwei, and to protect the rich agriculture in the vicinity a double embankment has been made. The salt produced in this prefecture in very white. Salt production begins to the north of Chwen-sha. The sea water there is salt enough to boil. If salt water breaks through the embankment, the crops in the vicinity sustain an injury. There must be three or four years' rain before this mischief can be remedied. Boiling hastens evaporation and leaves a sediment of excellent white salt.

Salt at Soochow.

Chung-wai-pao, July 29th, 1901, reports that at Soochow the Chekiang salt traders, having to pay large sums to the government, quite recently decided to follow the example of the Hwai-an salt system. The salt traders of that salt district have added five cash to the price of a catty.

Salt in Kiang-si.

Chung-wai-pao, June 21st, 1899.—There is a head office for distribution of Hwai salt in Nan-chang, the capital of Kiangsi. There are branches at Wu-ch'eng and Ki-an. There are salt warehouses at Kiukiang, I-ning, Jui-chang, Fu-chow 撫, Jao-chow. The whole amount sold in a year is covered by 100,000 certificates, or at least 70,000 certificates. The largest sale takes place in the city of Nan-chang. Several hundred certificates may be got rid of in a day. On June 3rd the amount sold reached 1,009 certificates, a record number.

Salt administration in Kiangsi.—The *Shen-pao* of June 23rd, 1899, says the Hwai salt superintendent, Ta Yu-wen, at Kiukiang, has sent a despatch to Wen Mow-t'ien, appointing him keeper of the Kiukiang salt warehouse.

Salt Gabelle in Hupei.

The salt gabelle in provinces on the river was to be placed under a Customs' commissioner. But in the *Sin-wen-pao* for May 30th, 1899, it is stated that the Hupei Tu-siau office 督銷局 continues to send the likin salt collection to Yangchow in the old way. The divided management is inconvenient. On this account the Tu-siau office manager has entrusted the amount collected of the personal service tax for military pay 丁餉 to a Show-pei, Liu Tsao-fan, to convey to Yangchow to the conveyance treasury there.

Salt in Hupei is partly derived from Szchwen, but the chief portion comes from Kiangsu. In the *Chung-wai-pao* of July 5th, 1899, there is a memorial from Viceroy Chang on salt. He recommends that two cash should be added to the price. This would ensure a revenue of Taels 160,000 or thereabouts. Out of this sum he asks the Emperor to authorize the expenditure of Taels 120,000 in paying 1,000 new trained soldiers for Hupei province. This includes salaries of for eigners and the price of ammunition, beside meeting the deficit, Taels 8,000 per annum, in the old account for soldiers learning foreign drill. The viceroy also recommends the application of Taels 40,000 to pay the bannermen at King-chow who are in training, but have no official duties to discharge. In this sum ammunition is included. The viceroy adds that he will consult with the Tartar General at King-chow, Siang-heng, in regard to details and that the general and he will forward a united memorial later. If the Emperor approves the viceroy will at once forward despatches to the Liang-kiang and Szchwen viceroys asking them to assist in carrying out the rule, adding two cash to the Hupei price of salt. He follows the example of the Hunan governor, who in January proposed the addition of two cash a catty on salt in his province. This was approved by the Emperor.

In the *Shen-pao* of July 30th, 1899, a Hankow letter mentions that the Emperor has granted the prayer of Viceroy Chang's memorial. Two cash more will be charged for Szchwen salt at Ichang and for Hwai-an salt in Hupei. The salt superintendent Ch'en, the Hankow superintendent of the Hwai-an salt depôt, and the Ichang salt depôt superintendent have received orders to carry out the new rule. The increase will amount to Taels 170,000 or Taels 180,000.

Canton Salt Tax.

Shen-pao, October 21st, 1901.—In the endeavour to meet the indemnity of Taels 250,000,000, for which Taels 18,000,000 are required, it is found necessary to add to the salt tax. Recently Feng, a salt merchant, in a petition to the viceroy, stated the circumstances. The viceroy replied that the Nan-yang viceroy had, in a despatch, written on this subject not long since. I know, says the Canton viceroy, the difficulties under which the salt merchants labour, and their statements are undoubtedly true. But the provinces on the Yangtsz River add three or four cash to each catty. How can Canton not be uniform with them in making this small increase to the tax? As to the exact amount I will await a reply from the salt commissioner, who will inquire into the facts as they are at present and inform me.

Chao-sin Subscription Loans Repaid from Salt Revenue.

The salt conveyance treasury in 1899 paid each year to the salt merchants Taels 20,000 on account of their Chao-sin subscription certificates, as principaland interest. Further, in May of 1899 the same treasury advanced for the treasurer Taels 24,000 for foreign loans.

Fear of Competition from the Import of Foreign Salt.

On August 14th, 1901, the *Shen-pao* printed a letter from Nan-chang saying that the new rules regarding the Hwai-an salt are causing anxiety in many minds in Nan-chang, the capital of Kiangsi. The officers in charge of sales of salt are exerting themselves to retain the present system unchanged. The provinces of Hunan, Hupei, Kiangsi, and Auhwei will be able, in addition to two million taels already paid in to the government, to forward 650 taels for each 綱. This will amount in all to a third million. The cash shop proprietors are endeavouring to purchase 3,000,000 yin, hoping after a time to secure a profit. The price will be Taels 660,000. In Kiangsi salt is already dearer than it should be. The salt commissioner has decided not to sell one yin for less than Taels 22.1.0. Learning this the cash shop proprietors were disappointed. They fear that foreign salt will make its appearance on the Yang-tsz River. It will be difficult to increase the retail price in the face of foreign competition.

Slowness in Buying Salt Certificates.

Shen-pao, September 12th, 1901.—The Yangchow salt department addresses the salt merchants of Hupei, Hunan, Kiangsi, and Anhwei, saying the Board of Revenue is pressing us to forward money. We have very little in hand. The new salt is ready. Will you not bring your money and buy salt certificates? Why are you so slow to do this?

Workmen's Perquisites.

When the workmen engaged in the salt manufacture collect the brine which drops from the basket sieve it forms a black sauce, which is much used in curing pork and fish. Such cured fish and pork are in brisk demand. Since this is not the salt proper the workmen are allowed to retain it as a perquisite.

Contraband Salt Boats.

The salt boats are very numerous, and the people who own them are bold and threatening in their attitude to the officials. The magistrates do not dare to attack them, because they would be worsted in any encounter. The *Chung-wai-pao* of May 21st, 1899, states that on April 14th a mob of 2,000 men was raised by the owners of more than thirty contraband salt junks with others. The scene of this riot was on the east side of the river, a few miles from Shanghai. It took place on occasion of a play being performed at Kao-kia-hang, a village containing a temple known as Siao-hwang-miao. The Catholic Christians were attacked, and the reason is stated to be that messengers come and go now very frequently between the magistrates and the bishops, who allow the mob to destroy ecclesiastical property as they please and afterwards lay a claim for an indemnity, which is paid. The magistrates delay payment and then refuse. They represent the case to their superior and consult with other officers with whom they are associated. As soon as the despatch has left, the constable will appear in a perspiration through fast running. A riot is in progress and buildings are burnt while the magistrates are powerless. Recently Bishop Yao wrote to the Mixed Magistrate of the French Concession at Shanghai, who informed the superintendent, and also the city magistrate, requesting the latter to take action in the matter, who accordingly sent a message to the Chwen-sha magistrate, asking him to aid him in subduing the riot. He then went himself in his chair to see what could be done. Within two days the burning had ceased, all was as if nothing had happened. Such prompt action is most creditable to the magistrate.

Objections to the Import of Foreign Salt.

The claim to admit foreign salt is not acceptable to the Chinese. It would interfere with the profits of the salt monopolists and possibly diminish the sum they pay to the revenue. At present salt is too dear in China. In the *Sin-wen-pau* of July 19th, 1901, it is stated that the viceroys and governors have urged on Li Chung-t'ang, in his capacity as plenipotentiary, to discuss the point with the foreign Ministers. Their object is to add a considerable sum to the revenue. Li Chung-t'ang does nothing. He seems to be forgetful of this matter.

Number of Certificates.

The yin certificates of the Chang-lu salt administration at Tientsin are in number 166,046. Extra certificates amount to 150,000 to 200,000.

Shantung salt yin certificates are in number 500,500; Cheng-piao certificates, 171,240; extra yin certificates, 50,000; extra piao certificates, 83,180.

Shansi salt yin certificates, 381,302; extra yin certificates, 10,000; additional yin certificates, 140,000; Chi-lan-t'ai extra yin certificates, 87,500. The salt certificates of Yang and Chü cities are in number 42,151.

Hwai-pei, Hwai-nan regular Kang-yin, certificates, 1,422,394. The Shih-yin certificates are 270,098. Those called Kang certificates represent salt taken to a great distance. Places near at hand are supplied with Shih-yin salt. The next year's Kang-yin certificates are given out to the number of 200,000 to 500,000. The next year's Shih-yin certificates are given out to the number of 20,000 or 30,000. The Hwai-nan and Hwai-pei administration does not give out extra certificates. If this year's certificates are soon exhausted permission is given to obtain a portion of next year's supply of certificates. Upon them, however, must be written the words "previously given out." Sometimes the sale may be slow. Certificates may not be cancelled in two years or even three or four years. The salt administration act according to the requirements after considering the circumstances. It is not necessary to have a limit of time for the sale of the salt represented by the certificates.

The Chekiang salt administration distributes 704,699 regular yin certificates. Of Piau-yin there are 100,698 and of extra yin certificates 150,000.

In Canton and Kwangsi the regular yin certificates amount to 814,509.

The Fukien regular yin certificates are in number 545,062. The extra yin certificates amount to 387,423, the extra yin certificates are 123,000.

Process for Whitening Salt.

At the salt lake in Shansi each year, on the first of the second month (about March first), the workmen who manipulate salt enter the lake. The lake is divided into allotments of fifty mow each (eight acres). When the wind favours they spread the salt water of the lake over the ground to a depth of an inch or two. After a few hours the water surface is covered with salt efflorescence. This is, with wooden rakes, forced to the bottom of the water. The wind and sun together render it white. Each year in May and June, when the sun is hot, the surface of the lake has a frosted appearance. The south-east wind blows on this efflorescence. It becomes the best white salt in the form of crystals. With a little rain it assumes a still fresher appearance.

The nine modes of preparing salt are the following: 1. Sea water is boiled. This is done at Ki-chow, Newchwang, in Shantung, in Kiangsu, Chekiang, Fukien, and Canton. 2. Salt is raised from wells and boiled as on the sea coast. This is done in Szchwen, Yun-nan, and Kwei-chou. 3. On the north of the old Yellow River at Ping-chou, near Cheng-ting-fu, water is poured on earth where it is white. When wetted sufficiently this earth is boiled to produce white salt. 4. At Lan-chow, in Kan-su, when rain has softened the earth where the sun has shone on it, it looks like frosted alum. From this salt is collected. The same method is used at Feng-siang-fu. 5. Brine by evaporation coagulates and produces salt. 6. Salt collects on tree roots, and is called tree salt. 7. It also collects on grass, and is known as 蓬鹽 feng-yen. 8. The eighth kind is salt by evaporation. 9. Salt is lifted from any salt deposit.

Chekiang Salt in Kiangsu.

Chekiang salt is conveyed to stations in Kiangsu province, such as Liu-ho. At Liu-ho, salt which has been doubly soaked, is boiled and exported to Shanghai, where it is now publicly sold by traders conducting their business under permit of the salt administration. It is intended to supplant the smuggled salt now commonly sold at Shanghai. Liu-ho is a port on the Yangtsz to the north-west of Shanghai.

IMPROVEMENTS CONTEMPLATED IN THE SYSTEM OF SALT CERTIFICATES.

In the *Tsï-lin-hu-pao*, June 14th, 1899, a Tientsin letter describes proposed changes in the salt system. Wan Ta-chwen asks the salt chief commissioner to memorialize the Emperor to allow the following changes: 1. Since the Chihli certificates, the number of which is now fixed by the Board, are not all sold, it is proposed to have the number diminished by three in ten. The limit of time is five years. If the whole be disposed of the old number can be reverted to. 2. Traders will be chosen to pay the government treasury profit to a diminished amount of three parts in ten. This will suffice for the requirements of the treasury. Hitherto the rule has been for the old receivers to retire and yield the duty to new traders, who will be responsible for the amount payable. 3. The system of supplemental payments should terminate. It is requested that new rules may be established, according to which only the old amounts will be required. In regard to the supplemental amounts we beg that they may not be called for. 4. To every certificate we request that so many catties for loss of salt in conveyance may be added. New salt in the salt heaps is soft. In going from Tientsin to the place of consumption there is a loss of thirty or forty catties.

REVENUE FROM LIKIN.

Abolition of Likin Discussed in September, 1902.

By the treaty of commerce signed at Shanghai September, 1902, likin is abolished and surtaxes are substituted for it on exports and on imports. This will take effect January 1st, 1904, if the foreign powers concerned all agree to accept Sir James Mackay's treaty.

Origin of the Likin in 1852.

The first thought of the likin was due to Lui Yi-chien, who was in charge of Hwai-an and Yang-chow, and in A. D. 1852 obtained by this tax of two or three per cent. on goods *ad valorem* support for the troops necessary for the protection of the two prefectures mentioned. Hu Lin-yi, governor of Hu-pei, followed him, and by him and Tseng Kwo-fan the system was extended. It was by this aid that it became possible to restore to tranquillity the provinces overrun by insurgents, who resisted the government and disturbed the public peace.

After the extinction of the T'ai-p'ing rebellion the likin was still found necessary to pay the troops and other demands on the funds at the disposal of the provincial treasurers. This tax is levied on traders in charge of goods passing barriers. The name means percentage, or rather one part in a thousand the word li signifying one-tenth of a candareen. It does not fall on the people as a direct tax, but it increases the expense of living somewhat and all barrier taxes are liable to the evil of overcharges by the collectors. Sixteen years ago, says the *Daily News* of May 28th, 1901, the Chungking Trading Company was established, an agency for the purchase of Tibetan wool. This wool was intended for export to Europe, and was purchased at Ta-tsien-lu and Sung-pan on the frontier. There were five or six likin stations between each of these marts and Chungking. The total duty levied on wool amounted to not more than from two to three per cent. on the value ; traders submitted without much murmuring to the payment of this impost, but in 1886 there were anti-Christian riots in the province of Szchwen. The viceroy was obliged to pay heavy indemnities in satisfaction of French demands made on behalf of the injured Roman Catholic Christians. The viceroy recouped himself by doubling the likin on all produce destined for foreign countries and on imports of yarn and piece goods. The Chungking Trading Company obtained transit passes exempting them from likin charges, but the likin barrier officials still insisted on the payment of the increased likin on the way, and during the detention thieves carried off part of the cargo. These thieves were the boatmen and muleteers engaged to convey cargo. The likin officials were in league with the thieves, and at some stations hot water was regularly provided with which, after robbery, the deficient weight of wool was made up. The Chinese raised the likin to fifteen per cent. and thus killed the trade.

The likin operates unfavourably on export trade. Merchants could afford to pay fifteen per cent. *ad valorem* on imports and exports if likin charges were withdrawn. Likin charges should be collected by the Imperial Maritime Customs at the open ports. The cost of collecting fifteen per cent. would be no more than the cost of collecting five per cent. A proportion should be allowed to the provincial authorities out of this foreign Customs' collection. This would be necessary to recoup them for the loss of likin. The advantage would be great to China if as in the United States trade were everywhere free in the interior.

In 1898 by treaty right British subjects could free their goods from all inland taxation by purchasing a transit pass, the duty on which was $2\frac{1}{2}$ per cent. *ad valorem*. The import and export duties had been calculated on a basis of five per cent. *ad valorem*. Chinkiang supplies foreign goods to the country near Yang-chow as far as Tung-chow. Thus during 1895 grey shirtings went from Shanghai to Tung-chow viâ Chinkiang. Foreign goods ought to be taken direct to Tung-chow, which is near Shanghai, by steamer under transit pass in order to cheapen the price to the buyer.

The likin is charged here at eleven tael cents a piece of grey shirtings, that is to say, five per cent. *ad valorem*, and is repeated at intervals of twenty English miles. Mr. Bourne thinks the likin excessive charges are caused by an agreement between the likin collectorate and the commercial guilds to the detriment of trade.

The piece goods guild pays the likin office at Shanghai each year Taels 7,150 for 10,000 bales of piece goods sold during the year. The guild appoints four committee men and an accountant to collect seventy-five tael cents per bale on each piece goods shop. The same guild for piece goods sent to Soochow pays Taels 12,000 each year to clear the goods to that city. After the arrival of the goods in Soochow an octroi (lo ti) tax is charged on the trader who sells them. Cotton piece goods, eight tael cents a bale. Camlets, twenty cents a bale.

Likin in 1894.

In A. D. 1894 the likin collections amounted to Taels 12,952,000. This was the total amount. At Soochow and Shanghai, Taels 1,970,000 ; Shansi and Chihli, Taels 60,000 ; Canton Taels 1,750,000 ; Hupei, Taels 1,600,000 ; Chekiang, Taels 1,500,000 ; Fukien, Taels 1,220,000. Both Szchwen and Kiangsi collected less than a million. Hunan, Taels 600,000 ; Kuangsi, Taels 580,000 ; Nanking, Taels 550,000 ; An-hwei and Yunnan, Taels 300,000 to Taels 400,000.

Likin in 1898. Pei-yang Viceroy's Memorial.

The Pei-yang viceroy, Yung Lu, states in a memorial printed in the *Shen-pao*, August 13th, 1898, that the sums taken from the likin formerly used in payment of troops can no longer be so applied because the likin collection for Soochow, Shanghai, Sung-kiang, Kiukiang, Eastern Chekiang, and the salt taxes of Ichang, Hu-peh, An-hwei, have been made over to the foreign Customs to collect. He adds that the salt tax of Kiangsi amounts to Taels 336,000. The Hwai-an director 運庫 of the salt treasury sends to the Board annually Tls. 120,000; Shanghai sends each year Tls. 120,000, and in addition 80,000; the Soochow treasurer sends each year Tls. 120,000; the Chinkiang Customs sends by the new rule Taels 6,000. These amount in all to Taels 782,000.

Out of this sum it was arranged that Taels 80,000 of the Shanghai Customs' collection should be retained, as also Taels 80,000 of the amount to be forwarded by the treasurer and Taels 180,000 of the proceeds of the Kiang-si salt tax. The amount retained would be 340,000. After this time it will in consequence only be possible to send to Peking Taels 440,000. By order of the former Chihli viceroy the 支應局 Chï-ying Board of Yang-chow and the Hwai Brigade Financial Board 淮軍報銷局 consulted with the Exchange Committee of the Hwai Brigade. The result is seen in the amount requested for the troops as stated, viz., Taels 2,300,000 instead of Taels 2,560,000, the amount disbursed before disbanding a portion of the troops.

Szchwen Viceroy's Report on Likin.

On September 30th, 1898, in the *Hu-pao*, K'wei Chiün, the new viceroy of Szchwen, reports on likin. The likin collected at Soochow and Shanghai from the beginning of 1869 to the summer of 1897 he gives in a tabular form. He encloses from the Soochow treasurer the amount for the later half year of 1897. The treasurer states that the above mentioned two likin offices have not collected taxes on native opium. The Treasurer adds that a Hupu despatch states that two-tenths of the tea and sugar duties and the whole amount of the increased tobacoo and wine duties are to be reserved to pay the debt to the four nations—Russia, France, England, and Germany. This has been sent, and no remainder has been left. The governor adds that the likin collections was taken over April 1st by the foreign Customs' staff. The amount of the likin collection for this year previous to April 1st the governor will report as soon as possible.

Likin Officers Changed once a Year.

The likin barrier officers are changed once a year in Chekiang. A new wei-yuen is sent to each office at the end of November (*Shen-pao*, November 18th, 1898).

Shen-pao, June 19th, 1902.—The crop of opium this year is, says a correspondent at Chungking, only two parts in ten of a thorough good year; the poppy met with cold weather. The juice collected was very little in quantity. The price is double what is usual. In Kwei-chow the crop is much better, and the Canton dealers are all on their way to that province to obtain supplies. The Hunan and Hu-pei dealers are doing the same.

Tsung-li Yamen's Despatch on Likin as Security for Loan of 1898.

The likin tax has been in part placed under the supervision of the foreign Customs because it was selected to be employed as security in paying for the loan of £16,000,000 negotiated in 1898. The rate of interest is four and a half per cent. Sir Robert Hart was appointed to collect the likin in the central provinces. A telegram from the Tsung-li Yamên to the viceroy stated that the salt and likin taxes were the security for the loan. The salt offices in Hupei were to be abolished and the foreign Customs service would collect the taxes formerly levied by these offices. The same new arrangement was made in An-hwei province, when the likin was collected by the Tu-hsiao-chü, and in Chekiang, Kiangsu and Kiangsi (*Shen-pao*, March 30th, 1898).

Likin Payment for School at Huchow.

A letter in the *Chung-wai-pao*, August 15th, 1901, states that the Chekiang governor has ordered the likin head office to pay to a Chinese and foreign school at Huchow $1,000 annually out of the silk tax proceeds.

Hangchow likin.—Paper, charcoal, and wood for fuel are taxed to the amount of Taels 32,000. The authorities are pressing the contractors to pay a further amount to aid the revenue. They can ill-bear an additional burden. *Sin-wen-pao*, November 23rd, 1898.

Amoy Likin on Beancake.

Fukien.—At Amoy, said the *Shen pao* of November 8th, 1898, the likin levied on beancake amounts to Taels 15,000 a year. Lately this sum has not been forwarded. The treasurer threatened the collectors with dismissal if they did not make up the required annual payment.

Likin as Guarantee for the Japanese War Debt.

The likin of seven districts was set apart as guarantee for the Japanese war debt. The offices were : 1, that of Soochow and Sung-kiang for collecting likin on ordinary goods;

2, the Sung-kiang and Shanghai likin office for ordinary goods; 3, the east Chekiang salt office; 4, the Canton salt likin office; 5, the Hupei likin office for-duties on ordinary goods; 6, the Kiukiang office for duties on ordinary goods; 7, the Ichang office for salt likin.

Likin in Nanking.

The *Shen-pao* of September 2nd, 1899, says : Lately Kang Chung-t'ang was contemplating the dissolution of the Nanking likin office. The treasurer consulted with the office manager on the matter. They found that the receipts are less than the expenditure and concluded to unite in recommending an amalgamation of the likin office of Nanking with that of Wan-t'ow 灣頭 for economy in expenditure. This last place is near Chinkiang.

The *Shen-pao* of October 3st, 1899, contains a statement that the manager of the chief likin office in Nanking had been ordered by the governor to proceed to Chinkiang and establish a tax office for Tsing-kiang-p'u and Hwai-an-fu 淸淮統捐局. He has hired a house and formed a set of rules. These he posted in a proclamation, made official visits, returned in the steamer *Kiangyu* to Nanking, and there reported to the viceroy what he had done. The new tax office will be open for the receipt of subscriptions almost immediately.

Offer to Farm Likin at Hankow.

In the *Chung-wai-pao* of August 26th, 1899, an offer to contract for the Hupei likin for ten years is mentioned. The annual amount is Taels 600,000 for Hankow alone. A merchant offers to pay this sum yearly for the Hankow collection. His offer had not yet been accepted by the viceroy and governor.

LIKIN RECEIPTS REDUCED THROUGH THE OPENING TO TRADE OF YO-CHOW.

The *Chung-wai-pao* of June 22nd, 1899, says that the opening of Yo-chow to trade lessened the receipts of the likin offices in Hupei and Hunan. Viceroy Chang in May sent prefect Shi Ki-yün to Ch'ang-sha to consult with Governor Yü on the remedy for this. He returned in June and reported that the consultation had led to no result. A remedy cannot be found.

Yü Yin-lin, the Hupei governor, learned that the likin officers were asking from traders what they call extra tax, 小費 siao-fei, in addition to the proper duty. The governor in a despatch prohibited this and sent two inspectors to visit the likin stations above and below Hankow to learn from secret information the real facts and so enable the governor to terminate all overcharges.

SUPPLEMENT.

Likin at Soochow.

Ya Li Chü 牙釐局 is the office at Soochow for collecting both the broker's license tax and likin on all sorts of goods. They are the chief office for tax collection under the treasurer of the province. A Taotai is the manager. This office was established in 1864 by Li Hung-chang, at that time governor of Kiangsu. Money was needed for the expenditure on the army by which the Tai Ping insurrection was crushed. The office is also called 釐捐總局 Li Kiuen Tsung Chü. The land tax at that time on account of depopulation over large tracts of land was deficient in the required amount.

New Land brought under the Plough.

I Ku is the agricultural commissioner sent in 1902 to Mongolia to manage the opening up of cultivation on land near Kwei-hwa-ch'eng, previously unploughed. The occupiers will pay land tax after a limited period. A similar work has been undertaken by I Tê, President of the Board of War on land near Jehol.

Import of Copper in the eighteenth Century.

The King Shï Wen, under the year 1769, has a memorial on the import of copper from Japan to be employed in coining cash. The viceroy of Nanking, Kau Tsin, says that the mint of Soochow mixes the copper of Japan and of Yunnan, half of one and half of the other, to make new cash. Before the year 1764 there were fifteen vessels employed in importing copper from Japan to Chekiang and Kiangsu. In the years 1764, 1766 only eleven of them continued to trade in copper. But

Fan Ts'ing-tsi has also eight vessels in the trade. Each vessel carries 100,000 catties. We allow him four-tenths to trade with on his own account. He resigns to us six-tenths. Soochow and Hangchow each take 200,000 catties, Kiangsi receives 80,000 catties. We now learn that the Japanese mines yield less copper than formerly. The deeper the mine the less amount of copper is obtained. The Japanese could send by each vessel only 88,000 catties. The merchants decided to employ only six vessels, each carrying 10,000 catties. The whole amount of imported copper is 600,000. As before the two mints have six-tenths and the traders four-tenths. The Soochow and Hangchow mints in buying copper of the trader require less by 50,000 catties. To compensate for this diminution will the Emperor graciously allow the purchase from Fan Ts'ing-tsi of the deficient weight of copper, that is, a sufficiency of the metal to supply the mints of Soochow, Hangchow, and Nanchang with as much as they received from the eight vessels before?

Trade in Ulianghai.

When Ulianghai was annexed to China in the eighteenth century Chinese traders were forbidden to go there to trade in furs, hides, and deer horn. It was feared that the Mongol tribes there would object that they are now submissive and law-abiding. Circumstances have changed. Russian traders come to Uliassutai in large number, buy hides and furs and other articles and enrich themselves by selling them to the Chinese. It is better for China to allow Chinese traders to go there for trade during six months of the year. They should be allowed to travel in all parts of Ulianghai with passports obtained at Uliassutai. At that city (says the *Shen-pao* of January 3rd, 1903), a Board of International Trade is to be at once established. A revenue from imports and exports will in future be collected there, on furs hides, deer horn, etc. At various points in Ulianghai, barrier officers will collect likin on goods brought by Russian traders. This will lead to a substantial addition to the revenue.

Prohibition of Export of Rice.

In the *Chung-wei-pao* for January 12th, 1898, the Wuhu letter gives an account of the rice export. The export amounts to a thousand million piculs annually. In the year 1895 in the autumn, when the peace between China and Japan was settled, the prohibition of rice export was withdrawn. At that time Viceroy Liu appointed a new grain Taotai to reside at Wuhu and levy likin at the Ta-sheng-kwan, at Sz-yuen-k'ou, and at Ta-ho-k'ou, all belonging to the lower Yang-tse stages. This Taotai consulting with the Customs' Taotai at Wuhu, arranged that on each picul of 150 catties likin to the amount of one mace should be collected in Ts'ao-p'ing currency 漕平銀.* But in the foreign Customs' system on the picul of 100 catties one mace of silver at the Hai-kwan rate or 洋稅銀* was levied. As rice still rose in price Viceroy Liu sent despatches to Shanghai, Chenkiang and Wuhu, directing that the export of rice should be prohibited. Also the Wuhu Customs' Taotai was ordered to prevent the export of Wuhu rice to any port which would require its passing Chenkiang. In August the harvest in Anhwei and Kiangsu was good, and the price of rice was high at Canton. The Canton Governor Hsü was asked by the Defence Office manager to direct Canton importers of rice to obtain certificates, Hu-chao, from the Canton Defence Office. If supplied with these they could bring rice from Wuhu. He wrote consequently to Viceroy Liu asking him to appoint that the

*Weights and Measure.—The Tsao Ping Yin has sixteen taels to the catty. The Hai Kwan Yin has over sixteen taels to the catty. The Shanghai Yin has over fifteen taels to the catty.

export of rice from Wuhu to Canton should be controlled by nine regulations requiring careful examination of steamer cargoes and documents in each instance. The object in view was to prevent the rice on arriving at Hongkong from being diverted to any foreign port, thus raising prices at Canton. Viceroy Liu adopted this proposition, and on September 25th ordered the prohibition of rice export at Wuhu to be temporarily withdrawn. He also directed Canton exporters to obtain a Hu-chao from the Canton Defence Office to be shown at the Customs as authority for the export. Subsequently it was found that the Chenkiang arrangement was more convenient. Merchants there obtain a triplicate memorandum answering the same purpose. The Canton traders requested the Taotai to ask permission in their behalf to follow the Chenkiang system and issue at Wuhu a triplicate memorandum. Viceroy Liu consented to this modification, and on December 26th, 1898, the Wuhu Taotai, having already announced the change to Commissioner Simpson, issued a proclamation for the information of traders. The change of system now inaugurated embraces the following provisions: The trading firm acting for any river steamer at Wuhu when exporting rice to any Canton port, becomes responsible for a sum double the value of the exported rice. The captain of any sea going steamer, or the firm acting as steamer agent exporting rice, enters into a bond for Taels 10,000 on occasion of each voyage. The superintendent provides a triplicate certificate.

The central portion is detained by the Customs and given to the exporter. The upper portion is presented on Saturday at the superintendent's office. The lower portion remains at the Customs as security for the duty. By this system it is possible for the Customs on the arrival of the rice at any port to learn by inspection of the certificate if the export is *bonâ fide* without collusion. On the certificate the amount of rice and the date when the certificate was given, are stated.

It is stamped and returned to the Wuhu Customs' superintendent to be examined and cancelled. If within twenty-five days after the issue of the certificate it is not returned the money deposit is confiscated and the sureties will be required to pay the amount stated on the bond. The steamer also will never again be allowed to trade at Wuhu.

GINSENG.

Extract from a petition.—The petitioners are dealers in Corean ginseng. They say: "You confiscated the ginseng on which duty had all been paid. We know we deserved punishment, and we have paid the fine inflicted by you. This is really the first time of offending. Kindly allow the other drawbacks of last year to stand valid. In regard to them there is absolutely no fault. They here follow in detail:—

1898.—June	6.	By *Kwangli*, s.s., to Hongkong,	No. 66,	Corean Gingseng.	
,,	24.	,,	,,	,, 51	do.
August	23.	,,	,,	,, 89	do.
September	9.	,,	,,	,, 85	do.

Ginseng is at Chefoo charged five mace import duty a catty and at Chemulpo export duty $18 a catty. The Chefoo import was in 1901, 140 piculs. The revenue from this one import at Chefoo is then Taels 7,000 at the present time.

PROVINCIAL CONTRIBUTIONS TO ASSIST THE GOVERNMENT.

In 1898 the *Chau sin ku p'iau*, vide pages 51, 52, were offered to those who would purchase share certificates; the money to be repaid with the promise of five per cent. interest. The sums lent were only returned for a time. On January 9th, 1903, the *Chung-wai* journal published the following statement of government loans not repaid:—

1. Mo-ho river gold mines.—Taels 100,000 were levied on traders by appeal from the government. Neither prinicipal nor interest were received.

2. The Peking and Tientsin railway has now been placed under official management after having been constructed with money contributed by traders.

3. Money was borrowed at interest from traders in 1895. On receipt of an edict ordering repayment, a part was diverted to other uses and the remainder was retained and not distributed.

4. Loan in the provinces 昭信股票.—This loan in 1898 was paid for some time to the government. After two or three years it ceased to be collected. The government had no means of repaying it. The gifts of the princes and high officials were not expected to be repaid. But disappointment was felt by traders who expected to have the loan returned with five per cent. interest.

5. In 1901 the management of the Kai Ping coal mines was suddenly transferred to a company of Chinese and English. This has led to resentment on the part of the old shareholders.

6. At Soochow a trader Chu, manager of a silk factory is now in prison for debt. The capital subscribed by traders was taels 300,000. Having to pay this sum he is imprisoned for what he owes to the province treasury. This is severe treatment.

7. The telegraph office company and the China Merchants' Navigation Company have now been suddenly transferred to official management. Sheng Kung-pau has urged the government to pay three million taels for the telegraph property, otherwise the shares will all go into foreign hands.

INDEX

Advances from the provinces to the government, 42.
Anhwei expenditure, 14 ; taxes, 180.
Amortisation of indemnity, 85.
Annual revenue, 4.
Arms not to be imported, 85.
Army expenditure 18, 20, 21, 30, 35 ; army loans, 106.

Balances in hand in each province, 46 ; should go to Peking, 65.
Banishment of princes, 83.
Barrier charges near Shanghai, 169.
Bean cake likin, 231.
Boards in provinces that may be abolished, 79.
Board of Revenue expenditure, 19 ; balance in hand, 22 ; statistics, 8.
Broker's license, 81 ; in Hei-lung-kiang, 69 ; tax on brokers, 177 ; brokers' occupation explained, 172.
Bursaries, 36.

Camphor monopoly in Formosa, 175.
Canton expenditure, 16 ; indemnity, 104 ; salt tax, 219.
Cash, 1,200 to the tael, 79 ; cash shop tax in Foochow, 176.
Charities, 37.
Chau-sin-ku-p'iau, 160 ; repaid in 1899 from salt revenue, 220.
Chekiang, 15 ; Imperial factory expenditure, 76.
Chien-an mine, 64.
Chihli new expenditure, 13 ; foreign loans, 95, 100.
China Merchants' Company, 64, 76.
Chung-wai-pau (Universal Gazette) estimate of revenue, 55.
Coast and frontier expenditure, 17, 78.
Commutation tax in Honan, 141 ; varies in different provinces, 154 ; do. of salt to land personal service, 193.
Contraband salt boats, 221.
Contracts with tax collectors, 155.
Contributions to Peking army, 43 ; contributions in 1898, 51 ; in the provinces, 52 ; by Hwai-nan salt merchants, 54 ; International Bank, China Merchants, and Telegraph Companies, 115.
Copper and silver in their bearing on taxation, 149.
Corruption in administrative departments, 63.
Courier service, 36.
Customs' collection, native, at Amoy, 180 ; foreign do., 181.

Death penalty on princes, 83.
Debt of China, 1902, £230,000,000, 120.
Deed tax, taels 1,000,000 in Szchwen, 78 ; in Kiangsu, 167 ; at Soochow, 173.
Deficit in Chihli and Kwangsi, 45 ; Hupu deficit in 1899, 69, 76.
Distillery tax in Chihli, 178.
Distribution of hay and straw, 49.
Duties ad valorem, 87.

Estimate of value of houses, 101, 102.
Eunuchs' misconduct in reference to the Hupu, 70.
Ewo loan, 101.
Examinations, 35 ; suspended during five years in some provinces, 84.
Exchange value of silver determines the amount of cash paid as grain tax, 153.
Exemption from payment of duty, 181.
Expenditure in time of war, 6 ; in cash, 47 ; do. of the army in 1898, 72 ; do. of the empire in 1893, 57 ; do. in A.D. 1558, 70 ; recent expenditure in Peking and the provinces, 12, 72.
Export duties at Wuhu, 280.

Famine relief, 61 ; distress in 1898, 62 ; distribution, 75.
Feudal taxation, 131.
Foreign competition in sale of salt, 220, 222.
Foreign customs' collection, 27 ; diminishes native customs' receipts, 62.
Foreign administration of native customs increases foreign customs' collection, 68.

Forke, Dr., 1.
Free gifts to the revenue in Chekiang, 69.
Frontier defence during Japanese war, 60; subscriptions in 1899, 108.
Fukien expenditure, 15; salt tax, 196; salt made at sixteen points, 197; history, 197.
Functions in the provinces, 34.

German statement of the revenue, 66.
Gold mines, 64.
Government receipts, 22; expenditure, 33; detail under twenty-six heads, 56; total expenditure, 57; payments to government departments, 43.
Grain conveyance by canal and by sea abandoned, 148.
Grain junk tax, 147.
Grain tribute, 6; grain Taotais, 148; receipts, 48; distribution, 48; amount, 55; Kiangsu, 170; tax in Jehol, 81; in Fukien, 81; under the Manchus, 136; grain ordered to be sent as tribute, A.D. 1898, 140; conveyance and distribution, 144; Soochow, 169.
Granary system, 143; faults in Peking granaries, 144.
Grand canal traffic, tax upon, 55.
Guarantee for revenue, 86, 94; likin guarantee for war debt, 231.

Haikwan tael, its value, 85.
Han dynasty taxation, 131.
Hangchow likin, 231.
Hannan's estimate of revenue, 55.
Hippisley's statement of loan payments, 112.
Honan expenditure, 14; indemnity, 122.
Hoste, acting for China Inland Mission, 123.
House tax, 81, 167; at Soochow, 173; in Hankow, 177.
Hsü-tung *v.* Sü-tung.
Hukwang likin, 80.
Hunan expenditure, 16; share of indemnity, 120.
Hupei expenditure, 16; land tax, 136; salt tax, 218.
Hupu memorial on navy, 58; Hupu deficit in 1899, 69; secretaries' report on Kiangsi, 80.
Hwaian salt, 97; customs' Taotai, 61, 62.
Hwai-pei salt tax, 200.

Iku, 65.
Imperial tombs, 33.
Imperial household, 81.
Indemnity, 82, 85, 91, 92; to and after forty-four years, 94; origin of indemnities, 103; table of old and new indemnities, 120; claims of various nations, 122; assessed on villages, 91; in Shansi, 93; plan for payment in seventy years, 94; payment yearly up to 1940, 119; payment as arranged by bankers, 122; shares of indemnity as due to nations, 122.
International bank, 115.

Jamieson, revenue and expenditure of China, 8, 68.
Japanese statement of revenue of China, 67; Japan land tax, 160.
Jehol military expenditure, 21, 81.

Kaiping mine, 64.
Kansu, 103.
Kang-yi, 63, 75, 83, 173.
Ketteler memorial, 83.
Kiangsi expenditure, 15, 80; salt, 218.
Kiangsu expenditure, 89; payment of loan, 96; share of indemnity in 1902, 121; grain tribute, 145; amount of do., 147; Kiangsu salt, 224.
King-shï-wen, 135.

Lamp tax, 178.
Land tax receipts, 22; in Anhwei, 79, 81; different periods, 130; Shanghai topography states land tax, 133; B.C. 300 15 per cent., A.D. 330, 10 per cent., 134; Sung-kiang, 169; at Soochow 172.
Licenses, 81.
Li Hi-sheng, statistics of revenue, 9.
Likin, 9, 27, 59, 64, 77; in Szchwen, 78; in Kiangnan, 78; on salt, 79; reform, 74; revenue, 226; abolition of likin discussed, 226; origin of likin, 230; contract to levy likin, 232; likin in 1894, 228; in 1898, 229; memorials on likin, 229; administration, 230; likin security for loan, 230.
Loans in the provinces, 30, 31; do. of taels 3,000,000, 78; do. foreign, 80; loan of Arnhold, Karberg, 61; Russian and French, 98; English and German, 98, 111, 114; origin of loans, 103; loans to foreigners,

new rule, 107; Russian, 109; British, 110; loan refused, 111; Hongkong and Shanghai Bank, 111; Hippisley's statement of annual payments, 112; Corean loan, 112; French loan, 112; native loan of 1898, 113; statement by Chinese bank, 115, 117; five per cent. loans by Chinese subscribers, 160.
Loom tax in Soochow, 171.
Lo-ti tax, 77, 156.

Manchu high officers condemned, 63; Manchu taxation light, its causes, 143.
Massacre of missionaries in Shansi, Chihli, Chekiang, and Shantung in 1899, 1900, 102.
Melting and surplus tax, 25.
Memorials, Min-chè Viceroy, 60; Li-Ping-heng on opium, 162; Kiangsi governor, 61; Kiangsu governor, 61.
Ming dynasty taxation, 142; memorial on exemption from duty, 181.
Mints of Nanking and Shanghai, 79, 80
Miscellaneous expenditure, 40.
Miscellaneous taxes, 23, 81, 135.
Mo-ho mines, 64.
Moukden province, 17.

Nanking likin, 232.
Nanyang army, 5; navy, 79.
National debt of China, 120.
Native customs' collection, 26; local expenditure of native customs, 41; native customs' revenue in 1899, 61; falling off of receipts, 62; corruption bold and insatiate, 63; native customs on land routes, 63; at Amoy, 180.
Navy, 58; navy support from likin funds, 59; expenditure for navy, 73.

Octroi in Soochow, 171.
Oil shop tax in Foochow, 176.
Old balances, 32.
Opium duties, tax on, 56; Sir R. Hart's proposal, 162; price in Shantung, 163; increase in native opium revenue, 164; Spence's statistics of native opium, 165; native opium tax in Szchwen, 175; do. in Canton, 176.

Palace expenditure, 33.
Pawn-shop license, 81; pawn-shop tax in Foochow, 176.
Pay office, Tientsin, 78.
Payments to foreigners in provinces, 41; payments from provinces, 43, 93, 96; Hupu deficit, 76.
Peace protocol, 82, 90.
Pei-yang expenditure for army, 72.
Peking legation quarter, 37; Peking indemnity claims, 92, 105, 114; Peking army support from Hupei, 111.
Plenipotentiaries, 82.
Poppy field tax and extent of poppy cultivation in Shansi, 179.
Port dues, 156.
Postponed taxes for each province, 28, 81; at Jehol, 81.
Processes in preparing salt, 224.
Protection of foreigners. Edicts, 88; proclamation, 123; Chinese text, 125.
Protocol, 82, 90.
Provincial savings drawn on by the Board, 29.
Purchases in the provinces, 38.

Railway from Tientsin to Shan-hai-kwan, 10; railway administration, 76; Tsin-lu railway, 64; Lu-han railway, 64.
Receipts from ordinary taxes, 11; from new taxes, 11; by contributions, 11.
Receipts in silver, 22; from old balances in each province, 31.
Red Book statistics, 1; the same in the Red Book of 1820, 1842, 1896, 1, 180.
Reed tax, 134.
Relief distribution, 75.
Rents and profits, 24.
Repairs of buildings, 37
Revenue of the empire, 1893, 10; views of Mencius on revenue, 50; revenue in 1899, 126; revenue 62; revenue tables, 3, 13, 22, 66.
Revenue of each province, 1, 2, 3; revenue in cash, 46; hay and straw, 49.
Rewards, 37.
Rice changed for silver, 67; rice tax at Changshu, 174; in Kiangsu, 175.
Russian loan, 109.

Sacrifices in the provinces, 33.
Salaries in provinces, 34, 39.
Salt administration in Ming dynasty, 71; in eighteenth century, 191; certificates, 7, 189, 190, 221, 222, 225; salt sold by the poor, 183;

tax eleven millions to pay indemnity, 91; Chekiang salt, 216; Hunan salt. 207; Hwai-pei and Hwai-nan, 209; salt wells of Hwai-pei, 210; do. in Hupei, 213; in Szchwen, 214; Shantung salt, 214; An-hwei salt, 215.
Salt lake administration, 194.
Salt revenue, 26, 183; native customs' collection, 26.
Salt of Kiangsu sold in Kweichow, 71; of Chang-lu. 69.
Salt tax, its moral effect, 196; gradual increase in, 201; late additions. 203; salt tax, how applied, 205; Chang-lu salt department, 205; salt at Tientsin, 206; smuggling in Peking, 207; do. near Soochow, 207; tax paid in salt wedges, 209; use of salt tax to quell rebellions, 215.
Sand field tax, 77.
Savings drawn by Board from each province, 29; of two million taels, 78; by disbanding troops, 77; by reducing likin office expenses, 77.
Securities on loans, 109.
Shan-how office at Canton, 78.
Shansi expenditure, 14; indemnity, 93, 105; Governor's proclamation, 123.
Shanghai taxation, 132.
Shen-chwen cash to be used in rewards, 81.
Shensi, 15.
Sheng-king, 24.
Sheng-siuen-hwai, 64.
Shop tax, 166; in Foochow, 176; in Hankow, 177.
Silk factory in Chekiang, 76.
Silver sent from native customs, 5; from each province, 25; silver treasury at Yangchow, 217; silver in place of grain, 139; scarcity of silver caused by foreign trade, 140; silver payment in A.D. 1799, 152.
Smuggling, 62, 69; of salt enormous, 184.
Soldiers' land, 135.
Soochow taxation, 128; 132, salt at Soochow, 217.
Special contributions, 160.
Spence's native opium statistics, 165.
Steam navigation company, 7.
Sü-tung v. Hsü, 64, 83.
Subscriptions from each province, 28.
Subsidies to Board of Revenue and to provinces, 40.
Sugiyama's murder, 84.
Sung dynasty taxation, 142; Sung-kiang salt, 217.
Supplementary tax from provinces, 55.

Taku forts destroyed, 87.
Tariff of likin, 78.
Tax revision, 128; tax offices near Shanghai. 128; amount of taxes in China, 129; remission of taxes. 29, 61, 130; principle adopted in levy of taxes, 130; Chinese names of taxes, 134, 136; reed land tax, 135; tax at Shanghai, 133; various taxes, 134.
Taxation, six canons of, 127; right of, 126; forms, 127; changes in taxation under the Manchus, 185; its lightness, 141; at Soochow, 171; in Shantung, 178; in Mouk-den province, 181
Tea tax, 162.
Telegraph company, 76, 78.
Tientsin indemnity, 92.
Timber yard tax in Shanghai, 177.
Tithes, their origin, 50.
Titles restored, 84; sold to aid the revenue, 137.
Tobacco tax in Hei-lung-kiang, 69.
Tonnage at Woochang, 80; Haichow, 62.
Transference of funds from province to province, 44.
Transit passes, 62.
Treasury notes as currency, A.D. 1300, 157.
Treaties are to be amended 88.
T'sen Ch'un-ts'iuen's proclamation of protection for missions, 123.
Tung Fu-hsiang, 84.
Tuan, Prince, banished, 83.

Universal Gazette statement of the revenue, 55.

Wai-wu-pu, 89.
Waste land tax, 137.
Wenchow customs, 15.
Whangpu river conservation, 89.
Whitening salt described, 224.
Wine tax in Chekiang, 76; at Chen-kiang, 175.
Workmen's perquisites, 221.

Ya li chü, 172.
Yarn tax, 166.
Yellow River repairs, 77, 104.
Yü Hien executed, 84.
Yuen dynasty tea tax, 157.
Yung Lu, 106.

Titles in the Modern Chinese Economy Series

THE LATE IMPERIAL PERIOD

(late nineteenth and early twentieth centuries)

1. Ball, Samuel. **An Account of the Cultivation and Manufacture of Tea in China.** London, 1848.

2. Chen, Jerome. **State Economic Policies of the Ch'ing Government, 1840–1895.** New York, Garland, 1979.

3. Edkins, Joseph. **The Revenue and Taxation of the Chinese Empire.** Shanghai, 1903.

4. Fortune, Robert. **Three Years' Wanderings in the Northern Provinces of China.** London, 1847.

5. King, Paul. **In the Chinese Customs Service: A Personal Record of Forty-Seven Years.** London, 1924.

6. Parker, E.H. **China: The History, Diplomacy, and Commerce from the Earliest Times to the Present Day.** London, 1917.

7. Parsons, William Barclay. **An American Engineer in China.** New York, 1900.

8. Wilkinson, Endymion Porter. **Studies in Chinese Price History.** [Ph.D. Dissertation, Princeton University, 1970.] New York, Garland, 1979.

9. Wright, Stanley. **Kiangsi Native Trade and Its Taxation.** Shanghai, 1920.

THE AGRARIAN ECONOMY

10. Buck, John Lossing. **Three Essays on Chinese Farm Economy.** New York, Garland, 1979.

11. **Economic Facts.** [published by the Department of Agricultural Economics of the University of Nanking, Chengtu.] September 1936–January 1946. Nos. 1–53. Four volumes.

12. Lamb, Jefferson D.H. **The Development of the Agrarian Movement and Agrarian Legislation in China.** Shanghai, 1934.

13. Roll, Charles Robert, Jr. **The Distribution of Rural Incomes in China: A Comparison of the 1930s and 1950s.** [Ph.D. Dissertation, Harvard University, 1974.] New York, Garland, 1979.

14. Tang, Chi-Yu. **An Economic Study of Chinese Agriculture.** Cornell, 1924. [Ph.D. Thesis.]

15. Wagner, Wilhelm. **Die Chinesische Landwirtschaft.** Berlin, 1926.

FOREIGN TRADE AND INVESTMENT

the Rise of the Modern State, and Their Impact upon the Hinterland

16. Arnold, Julean. **Commercial Handbook of China.** Washington, 1919, 1920. Two volumes.

17. Burrill, Harry R. and Raymond F. Crist. **Report on Trade Conditions in China.** Washington, 1906.

18. Chen Han-seng. **Industrial Capital and Chinese Peasants: A Study of the Livelihood of Chinese Tobacco Cultivators.** Shanghai, 1939.
Bound With
The China Institute of Economic and Statistical Research. **A Study of the Rural Economy of Wuhing, Chekiang.** Shanghai, 1939.
Bound With
Chin Chien Yen. **Wool Industry and Trade in China.** Tientsin, 1937.

19. **The Commercial, Industrial and Economic Situation in China.** London, 1926, 1927, 1928, 1930.
Bound With
Moser, Charles K. **Where China Buys and Sells.** Washington, 1935.

20. Wagel, Srinvas R. **Finance in China.** Shanghai, 1914.

TWENTIETH-CENTURY ECONOMIC DEVELOPMENT

21. The American Presbyterian Mission. **The Isle of Palms: Sketches of Hainan.** Shanghai, 1919.

22. China International Famine Relief Commission. **Herr Raiffeisen Among Chinese Farmers.** Peiping, 1930.

23. Duncan, Robert Moore. **Peiping Municipality and the Diplomatic Quarter.** Peiping, 1933.

24. Hosie, Alexander. **Manchuria: Its People, Resources and Recent History.** London, 1904.

25. Institute of Pacific Relations. **Economic Trends and Problems in the Early Republican Period.** 1931.

26. Kann, Edward. **The History of China's Internal Loan Issues.** Shanghai, 1934.
Bound With
B. Lyn Yu Shen: **China's Currency Reform: A Historical Survey.** Shanghai, 1941.

27. King-yi Hsu. **Political Mobilization and Economic Extraction: Chinese Communist Agrarian Policies During the Kiangsi Period.** New York, Garland, 1979.

28. Kraus, Richard A. **Cotton and Cotton Goods in China, 1918–1936.** [Ph.D. Dissertation, Harvard University, 1968.] New York, Garland, 1979.

29. Myers, Ramon H., ed. **Selected Essays in Chinese Economic Development.** New York, Garland, 1979.

30. Remer, C.F. **Readings in Economics for China.** Shanghai, 1933.

31. Sakatani, Baron Y. **Manchuria: A Survey of Its Economic Development.** [Revised by Grover Clark, prepared for the Division of Economics and History of the Carnegie Endowment for International Peace.] 1932.

32. Woodhead, H.G.W. **Extraterritoriality in China: The Case Against Abolition.** Tientsin, 1929.
Bound With
Fong, H.D. **The Growth and Decline of Rural Industrial Enterprise in North China.** Tientsin, 1936.
Bound With
Ho, Franklin L. and Hsien Ding Fong. **Extent and Effects of Industrialization in China.** Tientsin, 1929.

LABOR AND THE ECONOMY

33. Epstein, Israel. **Notes on Labor Problems in Nationalist China.** New York, 1949.

34. Fang Fu-an. **Chinese Labour: An Economic and Statistical Survey of the Labour Conditions and Labour Movements in China.** Shanghai, 1931.

35. Wagner, Augusta. **Labor Legislation in China.** Peking, 1938.

THE WARTIME ECONOMY AND POSTWAR PROBLEMS

36. Ch'ao-ting Chi. **War-time Economic Development in China.** New York, 1939.

37. Dawson, Owen L. "Food." No. 6 in **Studies of Relief and Rehabilitation in China.** August 1943.
Bound With
Dawson, Owen L. "Rehabilitation Problems in Agriculture." No. 14 in **Studies of Relief and Rehabilitation in China.** August 1943.
Bound With
Problems of Economic Reconstruction in China Series. H.D. Fong, K.Y. Lin, and Tso-Fan Koh, **Principles of Postwar Economic Reconstruction in China** (Part I) and **Capitol Stock in China** (Part II). Quebec, China Council, 1942.

38. Phillips, Ralph W., Ray G. Johnson and Raymond T. Moyer. **The Livestock of China.** Washington, 1945.

39. Taylor, George E. **Japanese Sponsored Regime in North China.** New York, 1939.

40. United Nations Relief and Rehabilitation Administration. **UNRRA in China.** Washington, 1948.
Bound With
Ray, J. Franklin, Jr. **UNRRA in China: A Case Study of the Interplay of Interest in a Program of International Aid to an Underdeveloped Country.** New York, 1947.
Bound With
Committee on Foreign Affairs, House of Representatives. **Text of Proposed China Aid Bill and Background Information on Economic Assistance Program for China.** Washington, 1948.